The BOURBON TASTING *Notebook*

SECOND EDITION

Susan Reigler

SUSAN REIGLER
MICHAEL VEACH

Happy tasting,
Heather!
Cheers,
Susan
Bourbon Women
Louisville, August 2019

Acclaim Press
MORLEY, MISSOURI

Acclaim Press
— *Your Next Great Book* —

P.O. Box 238
Morley, MO 63767
(573) 472-9800
www.acclaimpress.com

Book Design: Devon Burroughs
Cover Design: M. Frene Melton

ISBN: 978-1-942613-93-0 | 1-942613-93-8
Library of Congress Control Number: 2018902095

Second Printing, Second Edition: 2018
Printed in the United States of America
10 9 8 7 6 5 4 3 2

Contents

For Joanna
and
For My BFF

PREFACE

Bourbon is still booming! This edition of *The Bourbon Tasting Notebook* contains 50% more bourbons than the first edition, so you will find here almost 350 bourbons to try, take notes about, and score.

Most of the added bourbons come from craft distillers and independent bottlers. But many of the major distilleries have released new bourbons, as well as new expressions of many of their brands, in the last several months. Many small distilleries that were sourcing product while they were waiting for their own bourbon to mature, have started releasing that newly aged spirit. This somewhat blurs the line between Independent Bottlers and Craft Distillers and we have tried to make the distinction in the notes about the bourbons.

Additionally, some of the bottles we have in the book are no longer being made, or were limited releases. We have kept them (and noted when this is the case) because you may come across them in one of the larger bourbon bars around the country. (Tip: Always ask if a bar or restaurant has a private selection bottling. It will be intriguing to compare it to the regular expression of the brand.)

Finally, we could not have put together this edition as quickly as we did without the help of Chris Zaborowski and Richard Splan, the owners of Westport Whiskey & Wine in Louisville. They generously allowed us to sample from the extensive bourbon collection in their tasting room. Thank you Chris and Richard!

Happy tasting, readers!

Cheers,
Susan & Michael

NUTS AND BOLTS

How to Use This Book

With a record amount of bourbon whiskey aging in warehouses and visits to Kentucky's bourbon distilleries topping half a million annually, it is obvious that bourbon is enjoying unprecedented popularity. Just as people serious about wine or craft beer or Scotch like to keep track of what they have tasted and what labels are their favorites, we know that bourbon lovers are the same.

So, our purpose in writing this tasting notebook was to give you, the bourbon enthusiast, a handy logbook for keeping track of your sampling. Unlike the authors of many other beverage tasting guides, we have not attempted to say which bourbons are best or to assign ratings. We are leaving that up to you!

Taste is a highly subjective thing. For example, while we very often liked the same bourbons, we almost as often liked them for different reasons, detecting slightly different flavors, or similar flavors at different stages of a tasting. (Mike may have picked up a particular spicy or fruity note on the nose that Susan didn't experience until the finish, and vice versa.)

We also want you to know that we tasted no more than five or six bourbons per session, so our palates would stay fresh. The following information is given for each bourbon:

Proof: Ranging from 80 proof to barrel proof.

Age: When stated on the label, we included. If not, you'll see NAS for No Age Statement. Some distilleries will state on their websites or on tours that their whiskies are aged over a certain time span and we have included that information when we have been told.

Type: Most are straight bourbons meaning they have been aged at least two years and what's in the bottle is all bourbon. A handful of products were blended, that is, neutral grain spirit was added to the whiskey. These are designated "bourbon a blend."

Style: When the bourbon has a particular style, such as extra aged, barrel proof, or wheated, that style is noted. Otherwise, style is "Traditional."

Mash Bill: Some distilleries share their grain recipes. We give them where we know them. Others will say they use one or several and we describe this in general terms in the introductions. For example, Wild Turkey uses the same mash bill for all of its bourbons and simply states it is "high in rye."

Color: From lightest to darkest: Pale Straw, Light Straw, Straw, Dark Straw, Light Amber, Amber, Dark Amber, Bronze. (Straw has yellow hues. Ambers contain reddish ones.) Often, but not always, the longer the bourbon has aged, the darker the color. Higher proof bourbons may be darker, too.

Price: Price scale is based on what you would pay for the bourbon in Kentucky or, in the case of a bourbon not made in Kentucky, its state of origin. In any case, the price is relative and subject to change. Prices may be higher in other markets.

$ = $15 and under
$$ = $16-$25
$$$ = $26-$35
$$$$ = $36-$55
$$$$$ = $56-$99
$$$$$$ = $100 and more

Nose: We let the bourbon warm in a Glencairn tasting glass before nosing to detect characteristic aromas. To buy your own Glencairn glasses, go to a local liquor store or www.whiskyglass.com. You can also use any tulip shaped glass, such as a white wine or sherry glass, or a snifter.

Taste: We usually sipped without water, but we sometimes added a few drops of water to higher proof bourbons, especially those bottled at barrel proof.

Finish: The flavors revealed on the palate after the bourbon has been swallowed.

Notes: Our general comments about the whiskey, which may include overall impressions, suggestions for enjoyment, and other information.

We have not assigned numerical ratings to the bourbons. We are leaving that to you, since only you know which bourbons you like and for what reasons. Space is provided for your notes and ratings for each.

We have listed the bourbons by distillery and alphabetically within each distillery listing. A few special bottlings, such as annual limited releases, were tasted. Bear in mind that these can vary from year to year. We have not included whiskies to which flavoring has been added, such as Red Stag. By law, these are no longer bourbons. Major Kentucky distilleries, since they make more than 95% of bourbons, are listed first. Craft bourbons are listed alphabetically after the big companies. Independent bottlers, who bottle whiskey made at other distilleries, are last, and are also alphabetical.

To help you make comparisons, we have indexed the bourbons by proof and style. A checklist is also included, so you can keep track of what you have tasted.

Bourbon Defined

All bourbon is whiskey, but not all whiskey is bourbon. To understand bourbon's place in the world of whiskey, you must first understand "what is whiskey?" The word "whisky" is an Anglicized form of the Gaelic word "uisge beatha" or "water of life"; in Latin, "Aqua Vita", is the term used for all distilled spirits five hundred years ago. "Uisge" came to be the spirit distilled from the beers of Scotland and Ireland, as opposed to the brandies from the continental distilleries.

Today, the modern definition of whiskey is very simple — it is a distilled spirit made from a fermented cereal grain or a "beer". This "beer" is distilled at no higher than 190 proof and the spirit is placed in an oak container to age. Once removed from the oak, a whiskey must be bottled at no less than 80 proof. These simple rules define whiskey as a category. Different styles of whisky set additional rules such as age or geographical requirements. As long as these basic rules are not broken, then it is a "whiskey".

Bourbon is a whiskey with refined rules setting it apart from other whiskey styles. These rules evolved over the past two hundred years, creating the product we know today as "bourbon". The bourbon rules are the whiskey rules but narrowed and refined as follows:

1. Bourbon has to be at least 51% corn. This is a minimum amount of corn and there

is no upper limit for the amount of corn. Bourbon can be made from 100% corn, if that is what the distillers wants.

2. Bourbon cannot be distilled at higher than 160 proof. This allows more flavors from the grain and yeast to come through in the final distillate.

3. Bourbon has to go into a brand new, charred oak container at no more than 125 proof, and only pure water can be added to adjust the proof.

4. Bourbon has to be bottled at least at 80 proof.

5. Bourbon has to be a product of the United States.

There is no age requirement for bourbon. As soon as the distillate enters the barrel, it is "Bourbon". There are a few non-bourbon rules that must be adhered to in order for it to be called "Straight Bourbon".

1. To be called, "Straight" the whiskey has to be aged for two years in a new oak container.

2. Nothing other than pure water can be added to the whiskey to adjust the proof. No artificial coloring or flavoring is allowed.

3. If the distiller wants to bottle a bourbon without an age statement, then the whiskey inside the bottle has to be at least four years old.

These rules are the rules for making bourbon whiskey. They are more narrowly defined than the rules for "Whiskey", but they still have plenty room to allow distillers to create their own unique product.

There are six ways that the flavor can be varied using these rules. The distilleries use these variations to create their own flavor profiles for their brands. Here are the flavor variations:

1. **Grain**: The grain is a major source of flavor for bourbon. Bourbon has to be at least 51% corn, but the amount of corn is a factor in defining the flavor of the final product. Traditionally, bourbon uses a percentage

of rye to help flavor the whiskey, and the amount of rye in the mash bill will determine spice and fruit notes in the bourbon. Some brands such as Maker's Mark, Weller and Old Fitzgerald use wheat instead of rye in their mash bill, giving the bourbon a softer profile with more nuttiness in the flavor. Barley malt was needed to make bourbon in the days before artificial enzymes in order to convert starches into sugars for fermentation. If a distiller is using less than 10% barley malt, they are also using artificial enzymes for this product. Barley malt gives the bourbon some sweet nutty flavors in the distillate.

2. **Water**: The source of water has an impact on the flavor of bourbon. Some distilleries use spring water from deep limestone wells that are full of minerals that will add flavor to the spirits produced. Others use the local city water that has been treated through a process of reverse osmosis (RO water), removing all minerals and leaving just pure water. The important part of the Kentucky water is that it is iron free water, as iron adds a bad flavor to distilled spirits.

3. **Fermentation**: There are thousands of different variations of yeast, and each strain produce different flavors of alcohol. The Four Roses distillery has five different strains of yeast: Light Fruit, Heavy Fruit, Spicy, Herbal, and Floral. Each strain produces these flavors during fermentation. Brown-Forman has yeast strains for Early Times, Old Forester and Jack Daniels. The yeast they use for Woodford Reserve started as Old Forester yeast, but mutated to create the flavors found in Woodford. Yeast plays an important part of creating the flavor profiles in bourbon, as each distillery uses different strains of yeast and often in different ways. Some distillers use jug yeast grown at the distillery, while others use dried yeast purchased from a yeast producing company. Many distilleries allow for a three day fermentation while others will go four, five or even six days of fermentation. These practices all affect the flavor of the final spirit.

4. **Distillation**: This includes the type of stills used to make the distillation. Most distilleries use a column still with a pot still doubler. Some use a Thumper. Woodford Reserve uses pot still and triple distills the spirit. Many craft distilleries are using small hybrid stills that act as a pot still with a small rectifying column attached. The materials used to make the stills are important. Stills may be all copper, or they may be stainless steel with copper heads, or they may be 100% stainless steel with copper wool placed inside the column. Besides the equipment used, the distillation proof of the spirit is a factor in the flavor. The higher the distillation proof, the less flavor from the first three factors are carried into the spirit produced.

5. **Maturation**: This includes many factors such as the barrel, warehouse and the number of years aged. With the barrel, the distiller has to consider the level of char on the inside of the barrel and whether to "toast" the wood deeply before charring. The warehouse used also has an impact on flavor. Is it constructed of brick or stone or is it an iron clad warehouse with little insulation value to its walls? Is it heat cycled in the winter? Is it a warehouse with barrel racks or are the barrels being stored on pallets? Is it a single story warehouse or multi-storied? If it is multi-storied, what floor of the warehouse is the barrel stored? Is the barrel stationary once it is entered into the warehouse or does the distillery rotate barrels from level to level? Is the warehouse on a hillside in the country or in the heart of town? Finally, the distiller must decide how long to leave the barrel of bourbon in the warehouse before bottling the final product.

6. **Bottling**: Not only is age important in the flavor of the final product, but so are the bottling practices. The distiller has to decide the final proof in which to bottle the product. The type of filtration will have an effect on the flavor, even if the choice is not

to filter at all. Is the product going to be a bonded product, with all of the whiskey coming from the same distillery and made in the same season, or is it going to be a mixture of different ages and possibly even bourbon from a different distillery? Four Roses uses 10 different bourbons that they make at the same distillery to create their Four Roses Yellow Label. Is the final product a small batch product made from a limited number of barrels or even a single barrel product? These factors all help determine the final flavor profile of the bourbon that is bottled and sold to the consumer.

Even though all bourbon distilleries follow the bourbon regulations, each distiller manipulates these six flavor variables to create their own unique flavor profile for their brands. Many times, a distillery will use bourbon made with the first four variables the same but will use maturation and bottling to create multiple brands of bourbon, each with its own flavor profile.

Experiment with glassware by taking several different styles of glass and pour the same bourbon in each and then nose the bourbon in each glass. Make a note as to how the aromas are different in each glass.

Tasting Bourbon

Tasting bourbon is not a complex process, but the taster should have some understanding of what is happening so that he or she can determine the "why I like this" instead of simply saying "this is good". The first step in this process is to understand glassware, since the type of glass will change the tasting experience. For this book, the Glencairn Whisky Tasting Glass was used to taste the bourbons. It was chosen because it is a very good design for tasting whiskey and it is available for purchase at a reasonable price in most distillery gift shops, in many liquor stores, or from online sources, allowing you to acquire the glass for yourself. What makes the glass a good choice is the fact that the inward taper of the glass funnels aromas to the nose. If a Glencairn glass is not available, then a brandy snifter or tapered wine glass will work.

When tasting bourbon, you want to use your senses of sight, smell and taste. Each sense will help you to better understand what you are drinking. We will start with the sense of sight and color.

1. **Color**: Color will tell you something about the age and proof of the bourbon. As the spirit ages in a barrel, it gets darker in color as it picks up wood tannins from the charred oak. This color will vary from a light straw yellow to a dark amber red with age. Bourbon has no artificial caramel coloring added, so all of the coloring comes from aging in every bourbon, no exceptions. Adding water to adjust the proof will then lighten the color of the bourbon, so the whiskey at barrel proof will be much darker than the same whiskey at 80 proof. Not only is the water lightening the color, but also the whiskey is more heavily filtered at lower proof, removing more color in the process.

2. **Nose**: The aromas found in a bourbon will tell the taster much about what to expect to find in the taste. There are several different categories of aromas that are detected in bourbon. Not every bourbon will have aromas in every category, because every bourbon is different. Here are the categories:

   a. Candy Shop: These are the sweet candy-like aromas found in bourbons and usually created in aging whiskey. This category includes caramel, vanilla, toffee, maple syrup, chocolate – milk and dark varieties and pralines.

   b. Wood Shop: These are aromas from the barrel, but also the nut aromas that often come from the grains. This category includes oak, cedar, charcoal smoke, pecan, hazelnut, walnut, hickory nut, and sawdust or fresh cut wood.

   c. Fruit Stand: Flavors that often comefrom the yeast, but grain recipe can have some contribution to these aromas. They include apple (green and ripe), pear, cherry, berry (raspberry, blueberry, strawberry, banana, apricot, peach, date), citrus (orange, lemon, grapefruit, lime), and grape or wine aromas.

d. Flower Shop: Floral aromas often created in fermentation from the yeast. These include rose, lilac, honeysuckle and orange blossoms.

e. Herbal Shop: Aromas most often created in fermentation, but also in the aging process. This category includes mint, tobacco, licorice or anise and other herbal aromas.

f. Spice Rack: These flavors come from the grain, fermentation and aging of bourbon. They include clove, nutmeg, cinnamon, allspice, and pepper (black and white).

Adding water experiment: Take a straw or dropper and add water to a glass of bourbon three drops at a time and note how the water changes the aromas and flavor of the bourbon at each stage.

Bad aromas can be found in bourbon, but it is hoped the distiller detected them in samples and never let such whiskey into the bottle. Still, sometimes the cork will be bad, giving a bottle of bourbon a bad musty aroma and taste. Bad flavors include must, mold, dirt, cabbage or skunk (caused by sulfur) and acetone or chemical aromas.

3. **Taste**: There are many different ideas about how you must taste bourbon. Some will say to open your mouth after swallowing, while others will say to chew on the bourbon. The correct way to taste is whatever is most natural for the taster. The important thing to remember is to let the bourbon to flow over the tongue, covering taste buds in every region of the mouth. That is why swallowing the bourbon is important,

because 40% of the taste buds are locate in the esophagus and that is where a lot of the finish takes place. The flavors found can be split into the same six categories that are found in the nose, but they may be very different from what was detected on the nose. Adding a little water or letting the bourbon breath can often change the taste of a bourbon.

4. **Finish**: The Finish is the aftertaste left after swallowing the bourbon. This can be very long or very short, depending upon the bourbon. It can be very sweet with candy, fruit or sweet spice flavors or very dry with wood tannins and peppery spices. It is not uncommon for the finish to start one way and change to another before it is over.

> *Pour a glass of bourbon and taste it immediately. Then let the bourbon sit for five minute intervals between tastes and note how the aromas and flavors change.*

Hosting a Bourbon Tasting for friends and family can be a very entertaining event. It is a very easy event to put together, and here are some steps to take to make the process easy.

1. Choose a theme for the tasting. Themes make the tasting a learning experience as well as a fun night of enjoying bourbon. There are many themes that can be used for a tasting. Some favorites include: a) Traditional bourbon made with rye and "wheated" bourbon; b) Same brand, different age; c) Same brand, different proof; d) Different brand, same distillery; e) Bourbon, Rye, Tennessee whiskey comparison. There are many more themes that can be used for a tasting, so feel free to experiment with different themes.

2. Choose glassware. The glassware should be the same for every taster so that they are getting the same experience with the bourbon.

3.   Make sure the tasting area is clear of interference from strong smelling candles, tobacco smoke, cooking odors and other aromas that can disrupt the experience. Some even prefer to keep other outside distractions to a minimum and turn off televisions and music in the area.

4.   Make sure that there is plenty of water available for those who wish to add a little water to the bourbon and to cleanse the palate between tastings.

5.   Follow the steps provided above and make note of the tasting experience by either writing it down in your notebook or at least discussing the tastes and aromas amongst the group.

The tasting can also involve food. Traditionally, only a bland food such as a cracker is used to cleanse the palate between products. However, Ouita Michel, the chef-in-residence at Woodford Reserve Distillery has developed a flavor wheel of foods to help people understand how bourbon can be enjoyed with food. She takes a small plate and places sample bites of Parmesan cheese, dried cranberries or cherries, roasted hazelnuts or pecans, a fresh orange slice, a piece of dark chocolate and a spoon of sorghum. She has varied these foods from time to time and has used olives, orange zest, malt syrup, and other foods on the wheel as well. The point of the wheel is to take a sip of bourbon before eating anything on the plate. This establishes a flavor profile for the bourbon in the taster's mind. The taster then picks up a sample of the food and eats it, followed by another sip of the bourbon. The changes of flavor in the bourbon and or the food are then noted. This helps her as a chef to decide what foods are best paired with bourbon, as well as how bourbon can be used in her recipes. This type of tasting can be used with any of the themes listed above or even become a tasting theme in itself.

THE MAJOR PRODUCERS

BEAM SUNTORY

Bourbon Distilleries: Jim Beam, Clermont, Ky. •
Jim Beam, Boston, Ky. • Maker's Mark, Loretto, Ky.

The Beam family has been distilling in Kentucky since 1795. James B. Beam opened a distillery at the end of prohibition and Jim Beam Bourbon was introduced at that time. T. Jeremiah Beam, the son of James B. Beam, started as treasurer of James Beam Distilling Company in 1934 and it opened the distillery in Clermont, Kentucky. In 1944, he became the president of the company. James B. Beam passed away in 1947.

In 1954, to expand their production, the company acquired the Churchill distillery in Boston, Kentucky. In 1967, American Tobacco Company purchased the company. T. Jeremiah Beam passed away in 1977.

In 1987, James Beam Distilling Company acquired National Distilleries and the Old Grand Dad and Old Crow Brands. In 1992, the company introduced the "small batch" collection of Bourbons based upon Booker's Bourbon, an unfiltered, barrel proof Bourbon that Booker Noe had been giving as gifts since 1989. Beam was purchased in 2014 by Suntory of Japan.

While Beam Suntory does not release its mashbills, the website Modern Thirst (https://modernthirst.com) has been tracking down grain recipes for several years. According to the site, but unconfirmed by the company, the mashbill for most of the Jim Beam products is 75% corn, 13% rye, 12% malted barley. The mashbill for the "high rye" bourbons such as Basil Hayden and Old Grand-Dad is 63% corn, 27% rye, 10% malted barley. The Maker's Mark mashbill is 70% corn, 16% wheat, 14% malted barely. We offer these as guidelines only.

Baker's

Proof:	107
Age:	7 years
Type:	Straight
Style:	Small Batch
Mash Bill:	Not available
Color:	Straw
Price:	$$$$

Mike

Nose: A hint of chocolate and caramel with ripe apple fruit.

Taste: Apples and caramel with some peppery spices. Water brings out the caramel and chocolate.

Finish: Very quickly gets astringent with an alcohol burn. Then gets a little sweet at the very end. Water helps the finish.

Susan

Nose: Vanilla, dash of cocoa, ripe banana.

Taste: Cocoa evolves into saddle leather and caramel apples. Creamy mouthfeel.

Finish: Sweetly spicy and smooth. No burn.

Notes

Part of the Jim Beam Small Batch Collection. Excellent with chocolate desserts.

My Score

Notes: _____

_____

_____

Appearance (1-5)	____	Nose (1-25)	____
Taste (1-25)	____	Finish (1-25)	____
Complexity (1-10)	____	Overall Impression (1-10)	____

SCORE ____

Basil Hayden's

Proof:	80
Age:	NAS
Type:	Straight
Style:	Small Batch
Mash Bill:	High rye
Color:	Light Straw
Price:	$$$$

Mike

Nose: Very light nose. A little vanilla and caramel with faint oak in the background. Very faint!

Taste: Corn and vanilla, with a bit of spice. No burn and very little heat.

Finish: Very simple and short. The oak lasts longest, giving it a bit of spice.

Susan

Nose: Very light nose, with a little vanilla and corn and light – very light – spice.

Taste: Vanilla and light spices, which matches the nose.

Finish: Smooth finish starts sweet and dries to the faintly spiced oak. Short, though.

Notes

Part of the Jim Beam Small Batch Collection. Why pay a premium for 80 proof bourbon? That's very expensive, though tasty, water!

My Score

Notes: _____

_____

_____

Appearance (1-5)	____	Nose (1-25)	____
Taste (1-25)	____	Finish (1-25)	____
Complexity (1-10)	____	Overall Impression (1-10)	____

SCORE ____

Booker's

Proof:	127
Age:	6-8 years
Type:	Straight
Style:	Small Batch, Barrel Proof
Mash Bill:	Not available
Color:	Amber
Price:	$$$$

Mike

Nose: Caramel and a hint of milk chocolate. Fine leather and oak.

Taste: Hot! Needs water. A little water opens it up and brings out caramel and apples with some pepper spice, with fine leather and tobacco.

Finish: Nice and long with the water. Lots of Caramel sweetness leading into dry oak.

Susan

Nose: Woodshop with underlying caramel, vanilla and cream.

Taste: Vanilla, hazelnuts and dark chocolate. Drop of water reveals apple fruit. Remarkably smooth for barrel proof.

Finish: Long and sweet. Finishes with dry oak.

Notes

Part of the Jim Beam Small Batch Collection. Proof varies with each release, but is always barrel proof. Booker Noe himself drank this with water and who are we to disagree?

My Score

Notes: _____

_____

_____

Appearance (1-5)	____	Nose (1-25)	____
Taste (1-25)	____	Finish (1-25)	____
Complexity (1-10)	____	Overall Impression (1-10)	____

SCORE ____

Bourbon de Luxe

Proof:	80
Age:	4 years
Type:	Straight
Style:	Traditional
Mash Bill:	Not available
Color:	Pale Straw
Price:	$

Mike

Nose: Very simple nose with candy corn and with leather. A hint of honeysuckle blossoms

Taste: Very, very thin. A little vanilla and corn and not much else.

Finish: Fairly short with some oak tannins and pepper ice.

Susan

Nose: Honeyed vanilla and sweet caramel with a touch of sweet spice.

Taste: Vanilla and caramel corn, but an unfortunate mustiness revealed itself mid-palate.

Finish: Short and warm. Disappeared quickly.

Notes

You certainly get what you pay for with this bottom shelf brand.

My Score

Notes: _____

_____

_____

Appearance (1-5)	____	Nose (1-25)	____
Taste (1-25)	____	Finish (1-25)	____
Complexity (1-10)	____	Overall Impression (1-10)	____

SCORE ____

Devil's Cut

Proof:	90
Age:	NAS
Type:	Straight
Style:	Special Finish
Mash Bill:	Not available
Color:	Straw
Price:	$$

Mike

Nose: Vanilla and a bit of pitted fruit – cherry or date. A little leather and tobacco with oak.

Taste: Oak. Lots of oak making it almost too bitter. Caramel and fruit hide in the background.

Finish: Long and woody. Almost astringent.

Susan

Nose: Vanilla, black pepper, ripe banana and touch of caramel and leather.

Taste: Cinnamon spice with vanilla notes. Reminds me of red hot imperial candies.

Finish: Sweet cinnamon lingers in a fairly long finish showing pepper at the end.

Notes

The name refers to the bourbon that soaked into and is rinsed from the red layer of the barrel and added to the dumped whiskey. Opposite of the "angels' share" that evaporates during aging.

My Score

Notes: _____

_____

_____

Appearance (1-5) _____   Nose (1-25) _____

Taste (1-25) _____   Finish (1-25) _____

Complexity (1-10) _____   Overall Impression (1-10) _____

SCORE _____

Jim Beam

Proof: 80
Age: NAS
Type: Straight
Style: Traditional

Mash Bill: Not available
Color: Light Straw
Price: $$

Mike
Nose: Corn and vanilla. Very light nose. A hint of honey.
Taste: Very little heat. A bit thin and watery. Corn, vanilla, and oak. Very little spice, but what is there is sweet.
Finish: Not complex. A little sweet vanilla and oak tannins.

Susan
Nose: Caramel corn and pear with a dash of cinnamon. Not complex.
Taste: Sweet vanilla and frosted corn flakes. Not complex, but a pleasant sip.
Finish: Short, with a distinct cinnamon note at the very end.

Notes
Largest selling bourbon in the world. While there is no age statement on the label, the Jim Beam Black at 8 years states that it is "double aged." So is White Label 4 years old?

My Score

Notes: _____

_____

_____

Appearance (1-5) _____   Nose (1-25) _____

Taste (1-25) _____   Finish (1-25) _____

Complexity (1-10) _____   Overall Impression (1-10) _____

SCORE _____

Jim Beam Black

Proof:	86
Age:	8 years
Type:	Straight
Style:	Traditional
Mash Bill:	Not available
Color:	Golden Straw/Pale Gold
Price:	$$

Mike

Nose: Caramel corn and oak with a whisper spice – pepper.

Taste: Nice mouthfeel with a little heat and no burn. Caramelized pears and honey with some sweet spices – nutmeg and allspice.

Finish: long and sweet with spices and oak.

Susan

Nose: Vanilla/caramel with a dash of pepper and cinnamon.

Taste: Caramel, apple, and licorice. Cinnamon fades to black pepper.

Finish: Long with fruit at the beginning evolving into dry pepper spice at the end.

Notes

Other than for sipping on its own, try it with a cigar or pipe. Excellent value.

My Score

Notes: _____

_____

_____

Appearance (1-5)	____	Nose (1-25)	____
Taste (1-25)	____	Finish (1-25)	____
Complexity (1-10)	____	Overall Impression (1-10)	____

SCORE ____

Jim Beam Bonded

Proof:	100
Age:	NAS, at least 4 years
Type:	Straight
Style:	Bonded
Mash Bill:	Not available
Color:	Light Amber
Price:	$$

Mike

Nose: Caramel and vanilla with some corn and oak. Very simple, but nice, nose.

Taste: Candy corn and pepper with some fine tobacco and oak.

Finish: Starts sweet with caramel/vanilla and lasts a long time drying to oak tannins.

Susan

Nose: Bananas, whiff of cinnamon. Vanilla.

Taste: Sweet vanilla and a little cherry. Sweet spices include nutmeg.

Finish: Long, sweet, ending in sweet oak.

Notes

Nice addition to the small, but welcome, band of bottled-in-bond bourbons. Good value.

My Score

Notes: _____

_____

_____

Appearance (1-5)	____	Nose (1-25)	____
Taste (1-25)	____	Finish (1-25)	____
Complexity (1-10)	____	Overall Impression (1-10)	____

SCORE ____

Jim Beam Distiller's Masterpiece

Proof:	100
Age:	NAS
Type:	Not Straight
Style:	Special Finish
Mash Bill:	Not available
Color:	Dark Straw
Price:	$$$$$$

Mike

Nose: Chocolate and caramel dominate the nose.

Taste: Fruity with berries and corn, some caramel and oak.

Finish: Long. Starts sweet but dries out to oak and pepper finish.

Susan

Nose: Caramel and stir-fry vegetables.

Taste: Much sweeter than the nose! Caramel, orchard fruit, baking spices and some toasted marshmallow.

Finish: Warm, smooth, long, lingering.

Notes

Beam's entry into the ultra premium bourbon market. Retailing around $200 per bottle, the whiskey is finished in PX sherry casks. Advertising says it is "extra aged" but there is no age statement.

My Score

Notes: _____

_____

_____

Appearance (1-5)	____	Nose (1-25)	____
Taste (1-25)	____	Finish (1-25)	____
Complexity (1-10)	____	Overall Impression (1-10)	____

SCORE ____

Jim Beam Signature Craft

Proof: 86
Age: 12 years
Type: Straight Bourbon
Style: Small Batch, Extra Aged

Mash Bill: Not available
Color: Straw
Price: $$$$

Mike
Nose: Caramel corn and apricots.
Taste: Caramel and fruit – apricots and dates, with a bit of spice.
Finish: Long. Starts sweet but gets some nice oak and spice as it lasts.

Susan
Nose: Vanilla and graham crackers, some ripe apple.
Taste: Oaky entry, then vanilla and a little leather and tobacco.
Finish: Dry, but with a sweet caramel note at the end.

Notes
Very pleasant sip. Look for this in well-stocked bourbon bars. Beam is releasing several expressions in the Signature Craft series.

My Score

Notes: _____

_____

_____

Appearance (1-5) ____   Nose (1-25) ____

Taste (1-25) ____   Finish (1-25) ____

Complexity (1-10) ____   Overall Impression (1-10) ____

SCORE ____

Jim Beam 12-Year-Old Signature Craft

Proof:	86
Age:	12 years
Type:	Straight
Style:	Small Batch, Extra Aged
Mash Bill:	Not available
Color:	Straw
Price:	$$$$

Mike

Nose: Very light on the nose. Caramel and a hint of fruit – pears.

Taste: Sweet caramel and fruit – apples and pears – hint of oak.

Finish: Short and sweet. not very interesting.

Susan

Nose: Faint vanilla. Not much else. Perhaps a bit of corn.

Taste: Smooth for its age. Sweet corn and light vanilla on the palate.

Finish: Very short. Not hot, though.

Notes

Perhaps a bit pricey for what's in the bottle.

My Score

Notes: _____

_____

_____

Appearance (1-5)	____	Nose (1-25)	____
Taste (1-25)	____	Finish (1-25)	____
Complexity (1-10)	____	Overall Impression (1-10)	____

SCORE ____

Jim Beam Single Barrel

Proof:	95
Age:	NAS, bottled 6-18-14
Type:	Straight
Style:	Single Barrel
Mash Bill:	Not available
Color:	Light Straw
Price:	$$$

Mike

Nose: Corn, vanilla and floral notes with a hint of oak.

Taste: Sweet corn and vanilla, pepper spice and fine tobacco.

Finish: Starts peppery, but dries out with oak tannins for a very nice finish.

Susan

Nose: Very floral, lots of vanilla.

Taste: Nutty. Snickers Bar in a glass.

Finish: Warm with no burn. Long and spicy.

Notes

Fascinatingly different from the regular Jim Beam profile. Goes well with a pipe of tobacco.

My Score

Notes: _____

_____

_____

Appearance (1-5)	____	Nose (1-25)	____
Taste (1-25)	____	Finish (1-25)	____
Complexity (1-10)	____	Overall Impression (1-10)	____

SCORE ____

Knob Creek

Proof:	100
Age:	9 years
Type:	Straight
Style:	Small Batch
Mash Bill:	Not available
Color:	Light Amber
Price:	$$$

Mike

Nose: Caramel corn and honey with oak and leather. Just a hint of fruit – apricot.

Taste: A bit hot with caramel and pepper spice.

Finish: After the heat, it gets some nice fruit and caramel and lasts a fair amount of time, Getting drier with oak tannins.

Susan

Nose: Vanilla, light spice and a little sweet cheery fruit.

Taste: Vanilla predominates with caramel showing up mid-palate. Pepper and a flash of fruit.

Finish: Medium long. Fruit quickly fades to dry, almost hot, finish.

Notes

Part of the Jim Beam Small Batch Collection. Look for retailers' single barrel selections. They are often superior to the standard bottling.

My Score

Notes: _____

_____

_____

Appearance (1-5)	____	Nose (1-25)	____
Taste (1-25)	____	Finish (1-25)	____
Complexity (1-10)	____	Overall Impression (1-10)	____

SCORE ____

Maker's Mark

Proof:	90
Age:	NAS
Type:	Straight
Style:	Wheated
Mash Bill:	Not available
Color:	Dark Straw
Price:	$$$

Mike

Nose: Vanilla and caramel with a bit of apple fruit and oak.

Taste: A bit thin, but sweet with caramel and green apples. Pecans and oak wood.

Finish: Very nice oak tannins and apple. Lasts longer than the thin taste would indicate.

Susan

Nose: Light caramel and vanilla with faint pear note and oak.

Taste: Sweet corn and nuts, light vanilla and oak. Pleasant mouthfeel, but a bit of a burn.

Finish: Medium long and peppery with quite a bit of oak tannin at the end.

Notes

A good, solid bourbon to sip neat, but also works well in a variety of cocktails.

My Score

Notes: _____

_____

_____

Appearance (1-5) _____   Nose (1-25) _____

Taste (1-25) _____   Finish (1-25) _____

Complexity (1-10) _____   Overall Impression (1-10) _____

SCORE _____

Maker's Mark Cask Strength

Proof: 113.2
Age: NAS, but Bill Samuels told us 6 years
Type: Straight
Style: Barrel Proof, Wheated

Mash Bill: Not available
Color: Amber
Price: $$$$$

Mike
Nose: Vanilla, caramel, apples and pecans. Not complex, but nice.
Taste: Very nice chewy mouthfeel with warmth in the throat. Caramel and apples with a hint of honey and oak.
Finish: Long and nice with oak and a hint of pepper.

Susan
Nose: Lots of oak, with ripe apples and notes of caramel.
Taste: Sweet and smoky, like good barbecued pork, or even bacon!
Finish: Sweet and oaky, but no woody bitterness.

Notes
A welcome addition to the Maker's portfolio. Available in 375ml and 750ml bottles.

My Score		
Notes: _____		
_____		
_____		
Appearance (1-5) ____	Nose (1-25) ____	
Taste (1-25) ____	Finish (1-25) ____	
Complexity (1-10) ____	Overall Impression (1-10) ____	
SCORE ____		

Maker's 46

Proof:	94
Age:	NAS
Type:	Straight
Style:	Wheated, Special Finish
Mash Bill:	Not available
Color:	Amber
Price:	$$$

Mike
Nose: Vanilla and caramel with oak wood. A hint of fruit – apples and cherry.

Taste: Fruity – apples and cherries with vanilla and oak. A bit of peppery spice.

Finish: Dry oak and spice, but rather short. Ends on the bitter side.

Susan
Nose: Herbal, grassy with prominent wood and dried fruit and nuts.

Taste: Nutty with a dash of cinnamon and dried fruit. But oak predominates.

Finish: Short and warm. Lots of black pepper and and woody tannins.

Notes
Note this expression of Maker's is higher proof than the regular. After the regular warehousing, it is aged several months longer in barrels containing seared French oak staves.

My Score

Notes: _____

_____

_____

Appearance (1-5)	____	Nose (1-25)	____
Taste (1-25)	____	Finish (1-25)	____
Complexity (1-10)	____	Overall Impression (1-10)	____

SCORE ____

Old Crow

Proof: 80
Age: 3 years
Type: Straight
Style: Traditional

Mash Bill: Not available
Color: Pale Yellow
Price: $

Mike

Nose: Very light nose. Vanilla and corn and not much else.

Taste: Very thin, but some nice vanilla and corn flavor. Not hot at all.

Finish: Longer than expected with sweet vanilla at first, turning into a nice oak dryness.

Susan

Nose: Simple. Sweet corn and hay. Whiff of green apple.

Taste: Corn, nuts, malted barley. No depth.

Finish: Starts sweet, but quickly fades to a slightly peppery, dry finish.

Notes

Lawn mower bourbon with ice and soda? Alas, this historic brand is a pale version of the original.

My Score

Notes: _____

_____

_____

Appearance (1-5) ____   Nose (1-25) ____

Taste (1-25) ____   Finish (1-25) ____

Complexity (1-10) ____   Overall Impression (1-10) ____

SCORE ____

Old Crow Reserve

Proof:	86
Age:	4 years
Type:	Straight
Style:	Traditional
Mash Bill:	Not available
Color:	Dark Straw
Price:	$

Mike

Nose: Corn and light caramel with some leather and oak.

Taste: A little thin, but some nice caramel and corn with a bit of pepper spice and tobacco.

Finish: Very nice with dry oak and pepper spice.

Susan

Nose: Straightforward. Caramel, light vanilla and oak.

Taste: Vanilla again, with a faint note of cocoa and sweet spice.

Finish: Short and smooth with a touch of pepper.

Notes

Very nice as an inexpensive bourbon to use with mixers.

My Score

Notes: _____

_____

_____

Appearance (1-5)	____	Nose (1-25)	____
Taste (1-25)	____	Finish (1-25)	____
Complexity (1-10)	____	Overall Impression (1-10)	____

SCORE ____

Old Grand-Dad

Proof:	80
Age:	NAS
Type:	Straight
Style:	Traditional
Mash Bill:	High rye
Color:	Straw
Price:	$

Mike

Nose: Fruit and caramel – cherries and citrus. Just a bit of oak in the background.

Taste: Cherries and dates. Quite a bit more complex than expected. Caramel, oak and spice – cinnamon.

Finish: A bit short, but pleasant with oak and and spice.

Susan

Nose: Sweet vanilla, almost crème brûlée with buttery pear.

Taste: Surprisingly herbal after the nose. Vanilla and some cinnamon and caramel.

Finish: Medium length and warm. No burn.

Notes

A great bourbon to enjoy with a meal. President Harry Truman had a shot with breakfast every morning. Excellent bargain.

My Score

Notes: _____

_____

_____

Appearance (1-5) _____   Nose (1-25) _____

Taste (1-25) _____   Finish (1-25) _____

Complexity (1-10) _____   Overall Impression (1-10) _____

SCORE _____

Old Grand-Dad Bonded

Proof:	100
Age:	NAS, but at least 4 years
Type:	Straight
Style:	Bonded
Mash Bill:	High rye
Color:	Pale Amber
Price:	$$

Mike

Nose:	Cherries and orange peel with some nutmeg and cinnamon.
Taste:	Nice mouthfeel with no burn and a little heat. Caramel and citrus fruit with spices – cinnamon.
Finish:	Long and spicy with sweet caramel and dry oak.

Susan

Nose:	Chocolate and caramel with honey and citrus and a little sweet spice.
Taste:	Toffee and candies nuts. Rich vanilla and caramel mid-palate with orange and cinnamon notes. Rich mouthfeel.
Finish:	Smooth and sweet. Semi-dry ending.

Notes

A very good sip with food or a cigar. Lovely with chocolate, too. Excellent value.

My Score

Notes: _____

_____

_____

Appearance (1-5)	____	Nose (1-25)	____
Taste (1-25)	____	Finish (1-25)	____
Complexity (1-10)	____	Overall Impression (1-10)	____

SCORE ____

Old Grand-Dad 114

Proof:	114
Age:	NAS
Type:	Straight
Style:	High proof
Mash Bill:	High rye
Color:	Deep Amber
Price:	$$

Mike

Nose: Very complex. Cherries, dates and a bit orange peel, caramel and sweet spice. I could spend an hour just smelling this bourbon.

Taste: Almost chewy. Nice thick mouthfeel with caramel and fruit- citrus and apricots with some leather and tobacco.

Finish: Nice and long, starts sweet with fruit but gets dry with oak tannins.

Susan

Nose: Vanilla, dash of cocoa, fruit basket and sweet baking spices. Fair amount of alcohol, which is not surprising given the proof, but not unpleasant by any means.

Taste: Baked crème caramel. Touch of water brings out the vanilla and orange peel while taming the tannins.

Finish: Citrus fruit dries into light tannins.

Notes

Water weakens the flavors without opening new ones.

My Score

Notes: _____

_____

_____

Appearance (1-5) _____   Nose (1-25) _____

Taste (1-25) _____   Finish (1-25) _____

Complexity (1-10) _____   Overall Impression (1-10) _____

SCORE _____

Old Tub

Proof: 100
Age: 4 years
Type: Straight Bourbon
Style: Bottled-in-Bond

Mash Bill: Not available
Color: Dark Straw
Price: $$$

Mike
Nose: Corn, vanilla and a bit of tobacco and leather.
Taste: Corn and caramel with some pepper spice.
Finish: Nice – some pepper, spice, and oak.

Susan
Nose: Vanilla, citrus, buttered popcorn.
Taste: Fruit cake with caramel and a touch of mint. Very smooth.
Finish: Medium long and warm with a dash black pepper/ sweet oak at the end.

Notes
This can only be purchased at the Jim Beam American Stillhouse located on the distillery grounds in Clermont, Kentucky. Worth getting a 375ml bottle (Its only packaging.) when you are visiting.

My Score		
Notes: _____		
_____		
_____		
Appearance (1-5) ____	Nose (1-25)	____
Taste (1-25) ____	Finish (1-25)	____
Complexity (1-10) ____	Overall Impression (1-10)	____
SCORE ____		

Urban Stillhouse Select

Proof:	100
Age:	NAS
Type:	Straight Bourbon
Style:	Extra Aged
Mash Bill:	Not available
Color:	Straw
Price:	$$$$

Mike

Nose: Corn and vanilla with a hint of tobacco.

Taste: Caramel and corn with some apple fruit and pepper spice.

Finish: Nicely balanced oak and caramel.

Susan

Nose: Ripe apples and pecans with lashing of caramel.

Taste: Rich mouthfeel. More nuts, fruit, caramel. Candy bar in a glass.

Finish: Dry and oaky. Pepper kick at the end.

Notes

Only available in the shop at the Jim Beam Urban Stillhouse in downtown Louisville. It is non-chill filtered and the bottle says "extra aged" without a specific age statement.

My Score

Notes: _____

_____

_____

Appearance (1-5) ____   Nose (1-25) ____

Taste (1-25) ____   Finish (1-25) ____

Complexity (1-10) ____   Overall Impression (1-10) ____

SCORE ____

Additional Beam Releases

Name: _____

Distillery: _____

Proof: _____ **Mash Bill:** _____

Age: _____ _____

Type: _____ **Color:** _____

Style: _____ **Price:** _____

My Score

Notes: _____

_____

_____

Appearance (1-5) _____   Nose (1-25) _____

Taste (1-25) _____   Finish (1-25) _____

Complexity (1-10) _____   Overall Impression (1-10) _____

SCORE _____

Name: _____

Distillery: _____

Proof: _____ **Mash Bill:** _____

Age: _____ _____

Type: _____ **Color:** _____

Style: _____ **Price:** _____

My Score

Notes: _____

_____

_____

Appearance (1-5) _____   Nose (1-25) _____

Taste (1-25) _____   Finish (1-25) _____

Complexity (1-10) _____   Overall Impression (1-10) _____

SCORE _____

BROWN-FORMAN & WOODFORD RESERVE

Bourbon Distilleries: Brown-Forman Distillery, Shively, Ky. • Woodford Reserve Distillery, Woodford County, Ky.

George Garvin Brown and his half-brother J.T.S. Brown, Jr. entered the whiskey business in 1870 and created the Old Forrester brand as the first Bourbon to be sold only by the bottle. This whiskey was aimed at sales to the medical market and sold bottled to guarantee the quality of the whiskey being prescribed by doctors to their patients. Doctor William Forrester endorsed the product and allowed Brown to use his name on the label. When Dr. Forrester retired, the second "r" was dropped from the name. J.T.S. Brown left the company a few years later to form his own company and George Garvin Brown forms what would eventually become Brown-Forman.

Brown-Forman was one of the six companies with a license to sell "medicinal alcohol" during prohibition. It was during prohibition when the company acquired the Early Times Brand and stocks of whiskey. Early Times is still a Bourbon in the Japanese market, but except for limited releases, it is now "Kentucky Style" whiskey (aged in used cooperage) in the U.S.

In 1997 Brown-Forman opened the Woodford Reserve Distillery and introduced Woodford Reserve Bourbon. The Pepper family founded the distillery in the early 19th century. In 1870s, James E. Pepper as a minor owned the distillery and his guardian was E. H. Taylor, Jr. In 1878 financial difficulties forced the sale of the distillery to Labrot and Graham. Brown-Forman acquired the distillery and its stocks in 1940 but closed and sold it to a local farmer in 1973. They purchased the distillery back in 1995 and opened it in 1997.

In addition to the bourbons listed here, a special Master's Collection edition of Woodford Reserve is released annually. Some have special finishes, such as having been aged in wine cooperage. Others have special recipes, such as using chocolate rye or four grains.

Coopers' Craft

Proof:	82.2
Age:	NAS
Type:	Straight
Style:	Toasted Wood Whiskey
Mash Bill:	75% corn, 20% rye, 10% malted barley
Color:	Light Straw
Price:	$$$

Mike

Nose: Caramel and fruit with some oak and leather.

Taste: Sweet caramel and apple fruit with pepper spice.

Finish: Short, but sweet and fruity. Brandy-like.

Susan

Nose: Fruit salad- bananas, orange. Caramel and sweet spice.

Taste: Drier on palate than nose. Lots of oaky spice, some apple and vanilla.

Finish: Medium and sweet, ending in oak.

Notes

This is Brown-Forman's first new whiskey since the introduction of Woodford Reserve in 1996. The company is the only whiskey distillery in the world that owns its own cooperage, and this new bourbon was aged in barrels toasted differently from those used for B-F's other bourbons.

My Score

Notes: _____

_____

_____

Appearance (1-5)	____	Nose (1-25)	____
Taste (1-25)	____	Finish (1-25)	____
Complexity (1-10)	____	Overall Impression (1-10)	____

SCORE ____

Early Times Kentucky Straight Bourbon Whisky Brown Label

Proof:	80
Age:	NAS
Type:	Straight
Style:	Export to Japan only
Mash Bill:	79% corn, 11% rye, 10% malted barley
Color:	Dark Straw
Price:	$$

Mike

Nose: Very light nose. Corn and caramel with with a hint of green apples and pepper.

Taste: Caramel corn and pepper spice. A lot of flavor for an 80 proof bourbon.

Finish: Starts sweet but dries out with some oak.

Susan

Nose: Very oaky. Vanilla and a little orange peel.

Taste: Maple candy, sweet corn, vanilla with notes of dried fruit.

Finish: Sweet. Fairly short but smooth. No burn at all.

Notes

Impressive product for its low proof. Would stand up very well in a cocktail.

My Score

Notes: _____

_____

_____

Appearance (1-5)	____	Nose (1-25)	____
Taste (1-25)	____	Finish (1-25)	____
Complexity (1-10)	____	Overall Impression (1-10)	____

SCORE ____

Early Times Kentucky Straight Bourbon Whisky Yellow Label

Proof:	80
Age:	NAS
Type:	Straight Bourbon
Style:	Export to Japan only
Mash Bill:	79% corn, 11% rye, 10% malted barley
Color:	Straw
Price:	$$

Mike

Nose: Rich corn and vanilla. a hint of oak. Very simple.

Taste: Candy corn and vanilla with only a hint of spice/pepper.

Finish: Surprisingly long. Starts sweet and dries out as oak tannins kick in.

Susan

Nose: Faint peach, light vanilla, suggestion of honeycomb.

Taste: Buttered corn, toffee apple, very slightly spicy.

Finish: Long and smooth with a touch of honey and a bit of pepper at the end.

Notes

Not a complex bourbon, but very nicely made and very pleasant for sipping neat. We were both impressed with the finish.

My Score

Notes: _____

_____

_____

Appearance (1-5) ____	Nose (1-25)	____
Taste (1-25) ____	Finish (1-25)	____
Complexity (1-10) ____	Overall Impression (1-10)	____
	SCORE ____	

Early Times 354

Proof:	80
Age:	NAS
Type:	Straight Bourbon
Style:	Straight
Mash Bill:	79% corn, 11% rye, 10% malted barley
Color:	Dark Straw/Yellow
Price:	$$

Mike

Nose: Very light – corn and vanilla.

Taste: Corn and vanilla with just a hint of pepper spice.

Finish: Fairly long with oak tannins and sweet vanilla.

Susan

Nose: Light notes of vanilla with a hint of cocoa. Candy corn predominates.

Taste: Caramel corn, light spices, hint of pecans.

Finish: Smooth and longer lasting than one would expect from an 80 proof bourbon.

Notes

Very pleasant light sipping bourbon. Would be especially nice in warm weather. No need to add water or ice. Limited release, but may be found at well-stocked bourbon bars.

My Score

Notes: _____

_____

_____

Appearance (1-5)	____	Nose (1-25)	____
Taste (1-25)	____	Finish (1-25)	____
Complexity (1-10)	____	Overall Impression (1-10)	____

SCORE ____

Old Forester

Proof:	86
Age:	NAS
Type:	Straight Bourbon
Style:	Straight
Mash Bill:	72% corn, 18% rye, 10% malted barley
Color:	Dark Straw
Price:	$$

Mike

Nose: Dark fruit – apricots and ripe apples with caramel, fine leather and pepper spice. Just a hint of oak.

Taste: Very nice mouthfeel with no alcohol burn. Apples, caramel, pepper spice, vanilla and hint of oak.

Finish: Long and dry with oak and pepper spice that leads to sweet vanilla.

Susan

Nose: Complex nose with vanilla, caramel, apple with faint nuttiness and oak.

Taste: Caramel and vanilla, with notes of chocolate, leather, apple and hint of tobacco.

Finish: Smooth, long, peppery (but not hot) finish. Sweet vanilla note at the very end.

Notes

A classic. If you are introducing someone to bourbon, this would be a fine one to use as a benchmark. As fine in a cocktail (makes a splendid Old Fashioned) as it is sipped neat or with a single ice cube.

My Score

Notes: _____

_____

_____

Appearance (1-5)	____	Nose (1-25)	____
Taste (1-25)	____	Finish (1-25)	____
Complexity (1-10)	____	Overall Impression (1-10)	____

SCORE ____

Old Forester Birthday Bourbon 2013

Proof: 94
Age: 12 years
Type: Straight Bourbon
Style: Small Batch, Extra Aged

Mash Bill: 72% corn, 18% rye, 10% malted barley
Color: Deep Amber
Price: $$$$

Mike

Nose: Rich caramel corn and vanilla. Some fruit – berries and apples, with sweet spices. A bit of fine leather in the background.
Taste: Sweet fruit – apples, berries with caramel and a hint of anise/nutmeg. Some oak wood and leather.
Finish: Long and sweet to start, but dries out nicely with oak tannins and spice.

Susan

Nose: Ripe cherries, vanilla, and sweet spices. Intriguingly complex.
Taste: Rich caramel, vanilla. The cherry in the nose carries over to the palate, joined by cinnamon and buttery corn.
Finish: Long and fruit-filled. Sweet oak tannins and a bit of spicy warmth at the end.

Notes

Brown-Forman releases this mingling of 12-year-old Old Foresters every year in September to commemorate founder George Garvin Brown's birthday (2 September, 1846). They vary from year to year, but are always worth seeking out.

My Score		
Notes: _____		
_____		
_____		
Appearance (1-5) ____	Nose (1-25)	____
Taste (1-25) ____	Finish (1-25)	____
Complexity (1-10) ____	Overall Impression (1-10)	____
SCORE ____		

Old Forester 1870

Proof:	90
Age:	NAS
Type:	Straight Bourbon
Style:	Small Batch
Mash Bill:	72% corn, 18% rye, 10% malted barley
Color:	Light Amber
Price:	$$$$

Mike
Nose: Very nice. caramel and vanilla with some fruit – berries and apple, sweet spices.

Taste: Nice mouthfeel, almost chewy with sweet caramel and fruit – apple and pear.

Finish: Long and spicy with pepper and oak.

Susan
Nose: Lots of OF's signature caramel plus cherries, pears, sprinkling of nutmeg.

Taste: Rich mouthfeel with smoked toffee and baked fruit – cherry pie.

Finish: Long and warm. No burn. Pleasant spicy ending.

Notes
Attempt to recreate George Garvin Brown's original batch from 1870, the founding date of the distillery, by sourcing three bourbons with different production dates, different barrel entry proofs, and different maturation periods.

My Score

Notes: _____

_____

_____

Appearance (1-5)	____	Nose (1-25)	____
Taste (1-25)	____	Finish (1-25)	____
Complexity (1-10)	____	Overall Impression (1-10)	____

SCORE ____

Old Forester 1897

Proof: 100
Age: At least 4 years
Type: Straight
Style: Bottled-in-Bond

Mash Bill: 72% corn, 18% rye, 10% malted barley
Color: Light Amber
Price: $$$$

Mike
Nose: Bananas, caramel, and vanilla.
Taste: Caramel, bananas, baking spice, Bananas Foster.
Finish: Dry with oak and pepper.

Susan
Nose: Caramel, cinnamon, pears.
Taste: Cinnamon coffee cake with a layer of vanilla icing.
Finish: Dry with oak and pepper. Long and peppery.

Notes
The second release in Brown-Forman's Whiskey Row Series. This one pays homage to the Bottled-in-Bond Act of 1897, America's first consumer protection law, meant to guarantee whiskey quality.

My Score
Notes: _____
_____
_____

Appearance (1-5) ____   Nose (1-25) ____
Taste (1-25) ____   Finish (1-25) ____
Complexity (1-10) ____   Overall Impression (1-10) ____
SCORE ____

Old Forester 1920

Proof:	115
Age:	NAS
Type:	Straight
Style:	Cask Strength
Mash Bill:	72% corn, 18% rye, 10% malted barley
Color:	Rich Amber
Price:	$$$$$

Mike

Nose: Apricots and berries, caramel, tobacco and a hint of baking spice.

Taste: Fruit and spice with caramel toffee. Water brings out the fruit and spice.

Finish: Dry oak and spice. Water makes it spicier.

Susan

Nose: Lots of caramel, sweet spices, ripe apple.

Taste: Rich toffee without water. With water, more nuts, apples, spice.

Finish: Long, oaky, spicy.

Notes

Excellent sip, but do add water/ice. The third release in Brown-Forman's Whiskey Row Series. "Prohibition Style" since Brown-Forman was one of six distillery's given a government permit to make "medicinal whiskey." Barrel proof before bottling was typically 120.

My Score

Notes: _____

_____

_____

Appearance (1-5)	____	Nose (1-25)	____
Taste (1-25)	____	Finish (1-25)	____
Complexity (1-10)	____	Overall Impression (1-10)	____

SCORE ____

Old Forester Signature

Proof: 100
Age: NAS
Type: Straight Bourbon
Style: Straight

Mash Bill: 72% corn, 18% rye, 10% malted barley
Color: Amber
Price: $$

Mike

Nose: Dark fruit – apricots and dates, apples and caramel. Just a hint of spice and oak. Fine leather and tobacco. Very complicated. The longer it breathes, the more that comes out on the nose.

Taste: Thick and chewy with only a little warmth in the back of the throat. Apples, caramel, cherries and peppery spice with hint of oak.

Finish: Long and pleasing with oak and pepper changing to caramel and vanilla.

Susan

Nose: Complex nose with caramel, vanilla, dark fruit, roasted corn and toasted pecans. Be patient. More layers emerge as it sits in the glass.

Taste: Caramel and vanilla, with notes of bright cherry and apple. Oaky without being woody.

Finish: Vanilla and caramel dominate the finish which shows a peppery, but not hot, note at the end.

Notes

Beautifully balanced. Has the character and complexity of a bourbon twice its price.

My Score		
Notes: _____		
_____		
_____		
Appearance (1-5) ____	Nose (1-25)	____
Taste (1-25) ____	Finish (1-25)	____
Complexity (1-10) ____	Overall Impression (1-10)	____
	SCORE ____	

Old Forester Single Barrel

Proof:	90
Age:	Varies, but over 6 years
Type:	Straight Bourbon
Style:	Single Barrel
Mash Bill:	72% corn, 18% rye, 10% malted barley
Color:	Light Amber
Price:	$$$$

Mike

Nose: Apricots and peaches with vanilla and caramel. Some sweet spices and oak.

Taste: Sweet fruit – apricots and apples with some cinnamon spice and fine tobacco.

Finish: A little peppery and dry with oak. Lasts a long time.

Susan

Nose: Caramel and candied almonds with ripe cherries. Faint cinnamon notes.

Taste: Caramel and vanilla predominate supported by oak tannins. Fruit and nuts linger in the background.

Finish: Long and warm. Dries to sweet oakiness.

Notes

Private selections for retail stores, restaurants, whiskey clubs, and even individuals. Can have very distinct flavors that may not show up in other Old Forester expressions.

My Score

Notes: _____

_____

_____

Appearance (1-5)	_____	Nose (1-25) _____
Taste (1-25)	_____	Finish (1-25) _____
Complexity (1-10)	_____	Overall Impression (1-10) _____

SCORE _____

Woodford Reserve Distiller's Select

Proof:	90.4
Age:	NAS
Type:	Straight Bourbon
Style:	Small Batch
Mash Bill:	72% corn, 18% rye, 10% malted barley
Color:	Light Amber
Price:	$$$

Mike

Nose: Rich caramel. Crème brulee with pitted Fruit – cherries and peaches. Apricots with a hint of oak and leather.

Taste: Caramel and fruit with some sweet spice and oak.

Finish: Long and sweet – caramel and vanilla with only a hint of oak and spice.

Susan

Nose: Intense vanilla and caramel with fruit and flowers, lightly nutty and spicy.

Taste: Creamy caramel and vanilla. The orange emerges as the fruit, with layer of nuttiness and nutmeg.

Finish: Lingering. Warmth ends with sweet vanilla and a whisper of the nutmeg.

Notes

Richly flavored and fine neat or with a splash. Makes an excellent Manhattan paired with the best vermouth you can find.

My Score

Notes: _____

_____

_____

Appearance (1-5) _____   Nose (1-25) _____

Taste (1-25) _____   Finish (1-25) _____

Complexity (1-10) _____   Overall Impression (1-10) _____

SCORE _____

Woodford Reserve Double Oaked

Proof:	90.4
Age:	NAS
Type:	Straight Bourbon
Style:	Small Batch, Extra Aged
Mash Bill:	72% corn, 18% rye, 10% malted barley
Color:	Amber
Price:	$$$$

Mike
Nose: Oak and dark, chewy caramel. Very simple nose.
Taste: Oak wood and bitter tannins. Apples with hint of caramel.
Finish: Long and dry with oak tannins. Only a hint of oak and spice.

Susan
Nose: Oak and dark, rich caramel. Not complex.
Taste: Oaky maple syrup. Some caramel apple.
Finish: Long. Vanilla kicks in at the very end.

Notes
Dumped into a second oak barrel that has been deeply toasted and lightly charred. It is then aged for an additional six months. Add a splash of water to tame the tannins.

My Score	
Notes: _____	
_____	
_____	
Appearance (1-5) ____	Nose (1-25) ____
Taste (1-25) ____	Finish (1-25) ____
Complexity (1-10) ____	Overall Impression (1-10) ____
SCORE ____	

Woodford Reserve Double Oaked Single Barrel

Proof: 90.4
Age: NAS
Type: Straight Bourbon
Style: Single Barrel, Extra Aged

Mash Bill: 72% corn, 18% rye, 10% malted barley
Color: Amber
Price: $$$$$

Mike
Nose: Caramel toffee and spice. A bit of oak and fruit – apples and apricots.
Taste: Apple pie with caramel – a bit of pepper spice and oak.
Finish: Long. Starts peppery but dries out with oak and hickory nuts.

Susan
Nose: Nutty caramel, brown sugar, oak, and dark cherries.
Taste: Oaky, yeasty, nutty. Rich, chewy mouthfeel and lots of sweet vanilla.
Finish: Very long. Begins with caramel sweetness and dries to light spice and light oak.

Notes
Single Barrel selections are private bottlings for retailers, restaurants, and such. Look for this in a bourbon bar with large number of bourbons and several private bottlings.

My Score
Notes: _____

_____

_____

Appearance (1-5) ____   Nose (1-25) ____
Taste (1-25) ____   Finish (1-25) ____
Complexity (1-10) ____   Overall Impression (1-10) ____
SCORE ____

Woodford Reserve Double Double Oaked

Proof:	90.4
Age:	NAS
Type:	Straight
Style:	Small Batch
Mash Bill:	72% corn, 18% rye, 10% malted barley
Color:	Amber
Price:	$$$$$

Mike
Nose: Crème brulee, fruit, oak, and baking spice.
Taste: Toffee and pitted fruit with some sweet spice.
Finish: Starts buttery caramel but dries out with oak and spice.

Susan
Nose: Maple and toffee with baked apples.
Taste: Smoky. Rich caramel, vanilla, dates.
Finish: Long with sweet oak and wood smoke. Spicier and less sweet that the regular Double oak.

Notes
A true after-dinner sip. Retailing in Kentucky for about $40 for 375ml bottle, hence the dollar sign number. This is Woodford Double Oak aged for yet another year in heavily-toasted, lightly-charred new oak barrels.

My Score

Notes: _____

_____

_____

Appearance (1-5)	____	Nose (1-25)	____
Taste (1-25)	____	Finish (1-25)	____
Complexity (1-10)	____	Overall Impression (1-10)	____

SCORE ____

Additional Brown-Forman Releases

Name: _____

Distillery: _____

Proof: _____ **Mash Bill:** _____
Age: _____ _____
Type: _____ **Color:** _____
Style: _____ **Price:** _____

My Score

Notes: _____
_____
_____

Appearance (1-5) ____ Nose (1-25) ____
Taste (1-25) ____ Finish (1-25) ____
Complexity (1-10) ____ Overall Impression (1-10) ____
SCORE ____

Name: _____

Distillery: _____

Proof: _____ **Mash Bill:** _____
Age: _____ _____
Type: _____ **Color:** _____
Style: _____ **Price:** _____

My Score

Notes: _____
_____
_____

Appearance (1-5) ____ Nose (1-25) ____
Taste (1-25) ____ Finish (1-25) ____
Complexity (1-10) ____ Overall Impression (1-10) ____
SCORE ____

DIAGEO

London-based Diageo PLC is the largest alcoholic beverage producer in the world. Brands include Johnnie Walker Scotch, Tanqueray gin, Smirnoff vodka, and Guinness stout. Its Bulleit bourbons have been contract distilled in Kentucky and are aged in warehouses on the site of the Stitzel-Weller Distillery in Louisville, which Diageo had purchased and closed in 1972. (It was reopened it for tours in 2014.)

In 2017, Diageo opened a new distillery in Shelby County, Kentucky where it has started producing its own Bulleit bourbon and Bulleit rye whiskies.

While Diageo is coy about its mash bills, Modern Thirst lists the recipes for the Bulleit bourbons as 63% corn, 27% rye and 10% malted barley. Also according to Modern Thirst, most of the Orphan Barrel series are whopping 86% corn, a mere 6% rye, and 8% malted barley.

Barterhouse

Proof:	90.2
Age:	20 years
Type:	Not Straight
Style:	Extra Aged
Mash Bill:	Not available
Color:	Light Amber
Price:	$$$$$

Mike

Nose: Caramel and oak with some leather and spice.

Taste: Caramel and apricots with sweet spices and leather. A bit thin in the mouth.

Finish: Short and dry with oak and a hint of fruit.

Susan

Nose: Sweet oak, ripe peaches, light vanilla. Rather tight.

Taste: Caramel, vanilla, berries, sweet oak. Some leather.

Finish: Short and warm, ending in oak.

Notes

Interestingly, water does not change the profile at all. One of Diageo's "Orphan Barrel" bourbons bottled in Tullahoma, Tennessee.

My Score

Notes: _____

_____

_____

Appearance (1-5)	____	Nose (1-25)	____
Taste (1-25)	____	Finish (1-25)	____
Complexity (1-10)	____	Overall Impression (1-10)	____
		SCORE ____	

Blade and Bow

Proof:	92
Age:	NAS
Type:	Straight
Style:	Solera Aged
Mash Bill:	Proprietary
Color:	Dark Straw
Price:	$$$$

Mike

Nose: Creamy vanilla and sweet spice, ripe apples and pears. Just a hint of oak.

Taste: Apples and vanilla, with sweet spices-nutmeg and cinnamon. Water brings out sweet fruit and spice.

Finish: Fairly short. Starts sweet and gets spicy with some oak tannins. Water lengthens finish.

Susan

Nose: Dark fruit, light mint, and sweet vanilla.

Taste: Pears, sweet licorice, almonds. Biscotti in a glass.

Finish: Sweet and smooth. Just a touch of oak at the end.

Notes

Certainly snifter-worthy. Tiniest bit of water amplifies fruit and oak. This purports to have some of the last of the stock distilled at the legendary Stitzel-Weller Distillery in Shively, Kentucky.

My Score

Notes: _____

_____

_____

Appearance (1-5)	____	Nose (1-25)	____
Taste (1-25)	____	Finish (1-25)	____
Complexity (1-10)	____	Overall Impression (1-10)	____

SCORE ____

Blade and Bow
22-Year-Old

Proof:	92
Age:	22 years
Type:	Straight
Style:	Limited Release
Mash Bill:	Proprietary
Color:	Amber
Price:	$$$$$$

Mike

Nose: Lots of fruit. Apples and pears with a hint of berries. Vanilla and caramel.

Taste: Nice mouthfeel – chewy and thick. Fruit and spice balanced by some caramel and chocolate.

Finish: Very simple and short. The oak lasts longest, giving it a bit of spice.

Susan

Nose: Very fruity with peaches, chocolate, and sweet oak.

Taste: Fruit forward with notes of cocoa, honey, and caramel.

Finish: Long and warm. Very smooth and sweet.

Notes

Water dilutes the flavor. Do not add water or ice! Retailing for $180 per bottle, if you can find it. Worth splurging on for a shot in a good whiskey bar, where it is more likely to be found than on a store shelf.

My Score

Notes: _____

_____

_____

Appearance (1-5)	___	Nose (1-25)	___
Taste (1-25)	___	Finish (1-25)	___
Complexity (1-10)	___	Overall Impression (1-10)	___

SCORE ___

Bulleit

Proof:	90
Age:	NAS
Type:	Straight Bourbon
Style:	Traditional
Mash Bill:	Proprietary, but high rye
Color:	Straw
Price:	$$

Mike

Nose: Cream soda vanilla, light fruit – ripe pears and apples – touch of oak.

Taste: Rich vanilla and fruit – pears and berries with a little sweet spice and oak.

Finish: Long and spicy. Oak tannins turn to sweet spices – clove, cinnamon, allspice.

Susan

Nose: Candied nuts and light caramel with floral and vanilla notes hovering over the oak.

Taste: Cinnamon spice, bright fruit, and vanilla custard. Hint of mint.

Finish: Long, lingering, pumpkin pie spices and a distinctly oaky note.

Notes

A flavorful bourbon that can be enjoyed neat, but will be excellent in traditional bourbon cocktails. Very versatile and a real bargain at its price point.

My Score	
Notes: _____	
_____	
_____	
Appearance (1-5) ____	Nose (1-25) ____
Taste (1-25) ____	Finish (1-25) ____
Complexity (1-10) ____	Overall Impression (1-10) ____
SCORE ____	

Bulleit Cask Strength

Proof:	119
Age:	NAS
Type:	Straight
Style:	Barrel Strength
Mash Bill:	Proprietary, but high rye
Color:	Dark Straw
Price:	$$$$

Mike

Nose: Fruit and spice, caramel and a hint of honeysuckle flower.

Taste: Caramel and berries, baking spices and oak.

Finish: Very nice balance and oak dryness and fruit.

Susan

Nose: Bananas Foster, sweet mint, vanilla.

Taste: Loads of vanilla and ripe fruit – berries. Some oaky spice.

Finish: Smooth and warm, even at barrel proof.

Notes

Oddly, water makes it a bit astringent, rather than opening it up.

My Score

Notes: _____

_____

_____

Appearance (1-5)	____	Nose (1-25)	____
Taste (1-25)	____	Finish (1-25)	____
Complexity (1-10)	____	Overall Impression (1-10)	____

SCORE ____

Bulleit 10-Year-Old

Proof: 91.2
Age: 10 years
Type: Straight Bourbon
Style: Small Batch, Extra Aged

Mash Bill: Proprietary, but high rye
Color: Amber
Price: $$$$

Mike
Nose: Floral (roses) and vanilla. Pitted fruit- cherries and apricot. Hint of sweet spice cherries and apricot. Hint of sweet spice in the background.
Taste: Nice chewy mouthfeel with sweet apricot and some sweet cinnamon spice.
Finish: Long and dry. Starts sweet, but dried very quickly by the oak. Very pleasant.

Susan
Nose: Fruity and floral (apple, cherry) with almonds and balanced vanilla and caramel notes.
Taste: Creamy on the palate. More sweet almond and faint spices, supported by oak.
Finish: Long and spicy with oak at the end.

Notes
Very flavorful. A splash of water brings out more of floral character. This is a bourbon over which to linger. Sip slowly.

My Score

Notes: _____

_____

_____

Appearance (1-5) ____   Nose (1-25) ____
Taste (1-25) ____   Finish (1-25) ____
Complexity (1-10) ____   Overall Impression (1-10) ____
SCORE ____

Forged Oak

Proof:	90.5
Age:	15 years
Type:	Straight
Style:	Extra Aged
Mash Bill:	Proprietary
Color:	Dark Straw
Price:	$$$$$

Mike

Nose: Caramel and oak with a hint of tobacco. Some light apricot and honey.

Taste: Very light. Almost a bit thin. Caramel and apricots with some nutmeg and pepper.

Finish: A bit dry with oak tannins. A little short, too.

Susan

Nose: Caramel, sweet tobacco, a little mint, light apricots.

Taste: Caramel and vanilla with candied nuts. But lightweight for 15 years.

Finish: Lingering and sweet until a sharp note of pepper at the very end.

Notes

This is one of the so-called Orphan Barrel releases by Diageo from stores aged at the historic Stitzel-Weller Distillery in Louisville. Originally distilled at the New Bernheim Distillery in Louisville, which used to be owned by Diageo, but is now Heaven Hill's distillery.

My Score

Notes: _____

_____

_____

Appearance (1-5) ____	Nose (1-25)	____
Taste (1-25) ____	Finish (1-25)	____
Complexity (1-10) ____	Overall Impression (1-10)	____
	SCORE ____	

I.W. Harper

Proof:	82
Age:	NAS
Type:	Straight
Style:	Traditional
Mash Bill:	Proprietary
Color:	Light Amber
Price:	$$$

Mike

Nose: Caramel and citrus fruit. Some honeysuckle and oak.

Taste: Nice mouthfeel. A bit chewy with caramel and honey, orange peel, and tobacco.

Finish: Long and drying with oak tannins and pepper. Pepper increases over the course of the finish.

Susan

Nose: Caramel, light cinnamon, ripe pears.

Taste: Rich mouthfeel. Butter caramel/toffee. Sweet spices and ripe orchard fruits.

Finish: Begins sweet and dries to a light pepper ending.

Notes

Proof is an interesting choice. A couple of degrees stronger than the export version. Label states it was distilled in Kentucky. No source named.

My Score

Notes: _____

_____

_____

Appearance (1-5) ____	Nose (1-25)	____
Taste (1-25) ____	Finish (1-25)	____
Complexity (1-10) ____	Overall Impression (1-10)	____
	SCORE ____	

I.W. Harper
Gold Medal

Proof: 80
Age: NAS
Type: Straight Bourbon
Style: Not available

Mash Bill: Proprietary
Color: Light Amber
Price: $$$$$ (Export only)

Mike

Nose: Citrus fruit and vanilla, with hint of oak and honey spice (cloves?) hiding in the background.
Taste: Very easy to drink with no alcohol burn. Yet flavorful, with sweet corn, apple and sweet clove and nutmeg.
Finish: Long and sweet with spices and fruit. Just a hint of oak.

Susan

Nose: Honey and nuts, with vanilla and orange blossom over the underlying oak.
Taste: Buttered popcorn. Very rich and smooth with citrus and light spiciness.
Finish: Long and warm, but no burn. Ends in honey and fruit.

Notes

Notably flavorful, complex and satisfying for an 80 proof bourbon! Can be enjoyed neat, but would make a fantastic Old Fashioned. Available only in Asian markets.

My Score		
Notes: _____		
_____		
_____		
Appearance (1-5) ____	Nose (1-25)	____
Taste (1-25) ____	Finish (1-25)	____
Complexity (1-10) ____	Overall Impression (1-10)	____
SCORE ____		

I.W. Harper
12-Year-Old

Proof: 86
Age: 12 years
Type: Straight Bourbon
Style: Extra Aged

Mash Bill: Proprietary
Color: Amber Shading to Orange
Price: $$$$$$ (Export only)

Mike
Nose: Citrus, fruit and vanilla with fine leather and oak, plus honey and nutmeg.
Taste: Very easy to drink with no alcohol burn. Caramel and honey with some sweet peach fruit and cinnamon.
Finish: Long finish starts sweet and ends in honey with a nice oak dryness.

Susan
Nose: Well-balance vanilla, honey, and caramel, with prominent citrus.
Taste: Rich toffee, light fruit and hint of leather, with underlying spice.
Finish: Long and warm and buttery, with a pleasantly dry ending.

Notes
Great bourbon to drink with a meal. Works well with savory food. Regrettably, only available in Asian markets.

My Score

Notes: _____

_____

_____

Appearance (1-5) ____   Nose (1-25) ____
Taste (1-25) ____   Finish (1-25) ____
Complexity (1-10) ____   Overall Impression (1-10) ____
SCORE ____

I.W. Harper 15-Year-Old

Proof:	86
Age:	15 years
Type:	Straight Bourbon
Style:	Extra Aged
Mash Bill:	Proprietary
Color:	Light Amber
Price:	$$$$$

Mike

Nose: Caramel and vanilla citrus and apricots.

Taste: Carmel and apricots with nutmeg and tobacco.

Finish: Long. Starts sweet and gets dry with oak and pepper.

Susan

Nose: Butterscotch, caramel, and oak, and fruity spice.

Taste: Lots of vanilla and caramel, caramel corn. Sprinkling of nutmeg.

Finish: Long and dry, with a peppery ending.

Notes

An elegant, snifter-worthy sip. This was Batch SS-1 FGS.

My Score

Notes: _____

_____

_____

Appearance (1-5)	____	Nose (1-25)	____
Taste (1-25)	____	Finish (1-25)	____
Complexity (1-10)	____	Overall Impression (1-10)	____

SCORE ____

Rhetoric

Proof: 90
Age: 20 years
Type: Straight Bourbon
Style: Extra Aged

Mash Bill: Proprietary
Color: Amber
Price: $$$$$

Mike

Nose: Honeysuckle and caramel with ripe pears and oak.
Taste: Sweet caramel and honey with pears, apples and some spice. Nice mouthfeel with no burn and nice warmth in the throat.
Finish: Starts sweet and dries nicely with a long oak finish.

Susan

Nose: Rich caramel, almonds, ripe apricots, buttered corn.
Taste: Ripe apples and peaches on the tongue. Fruit salad with nuts and vanilla. Very chewy.
Finish: Long and warm and buttery, with a pleasantly dry ending.

Notes

As it breathes it opens up with more oak and citrus. Water makes this sip even sweeter, bringing out honey notes. One of the "Orphan Barrel" releases from Diageo. Company says that it comes from "barrels discovered at the back of he rickhouse" on the Stitzel-Weller property in Louisville. It was bottled at George Dickel in Tullahoma, TN.

My Score

Notes: _____

_____

_____

Appearance (1-5) _____   Nose (1-25) _____

Taste (1-25) _____   Finish (1-25) _____

Complexity (1-10) _____   Overall Impression (1-10) _____

SCORE _____

Additional Diageo Releases

Name: _____

Distillery: _____

Proof: _____ **Mash Bill:** _____
Age: _____ _____
Type: _____ **Color:** _____
Style: _____ **Price:** _____

My Score

Notes: _____
_____
_____

Appearance (1-5) ____   Nose (1-25) ____
Taste (1-25) ____   Finish (1-25) ____
Complexity (1-10) ____   Overall Impression (1-10) ____
SCORE ____

Name: _____

Distillery: _____

Proof: _____ **Mash Bill:** _____
Age: _____ _____
Type: _____ **Color:** _____
Style: _____ **Price:** _____

My Score

Notes: _____
_____
_____

Appearance (1-5) ____   Nose (1-25) ____
Taste (1-25) ____   Finish (1-25) ____
Complexity (1-10) ____   Overall Impression (1-10) ____
SCORE ____

FOUR ROSES

Bourbon distilleries: Four Roses Distillery,
Lawrenceburg, Ky.

Paul Jones created the Four Roses brand after the Civil War in Atlanta, Georgia using whiskey from the Rose distillery in that city. When Prohibition made Jones leave the state in 1884, he moved to Louisville, Ky., bringing his brand with him. Paul Jones dies in 1895 and the business passes to his nephew. In 1922 The Paul Jones Company purchases the Frankfort Distilleries Company and their license to sell medicinal whiskey during Prohibition. The business became known as Frankfort Distilleries and Four Roses was their leading brand.

In 1943 Seagrams purchased Frankfort Distilleries and Straight Bourbons were phased out in favor of blended whiskey in the United States, but Four Roses remained a straight Bourbon in the overseas markets of Europe and Japan. In 2002 Seagrams was sold to Diageo who sold the Four Roses Brand and distillery to Kirin. Kirin immediately discontinued the Four Roses blended whiskey and brought the Bourbon back to the American market as well as the overseas markets.

Four Roses is unique among bourbon distilleries in that it uses two different mash bills (one high corn, one high rye) and five different yeast strains. By combining each of the two mash bills with each of the five yeast strains, Four Roses has 10 different bourbon recipes. They are used in different proportions in the different Four Roses expressions.

Mash bills: E - 75% corn, 20% rye, 5% malted barley
B – 60% corn, 35% rye, 5% malted barley

Yeast Strain Codes: V – Light Fruitiness
K – Slightly Spicy
O – Rich Fruitiness
F – Herbal
Q – Floral

The four letter recipes are OBSV, OBSK, OBSQ, OBSO, OBSF and OESV, OESK, OESQ, OESO, OESF. The First O in each stands for the Lawrenceburg distillery, once known as Old Prentice. At one time this was one of five distilleries owned by Seagrams, which is how Four Roses wound up with five yeast strains. The S indicates that Four Roses is a straight bourbon.

In our notes we indicate which recipes are used in each bourbon. Finally, it is also of interest that Four Roses is unique among the bourbon distilleries in that it uses one story warehouses. Apparently, the ten recipes introduce enough variables to the bourbons without having to worry about aging at different rates at different warehouse levels!

In addition to the bourbons for which we have provided tasting notes, the distillery does annual, dated limited releases of specially selected Small Batch and Single Barrel bottlings.

Four Roses Yellow Label

Proof: 80
Age: NAS
Type: Straight Bourbon
Style: Traditional

Mash Bill: All 10 recipes
Color: Dark Straw
Price: $$

Mike

Nose: Very floral (roses?), caramel and vanilla with light fruit. Just a hint of oak and spice.
Taste: Sweet with apples, pears and vanilla. Not hot at all. Nice mouthfeel.
Finish: Starts sweet but gets dry and peppery. Long lasting. One of the best finishes of any 80 proof bourbon.

Susan

Nose: Floral, light vanilla/caramel with underlying cinnamon notes.
Taste: Sweet vanilla with pear. Light and smooth on the tongue.
Finish: Starts sweet and dries towards the end. Lingering. No burn whatsoever.

Notes

A lot of presence for an 80 proof bourbon. Excellent to have on hand for making any of the classic bourbon cocktails.

My Score

Notes: _____

_____

_____

Appearance (1-5) ____   Nose (1-25) ____

Taste (1-25) ____   Finish (1-25) ____

Complexity (1-10) ____   Overall Impression (1-10) ____

SCORE ____

Four Roses Elliott's Select

Proof: 106
Age: 14 years
Type: Straight
Style: Single Barrel, Barrel Proof, Extra Aged
Mash Bill: OESK
Color: Light Amber
Price: $$$$$$

Mike

Nose: Crème brulee and fruit –ripe apples and berries – hint of spice.

Taste: Sweet berry fruit, vanilla and caramel with some oak.

Finish: Long and fruity with well-balanced oak.

Susan

Nose: Cinnamon, ripe berries and cherries with crème brulee. As it opens, cashews and pistachios emerge.

Taste: Fruit, caramel, vanilla and some milk chocolate.

Finish: Long, smooth, warm. A true Kentucky hug.

Notes

Brent Elliott's first signature release for Four Roses after succeeding Jim Rutledge as Master Distiller. This was Barrel 53-2Q.

My Score

Notes: _____

_____

_____

Appearance (1-5) _____   Nose (1-25) _____

Taste (1-25) _____   Finish (1-25) _____

Complexity (1-10) _____   Overall Impression (1-10) _____

SCORE _____

Four Roses Fine Old Bourbon Black Label

Proof: 80
Age: At least 6 years
Type: Straight Bourbon
Style: Export only to Japan

Mash Bill: OBSK, OESK
Color: Dark Straw
Price: $$$

Mike

Nose: Apples, pears and berries. Vanilla and nutmeg with oak in the background.
Taste: Sweet caramel and apple fruit with cinnamon spice and oak. No burn and almost chewy mouthfeel.
Finish: Starts sweet but becomes dry and spicy as the oak kicks in. A great finish for an 80 proof bourbon.

Susan

Nose: Very sweet. Spicy vanilla with a touch of mint.
Taste: Vanilla crème brûlée with sweet spices. Creamy on the tongue.
Finish: Moderately long finish. Very smooth with no burn at all. Lingering creaminess.

Notes

Very well-balanced bourbon. Fine for both sipping with a splash or an ice cube and for making cocktails.

My Score

Notes: _____

_____

_____

Appearance (1-5) _____   Nose (1-25) _____
Taste (1-25) _____   Finish (1-25) _____
Complexity (1-10) _____   Overall Impression (1-10) _____
SCORE _____

Four Roses Single Barrel

Proof:	100
Age:	NAS
Type:	Straight Bourbon
Style:	Single Barrel
Mash Bill:	OBSV
Color:	Amber
Price:	$$$$

Mike

Nose:	Sweet fruit. Berries and cherries with vanilla and caramel and a little spice.
Taste:	Sweet berries and pears with some berries and spices. No burn and this is a 100 proof bourbon.
Finish:	Long and sweet. Dry oak quickly becomes caramel and vanilla.

Susan

Nose:	Vanilla, apple, pear with touch of cocoa and light spices.
Taste:	Sweet vanilla and caramel with cinnamon sprinkled pear. Creamy mouthfeel.
Finish:	Stays sweet to the very end of a long finish. Lingering cinnamon.

Notes

Complex and sophisticated, this still a bargain at its price. Another bourbon to savor post-dinner.

My Score

Notes: _____

_____

_____

Appearance (1-5) _____   Nose (1-25) _____

Taste (1-25) _____   Finish (1-25) _____

Complexity (1-10) _____   Overall Impression (1-10) _____

SCORE _____

Four Roses Single Barrel Private Selection

Proof:	116.6
Age:	10 years, 7 months
Type:	Straight Bourbon
Style:	Single Barrel, Barrel Proof, Extra Aged
Mash Bill:	OESF
Color:	Amber
Price:	$$$$$

Mike

Nose: Very floral and minty – some caramel and tobacco/leather notes. Water brings out some honeysuckle.

Taste: Mint, caramel, apple fruit and tobacco. Water tames the mint and brings out fruit and liquorice.

Finish: Long and minty. Water makes the finish a bit sweeter with fruit and mint.

Susan

Nose: Spicy caramel, figs, dates, sweet tobacco. Water amplifies floral notes.

Taste: Add water to release sweet caramel, mint, with spicy oak and ripe figs.

Finish: Long, smooth, spicy with sweet saddle leather and fruit. Luscious.

Notes

Barrel proof single barrel selections are made by restaurants, bars, retailers, and bourbon clubs. They usually come with exact age statements. Four Roses enthusiasts will want to find all ten recipes. Addition of water reveals full complexity.

My Score

Notes: _____

_____

_____

Appearance (1-5)	____	Nose (1-25)	____
Taste (1-25)	____	Finish (1-25)	____
Complexity (1-10)	____	Overall Impression (1-10)	____

SCORE ____

Four Roses Small Batch

Proof: 90
Age: NAS
Type: Straight Bourbon
Style: Small Batch

Mash Bill: OBSO, OBSK, OESO, OESK
Color: Light Amber
Price: $$$

Mike
Nose: Lots of apples, pears and flowers with vanilla and caramel and just a bit of oak.
Taste: Sweet fruit – pears. Vanilla and caramel with oaky spiciness. Nice mouthfeel – almost chewy.
Finish: Long with sweet fruit. Ends with caramel and just a touch of oak.

Susan
Nose: Caramel and vanilla with fresh pears and apples. Has oaky undertones.
Taste: Dark berry fruit, spices with vanilla and caramel creamy on the tongue.
Finish: Long, rich finish ending in light oak and a sprinkling of black pepper.

Notes
A fine sipping bourbon. Take it neat or with a splash of water.

My Score
Notes: _____
_____
_____

Appearance (1-5) ____   Nose (1-25) ____
Taste (1-25) ____   Finish (1-25) ____
Complexity (1-10) ____   Overall Impression (1-10) ____
SCORE ____

Four Roses Super Premium Platinum Label

Proof:	86
Age:	80% at least 8 years/20% 10 years
Type:	Straight
Style:	Export only to Japan
Mash Bill:	OBSK, OESK, OBSV, OESV
Color:	Dark Straw
Price:	$$$

Mike

Nose: Very floral – roses and apple blossom. A little anise/licorice, spice and oak.

Taste: Peppery spices and caramel. Vanilla accompanies by oak and anise.

Finish: Very long and dry as the oak tannins and and peppery spice quickly hide the sweetness.

Susan

Nose: Honey, orange blossom, toffee with prominent oak.

Taste: Sweet spices, rich vanilla/caramel. There's a touch of pear.

Finish: Long and smooth with sweet licorice at the very end.

Notes

Complex and assertive for such a moderately strong proof. Pleasant neat, but also a good choice for cocktail mixing.

My Score

Notes: _____

_____

_____

Appearance (1-5)	____	Nose (1-25)	____
Taste (1-25)	____	Finish (1-25)	____
Complexity (1-10)	____	Overall Impression (1-10)	____

SCORE ____

Additional Four Roses Releases

Name: _____

Distillery: _____

Proof: _____   **Mash Bill:** _____
Age: _____   _____
Type: _____   **Color:** _____
Style: _____   **Price:** _____

My Score		

Notes: _____
_____
_____

Appearance (1-5) ____   Nose (1-25) ____
Taste (1-25) ____   Finish (1-25) ____
Complexity (1-10) ____   Overall Impression (1-10) ____
SCORE ____

- -

Name: _____

Distillery: _____

Proof: _____   **Mash Bill:** _____
Age: _____   _____
Type: _____   **Color:** _____
Style: _____   **Price:** _____

My Score		

Notes: _____
_____
_____

Appearance (1-5) ____   Nose (1-25) ____
Taste (1-25) ____   Finish (1-25) ____
Complexity (1-10) ____   Overall Impression (1-10) ____
SCORE ____

HEAVEN HILL

Bourbon Distilleries: Bernheim Distillery, Louisville, Ky. •
Evan Williams Bourbon Experience, Louisville, Ky.

The five Shapira brothers, – Gary, Mose, George, Edward and David – decided to go into the distilling business after the repeal of Prohibition. They purchased the land once owned by William Heavenhill near Bardstown and built a distillery. The distillery opened in 1935 and the brothers hired a Beam to make their whiskey. It is still a family owned business with Edward's son Max at the helm. In 1996 a fire destroyed the distillery in Bardstown and the company purchased the Bernheim distillery in Louisville from Diageo. In 2014, Heaven Hill opened a small craft distillery and tour on Main Street in Louisville where they make one barrel of whiskey a day.

Heaven Hill has the second-largest stock of aging spirits in Kentucky, after Jim Beam. It contract distills for a number of independent bottlers.

As a privately held company, Heaven Hill does not have to release its mash bills. But Modern Thirst has listed 78% corn, 10% rye, and 12% malted barley for the non-wheated, wide release bourbons. Wheated brands may be 68% corn, 20% wheat, and 12% malted barley. Limited release Parker's Heritage whiskeys have a variety of mash bills.

Cabin Still

Proof:	80
Age:	36 months
Type:	Straight Bourbon
Style:	Traditional
Mash Bill:	Proprietary
Color:	Light Straw
Price:	$

Mike

Nose: Corn and vanilla. A hint of oak. Not complex.

Taste: Corn and vanilla with some oak tannins.

Finish: Short, but gets some oak and pepper toward the end.

Susan

Nose: Some mint, sweet corn, caramel.

Taste: Sweet on the tongue. Again, mint with a little sweet spice.

Finish: Medium long. Stays warm and sweet.

Notes

Considering that you can find this bourbon for under $10, it is well worth trying. Nice, light sip that will be a good "summer bourbon" with an ice cube.

My Score

Notes: _____

_____

_____

Appearance (1-5) ____   Nose (1-25) ____

Taste (1-25) ____   Finish (1-25) ____

Complexity (1-10) ____   Overall Impression (1-10) ____

SCORE ____

Elijah Craig Single Barrel

Proof:	132.4
Age:	12 years
Type:	Straight Bourbon
Style:	Single Barrel, Barrel Proof, Extra Aged
Mash Bill:	Proprietary
Color:	Rich Amber
Price:	$$$$$

Mike

Nose: Caramel with a hint of milk chocolate, ripe pears and apples, fine leather, sweet spices.

Taste: Sweet fruit – apricots, pears, and berries caramel and vanilla with nutmeg. Very rich mouthfeel with little burn.

Finish: Long and spicy with sweet oak.

Susan

Nose: Ripe figs, crème brûlée, roasted corn, and alcohol of its high proof.

Taste: Add water! It reveals ripe apple, pears and roasted corn. Multi-layered.

Finish: Long, sweet, and smooth.

Notes

This may prove difficult to find. Heaven Hill keeps changing age and availability of its Elijah Craig expressions. By the way, all the stories about Baptist minister Elijah Craig having been the first to put whiskey in charred oak barrels are fun, but mythological.

My Score

Notes: _____

_____

_____

Appearance (1-5)	____	Nose (1-25)	____
Taste (1-25)	____	Finish (1-25)	____
Complexity (1-10)	____	Overall Impression (1-10)	____

SCORE ____

Elijah Craig 12-Year-Old

Proof: 94
Age: 12 years
Type: Straight Bourbon
Style: Small Batch, Extra Aged

Mash Bill: Proprietary
Color: Light Amber
Price: $$$

Mike
Nose: Crème brûlée, apricots, and oak. Fine tobacco and leather with a hint of spice.
Taste: Apricots and caramel with some oak wood and spice.
Finish: Long. Starts sweet but finishes with oak and a hint of rotten peach.

Susan
Nose: Ripe peaches, roasted corn, caramel candy with a touch of wood smoke.
Taste: Pitted fruits, soft vanilla and buttered popcorn. Buttery mouthfeel.
Finish: Long and warm. Very smooth.

Notes
Not especially high proof, but just a few drops of water will amplify the fruit character. Very nice neat, too. Excellent for the price.

My Score
Notes: _____

Appearance (1-5) ____   Nose (1-25) ____
Taste (1-25) ____   Finish (1-25) ____
Complexity (1-10) ____   Overall Impression (1-10) ____
SCORE ____

Elijah Craig 18-Year-Old

Proof:	86
Age:	18 years
Type:	Straight
Style:	Single Barrel, Extra Aged
Mash Bill:	Not available
Color:	Straw
Price:	$$$$$$

Mike
Nose: Caramel, vanilla, and old leather.
Taste: Caramel, vanilla, fruit and spice.
Finish: Oak with a hint of rotten peach.

Susan
Nose: Vanilla, pears, hard candy.
Taste: Vanilla custard, almonds, marzipan, with some orchard fruit.
Finish: Long, smooth and sweet.

Notes
This was barrel number 4146. A few short years ago you could buy this bourbon for about $45 a bottle. No more!

My Score

Notes: _____

_____

_____

Appearance (1-5)	____	Nose (1-25)	____
Taste (1-25)	____	Finish (1-25)	____
Complexity (1-10)	____	Overall Impression (1-10)	____

SCORE ____

Elijah Craig 21-Year-Old

Proof: 90
Age: NAS
Type: Straight Bourbon
Style: Single Barrel, Extra Aged

Mash Bill: Not available
Color: Dark Straw
Price: $$$$$$

Mike
Nose: Vanilla and peaches with baking spice. Corn husk, nuts, hay loft.
Taste: Corn, vanilla, and spice.
Finish: Spice with a hint of rotten peaches.

Susan
Nose: Corn husk, nuts, hayloft.
Taste: Very herbal. Not unpleasant, just different. There's a bit of chocolate, too.
Finish: Surprisingly sweet finish with a coconut note.

Notes
This was from barrel number 18. A complex sip; we obviously had very different impressions of this bourbon!

My Score		
Notes: _____		
_____		
_____		
Appearance (1-5) ____	Nose (1-25)	____
Taste (1-25) ____	Finish (1-25)	____
Complexity (1-10) ____	Overall Impression (1-10)	____
SCORE ____		

Elijah Craig 23-Year-Old

Proof:	90
Age:	23 years
Type:	Straight Bourbon
Style:	Single Barrel, Extra Aged
Mash Bill:	Proprietary
Color:	Dark Amber/Bronze
Price:	$$$$$$

Mike

Nose: Crème brûlée, apricot, oak, fine leather and little tobacco.

Taste: Sweet fruit – peaches and apricots – caramel and vanilla. A bit of nutmeg and fine tobacco.

Finish: Very simple and short. The oak lasts longest, giving it a bit of spice.

Susan

Nose: Honey, dates, fruit cobbler, and sweet oaky wood.

Taste: Honey, caramel apple, a flash of coconut Leather and tobacco balanced against fruit and spices.

Finish: Long and lingering with warm fruit. A masterpiece.

Notes

This was Barrel 26, filled on 26 February, 1990. The retail price hovers around $200, so worthy of the best glassware and the finest cigar. Let it sit in the glass for a bit for all the layers to develop.

My Score

Notes: _____

_____

_____

Appearance (1-5)	____	Nose (1-25)	____
Taste (1-25)	____	Finish (1-25)	____
Complexity (1-10)	____	Overall Impression (1-10)	____

SCORE ____

Evan Williams

Proof:	80
Age:	NAS
Type:	Straight Bourbon
Style:	Traditional
Mash Bill:	Proprietary
Color:	Dark Straw
Price:	$$

Mike

Nose: Corn and vanilla with some sweet spice and oak. Not overly complex.

Taste: Nice mouthfeel with no alcohol burn, but warmth in the throat. Sweet corn and vanilla with a bit of apple and spice.

Finish: Starts sweet, but quickly dries to a nice oak finish.

Susan

Nose: Sweet buttered corn and vanilla. Light.

Taste: Sweet and smooth with a pleasant buttery texture. Candied nuts and sweet spices on the palate.

Finish: Long, smooth, and sweet. No burn.

Notes

A very good everyday bourbon at an excellent price. Makes a good Old Fashioned.

My Score	
Notes: _____	
_____	
_____	

Appearance (1-5) ____	Nose (1-25) ____
Taste (1-25) ____	Finish (1-25) ____
Complexity (1-10) ____	Overall Impression (1-10) ____
SCORE ____	

Evan Williams Barrel Proof

Proof:	125
Age:	NAS
Type:	Straight Bourbon
Style:	Barrel Proof
Mash Bill:	Not available
Color:	Amber
Price:	$$$$

Mike

Nose: Corn and caramel with some fruit and spices.

Taste: Corn, vanilla, oak, and spice. Not hot, but warm in the throat.

Finish: Very nice. Starts oak dry but sweetens with caramel.

Susan

Nose: Vanilla, peaches, pistachios, new leather.

Taste: Very fruity entry. Then crème brulee and nuts.

Finish: Peppery at barrel proof, but water reveals caramel.

Notes

Definitely add a bit of water or let an ice cube melt to reveal the full complexity of this bourbon.

My Score

Notes: _____

_____

_____

Appearance (1-5) ____   Nose (1-25) ____

Taste (1-25) ____   Finish (1-25) ____

Complexity (1-10) ____   Overall Impression (1-10) ____

SCORE ____

Evan Williams Black Label

Proof:	86
Age:	NAS
Type:	Straight Bourbon
Style:	Traditional

Mash Bill:	Not available
Color:	Dark Straw
Price:	$

Mike

Nose: Honey, vanilla, corn. Some pear fruit.

Taste: Pears and caramel with sweet spices (nutmeg or allspice?).

Finish: Long. Starts sweet and dries to oak and pepper.

Susan

Nose: Sweet vanilla, dash of cinnamon, hint of cocoa.

Taste: Vanilla, ripe peach, sweet spices. Hint of sweet mint Rich mouthfeel.

Finish: Warm and quite smooth. No burn. Ends in sweet oak.

Notes

An outstanding bargain in bourbon. Nice with an ice cube. Excellent for mixing cocktails.

My Score

Notes: _____

_____

_____

Appearance (1-5) _____   Nose (1-25) _____

Taste (1-25) _____   Finish (1-25) _____

Complexity (1-10) _____   Overall Impression (1-10) _____

SCORE _____

Evan Williams White Label

Proof:	100
Age:	NAS
Type:	Straight Bourbon
Style:	Bonded
Mash Bill:	Proprietary
Color:	Dark Straw
Price:	$$

Mike

Nose: Vanilla/caramel with some apple and apricot, cinnamon and nutmeg and a hint of oak.

Taste: Great mouthfeel, almost chewy with no burn. Apples, cinnamon, caramel, vanilla. Fine leather appears last.

Finish: Very nice with a bit of sweetness leading into some oak. Medium long.

Susan

Nose: Sweet caramel corn, cotton candy, vanilla ice cream, sweet spices.

Taste: Crème brûlée with candied almonds. Very smooth, sweet sip.

Finish: Sweetness lingers, but not cloying. Touch of oak at the end.

Notes

Very approachable bottled-in-bond bottle and an excellent price.

My Score

Notes: _____

_____

_____

Appearance (1-5) ____   Nose (1-25) ____

Taste (1-25) ____   Finish (1-25) ____

Complexity (1-10) ____   Overall Impression (1-10) ____

SCORE ____

Evan Williams Single Barrel 2004

Proof: 86.6
Age: 10 years
Type: Straight Bourbon
Style: Single Barrel, Extra Aged

Mash Bill: Proprietary
Color: Light Amber
Price: $$

Mike

Nose: Sweet fruit – apricots and berries with caramel and oak.

Taste: Caramel and apricots with some peppery spice, old leather, and oak.

Finish: Long and dry. Starts fruity and spicy but dries to nice oak finish.

Susan

Nose: Caramel, cocoa, cinnamon, and orchard fruits.

Taste: Cherry and caramel with a little ginger. Buttered corn.

Finish: Long and sweet, ending in sweet oak.

Notes

Another bargain-priced goody from Heaven Hill. Sip neat, but also excellent for cocktails. This was Barrel 591.

My Score

Notes: _____

_____

_____

Appearance (1-5) ____   Nose (1-25) ____

Taste (1-25) ____   Finish (1-25) ____

Complexity (1-10) ____   Overall Impression (1-10) ____

SCORE ____

Evan Williams 12-Year-Old

Proof:	101
Age:	12 years
Type:	Straight
Style:	Extra Aged
Mash Bill:	Proprietary
Color:	Amber/Copper
Price:	$$$$$$

Mike

Nose: Caramel and apples with ginger and nutmeg, fine tobacco and leather. Water brings out the oak.

Taste: Caramel, apple, hint of chocolate. Nutmeg cinnamon with some tobacco. Water amplifies the chocolate.

Finish: Long, but not too long. Oak and some pepper. Water removes most of the pepper and enhances the oak.

Susan

Nose: Chocolate-covered caramel, cashews and ripe apples.

Taste: Honey, caramel, cocoa. Water reveals apples and more caramel.

Finish: Long, smooth and caramel sweet. Dries to sweet oak.

Notes

The retail price is more than $100. But this "Extra Smooth Sour Mash" delivers.

My Score

Notes: _____

_____

_____

Appearance (1-5)	____	Nose (1-25)	____
Taste (1-25)	____	Finish (1-25)	____
Complexity (1-10)	____	Overall Impression (1-10)	____

SCORE ____

Evan Williams 23-Year-Old

Proof:	107
Age:	23 years
Type:	Straight Bourbon
Style:	Extra Aged
Mash Bill:	Proprietary
Color:	Dark Amber
Price:	$$$$$$

Mike

Nose: Caramel and chocolate with some fruit and spice. Fine tobacco and oak.

Taste: Not very hot, with some sweet caramel, oak and a hint of must or mold.

Finish: Starts sweet and dries nicely with a long oak finish.

Susan

Nose: Honey and molasses with notes of pears and sweet spices.

Taste: Closed at first, but water brings out pear, apple, honey. Complex, with a little cinnamon and leather.

Finish: Long and warm and buttery, with a pleasantly dry ending.

Notes

A little water lessens the mustiness detected by Mike. Limited annual release and one of the most expensive bourbons on the market.

My Score

Notes: _____

_____

_____

Appearance (1-5) _____   Nose (1-25) _____

Taste (1-25) _____   Finish (1-25) _____

Complexity (1-10) _____   Overall Impression (1-10) _____

SCORE _____

Evan Williams 1783

Proof: 86
Age: NAS
Type: Straight Bourbon
Style: Small Batch

Mash Bill: Proprietary
Color: Medium Dark Straw
Price: $$

Mike

Nose: Very light. Corn and vanilla with a bit of spice.
Taste: A bit thin in the mouth – corn and vanilla with some apple fruit and pepper spice.
Finish: Short. A bit of corn sweetness but fades quickly with only a hint of oak.

Susan
Nose: Light caramel with herbal notes. A little burnt sugar and cocoa powder.
Taste: Nutty. Vanilla fades into corn and sweet spices.
Finish: Somewhat short, but a bright oak note at the end.

Notes
Evan Williams was a Louisville brick maker and distiller, who had one of the earliest commercial distilleries in Kentucky. Yes, the distilling license was granted in 1783.

My Score

Notes: _____

_____

_____

Appearance (1-5) ____   Nose (1-25) ____

Taste (1-25) ____   Finish (1-25) ____

Complexity (1-10) ____   Overall Impression (1-10) ____

SCORE ____

Fighting Cock

Proof:	103
Age:	6 years
Type:	Straight Bourbon
Style:	Traditional
Mash Bill:	Proprietary
Color:	Light Amber
Price:	$$

Mike

Nose: Vanilla and oak with leather and sweet spice. A little honeysuckle.

Taste: Thick, chewy mouthfeel. Ripe apple and pepper spice with fine tobacco.

Finish: This is where the fight comes in, with boatloads of spicy pepper and oak.

Susan

Nose: Big fruit and caramel nose with hazelnut and vanilla bean.

Taste: Nutty caramel and chocolate. Truly a Snickers Bar in a glass.

Finish: Buttered popcorn that rolls across the tongue and finishes in pepper and oak.

Notes

A very well-balanced bourbon and an excellent value with age and proof. "I like it. Too bad about the name," says Susan.

My Score

Notes: _____

_____

_____

Appearance (1-5)	____	Nose (1-25)	____
Taste (1-25)	____	Finish (1-25)	____
Complexity (1-10)	____	Overall Impression (1-10)	____

SCORE ____

Heaven Hill Old Style Bourbon Bottled-in-Bond

Proof: 100
Age: 6 years
Type: Straight Bourbon
Style: Bonded

Mash Bill: Proprietary
Color: Light Amber
Price: $$

Mike

Nose: Very light. A bit of vanilla/caramel or honey and some plums and sweet spice.
Taste: Plums or apricots with caramel and vanilla. Fine leather and oak. Nutmeg or allspice.
Finish: Starts sweet and with caramel and sweet spices and dries to nice, long oak finish.

Susan

Nose: Light vanilla and caramel with a little honey orange essence.
Taste: Vanilla and cherry. A little water amplifies these flavors.
Finish: Long and sweet, ending in spicy oak.

Notes

Mike: "I want this with a cigar!" Very good example of a bottled-in-bond bourbon at an excellent price. But only available in Kentucky and Indiana. Pick it up for your collection if you are in the area.

My Score

Notes: _____

_____

_____

Appearance (1-5) ____   Nose (1-25) ____
Taste (1-25) ____   Finish (1-25) ____
Complexity (1-10) ____   Overall Impression (1-10) ____
SCORE ____

Heaven Hill Old Style Bourbon Green Label

Proof:	80
Age:	36 months
Type:	Straight Bourbon
Style:	Traditional
Mash Bill:	Proprietary
Color:	Light Straw
Price:	$

Mike

Nose: Very light. Corn and vanilla with a hint of spiced oak.

Taste: Corn and vanilla with some pepper spice. Light, but not watery.

Finish: Medium long with some oak spiciness.

Susan

Nose: Sweet vanilla, light spices, ripe apple. Surprisingly present for age and proof.

Taste: Vanilla with a touch of oak. Not much fruit or spice on the palate.

Finish: Medium. Starts sweet and fades to warm, black pepper.

Notes

Lightweight and young, but this could be a very nice introductory bourbon for someone afraid that whiskey is "harsh." Very pleasant, if simple.

My Score

Notes: _____

_____

_____

Appearance (1-5) _____   Nose (1-25) _____

Taste (1-25) _____   Finish (1-25) _____

Complexity (1-10) _____   Overall Impression (1-10) _____

SCORE _____

Heaven Hill Select Stock

Proof: 128
Age: 8 years
Type: Special Finish
Style: Single Barrel, Barrel Proof

Mash Bill: Not available
Color: Light Amber
Price: $$$$$$

Mike

Nose: Crème brulee, fruit and hint of oak.
Taste: Caramel and raisins with some pepper spice.
Finish: Oak and alcohol. Water helps and makes the finish less astringent.

Susan

Nose: Vanilla and pears with dash of cinnamon.
Taste: Crème brulee, ripe pears, almonds.
Finish: Hot at barrel proof. Much sweeter with water.

Notes

Definitely add water! Bit warm in the mouth. Dash of water takes away the burn and leaves the flavors intact. Bourbon was finished in used cognac barrels. This was barrel #44823. Distilled 9-24-03. Bottled 5-5-14.

My Score

Notes: _____

_____

Appearance (1-5) _____   Nose (1-25) _____

Taste (1-25) _____   Finish (1-25) _____

Complexity (1-10) _____   Overall Impression (1-10) _____

SCORE _____

Henry McKenna

Proof:	80
Age:	NAS
Type:	Straight Bourbon
Style:	Traditional
Mash Bill:	Proprietary
Color:	Straw
Price:	$

Mike

Nose: Very light. Vanilla and candy corn with a hint of oak.

Taste: Bit thin and watery. Vanilla and corn, with some pepper spice. Little heat.

Finish: Starts sweet and dries nicely with a long oak finish.

Susan

Nose: Light. Some ripe peach and a little vanilla and sweet corn.

Taste: Candy corn and peppery spice. Not complex but pleasant.

Finish: Long and warm and buttery, with a pleasantly dry ending.

Notes

Nice, inexpensive whiskey for a mixed drink such as bourbon and ginger ale.

My Score

Notes: _____

_____

_____

Appearance (1-5)	____	Nose (1-25)	____
Taste (1-25)	____	Finish (1-25)	____
Complexity (1-10)	____	Overall Impression (1-10)	____

SCORE ____

Henry McKenna Bottled-in-Bond

Proof:	100
Age:	10 years
Type:	Straight Bourbon
Style:	Bonded, Single Barrel
Mash Bill:	Proprietary
Color:	Dark Straw
Price:	$$$

Mike

Nose: Caramel and vanilla up front. Old leather, ripe peach or apricot, and oak.

Taste: Very soft on the tongue with fruit and spice – nutmeg. A bit of honey and oak toward the end.

Finish: Starts sweet and dries nicely with a long oak finish.

Susan

Nose: Sweet, floral, with vanilla and caramel candy.

Taste: Caramel apple with sweet vanilla and powdered sugar. Drop of water brings out cherries and chocolate.

Finish: Long, smooth, and warm. No burn.

Notes

This was Barrel No. 1210. Don't be afraid to add a little water to bring out more fruit and spice.

My Score

Notes: _____

_____

_____

Appearance (1-5)	____	Nose (1-25)	____
Taste (1-25)	____	Finish (1-25)	____
Complexity (1-10)	____	Overall Impression (1-10)	____

SCORE ____

J.T.S. Brown
Bottled-in-Bond

Proof: 100
Age: At least 4 years
Type: Straight Bourbon
Style: Bottled-in-Bond

Mash Bill: Not available
Color: Light Straw
Price: $$

Mike
Nose: Vanilla and corn with a hint of oak.
Taste: Corn and vanilla with a hint of honey.
Finish: Dry and spicy with oak and pepper.

Susan
Nose: Vanilla, banana, nutmeg.
Taste: Caramel entry, but quite spicy on the tongue.
Finish: Short, peppery.

Notes
Perhaps a bit lightweight for a bottled-in-bond. But, very interesting to compare to other B.I.B. brands.

My Score

Notes: _____

_____

_____

Appearance (1-5) _____   Nose (1-25) _____

Taste (1-25) _____   Finish (1-25) _____

Complexity (1-10) _____   Overall Impression (1-10) _____

SCORE _____

Larceny

Proof:	92
Age:	NAS
Type:	Straight Bourbon
Style:	Wheated
Mash Bill:	Proprietary
Color:	Straw
Price:	$$

Mike
Nose:	Not complex. Vanilla/caramel with some apples and pears.
Taste:	Sweet with vanilla/caramel and apple and honey. Hint of pecan and sweet spices.
Finish:	Starts sweet with caramel and dries out with some nice oak tannins. Long and lightly dry.

Susan
Nose:	Touch of honey under the vanilla and caramel.
Taste:	Sweet vanilla custard. Some marzipan. A little nutmeg and cinnamon.
Finish:	Medium long and smooth with a touch of dry oak at the very end.

Notes
Good value in a wheated bourbon.

My Score

Notes: _____

_____

_____

Appearance (1-5) ____   Nose (1-25) ____

Taste (1-25) ____   Finish (1-25) ____

Complexity (1-10) ____   Overall Impression (1-10) ____

SCORE ____

Old Fitzgerald Bottled-in-Bond

Proof:	100
Age:	NAS
Type:	Straight Bourbon
Style:	Wheated
Mash Bill:	Proprietary
Color:	Dark Straw
Price:	$$

Mike

Nose: Vanilla and hazelnuts with some apple fruit and a whisper of oak.

Taste: Vanilla and apples with some oak and pecan. A bit of pepper spice toward the end. Nice warmth in the throat, but not hot.

Finish: Long and spicy with a nice oak dryness.

Susan

Nose: Honey, caramel, whiff of sweet spice. A hint of cocoa. Very smooth.

Taste: Honey, candied apples, vanilla, and buttered corn. A little water brings out cinnamon.

Finish: Lingering with light oak and pepper.

Notes

Elegant bonded bourbon that becomes fruitier and sweeter with a little bit of water. But don't add too much.

My Score

Notes: _____

_____

_____

Appearance (1-5) ____   Nose (1-25) ____

Taste (1-25) ____   Finish (1-25) ____

Complexity (1-10) ____   Overall Impression (1-10) ____

SCORE ____

Old Fitzgerald Prime

Proof: 80
Age: NAS
Type: Straight Bourbon
Style: Wheated

Mash Bill: Proprietary
Color: Light Straw
Price: $

Mike

Nose: Light. Corn, apples, vanilla.
Taste: Sweet vanilla and honey with apples pecans. Bit of pepper spice at the end.
Finish: Long and spicy with a nice oak dryness.

Susan

Nose: Sweet vanilla, ripe pears. Light.
Taste: Vanilla and ripe pear on the tongue, too. and Nice mouthfeel. Very smooth.
Finish: Lingering, with a sweet oak ending.

Notes

Great value in a wheated bourbon. Sip neat or with a small cube of ice.

My Score

Notes: _____

_____

_____

Appearance (1-5) _____   Nose (1-25) _____
Taste (1-25) _____   Finish (1-25) _____
Complexity (1-10) _____   Overall Impression (1-10) _____
SCORE _____

Parker's Heritage Collection Promise of Hope

Proof:	96
Age:	NAS
Type:	Straight Bourbon
Style:	Traditional
Mash Bill:	Proprietary
Color:	Amber
Price:	$$$$$

Mike

Nose: Very rich with caramel, dates, honey, sweet spices – nutmeg, cinnamon – and oak.

Taste: Almost like cognac, with pitted fruit – cherries and apricots. Cinnamon, fine tobacco and oak.

Finish: Long. Starts sweet with fruit and then gets a little more oak. Never looses sweetness.

Susan

Nose: Candies fruit and nuts. Sweet pecans, luscious vanilla and caramel. Sweet spices and new leather.

Taste: Chewy. Reminds me of cognac. Spicy tobacco and leather with rich vanilla and lots of peppery oak.

Finish: Long, warm and very, very smooth. Ends with sweet oak. Gorgeous.

Notes

Would be great with a steak and with a fine cigar afterwards. Gets better as it breathes! While there is no age statement on the bottle, the Heaven Hill website stated it was 10 years old.

My Score		
Notes: _____		
_____		
_____		
Appearance (1-5) ____	Nose (1-25)	____
Taste (1-25) ____	Finish (1-25)	____
Complexity (1-10) ____	Overall Impression (1-10)	____
SCORE ____		

Very Special Old Fitzgerald

Proof: 90
Age: 12 years
Type: Straight Bourbon
Style: Wheated, Extra Aged

Mash Bill: Proprietary
Color: Straw
Price: $$$

Mike
Nose: Great nose. Caramel, apples, pecans. Candied apple in a glass! Hints of milk chocolate and honey.
Taste: Nice warmth in the throat with caramel apples and peppery spice. Honey on the tongue quickly leads into other flavors.
Finish: Long and sweet with only a hint of oak tannins.

Susan
Nose: Honey, caramel, ripe apples, with rich vanilla aroma.
Taste: Caramel-coated fruit and nut bar. Honey on the tongue. Almost heartbreakingly smooth.
Finish: Long, honeyed with buttered sweet corn at the very end.

Notes
Another gem at great price. But getting hard to find. Also fine with a meal and a good smoke.

My Score

Notes: _____

_____

_____

Appearance (1-5) ____   Nose (1-25) ____

Taste (1-25) ____   Finish (1-25) ____

Complexity (1-10) ____   Overall Impression (1-10) ____

SCORE ____

William Heavenhill Bottled-in-Bond

Proof:	100
Age:	132 months (11 years)
Type:	Straight
Style:	Bonded, Small Batch
Mash Bill:	Not available
Color:	Dark Straw
Price:	$$$$$$

Mike

Nose: Caramel and peaches with oak tones.

Taste: Caramel corn and a hint of peach. Lots of oak, in a good way.

Finish: Dry and oaky with a hint of sweet caramel.

Susan

Nose: Caramel, dates, figs, light spice.

Taste: Dried fruit and oak. Think Fig Newton.

Finish: Long and warm with caramel at the end.

Notes

One of the limited editions sold in the Heaven Hill gift shops in Bardstown and Louisville. Each small batch was mingled from fewer than 12 barrels.

My Score

Notes: _____

_____

_____

Appearance (1-5) ____   Nose (1-25) ____

Taste (1-25) ____   Finish (1-25) ____

Complexity (1-10) ____   Overall Impression (1-10) ____

SCORE ____

William Heavenhill Cask Strength

Proof:	135.6
Age:	15 years
Type:	Straight
Style:	Extra Aged, Barrel Proof
Mash Bill:	75% corn, 13% rye, 12% malted barley
Color:	Rich Amber
Price:	$$$$$$

Mike

Nose: Chocolate caramel chew. Some apricot and spice. Water releases spice.

Taste: Chocolate and caramel with apricots and berries with oak. Water brings out the chocolate.

Finish: Dry with oak and chocolate. Water makes finish less oaky, more chocolate.

Susan

Nose: Caramel, vanilla, chocolate, dark dried fruit, pecans.

Taste: Vanilla, saddle leather, milk chocolate, pitted fruit. Water amplifies fruit and nuts.

Finish: Long, warm, sweet and complex.

Notes

One of the limited editions sold in the Heaven Hill gift shops in Bardstown and Louisville. Retail about $250. You may find it in the top bourbon bars in big cities. Know there were only about 350 bottles.

My Score

Notes: _____

_____

_____

Appearance (1-5)	____	Nose (1-25)	____
Taste (1-25)	____	Finish (1-25)	____
Complexity (1-10)	____	Overall Impression (1-10)	____

SCORE ____

Additional Heaven Hill Releases

Name: _____

Distillery: _____

Proof: _____   **Mash Bill:** _____
Age: _____   _____
Type: _____   **Color:** _____
Style: _____   **Price:** _____

My Score	
Notes: _____	
_____	
_____	
Appearance (1-5) ____	Nose (1-25) ____
Taste (1-25) ____	Finish (1-25) ____
Complexity (1-10) ____	Overall Impression (1-10) ____
SCORE ____	

Name: _____

Distillery: _____

Proof: _____   **Mash Bill:** _____
Age: _____   _____
Type: _____   **Color:** _____
Style: _____   **Price:** _____

My Score	
Notes: _____	
_____	
_____	
Appearance (1-5) ____	Nose (1-25) ____
Taste (1-25) ____	Finish (1-25) ____
Complexity (1-10) ____	Overall Impression (1-10) ____
SCORE ____	

KENTUCKY BOURBON DISTILLERS/ WILLETT

Bourbon Distilleries: Willett Distillery,
Bardstown, Kentucky

Thompson Willett and his bother John L. Willett founded the Willett Distillery after the repeal of Prohibition. It opened in 1936. By St Patrick's Day 1937, the first barrel of whiskey was rolled into Warehouse A. For a short period of time in the late 1970's the distillery was converted to a fuel alcohol plant.

On December 16, 1972, a Norwegian decanter craftsman, Even G. Kulsveen, married the daughter of Thompson Willett, Martha Harriett Willett. Together, Even & Martha purchased the property in 1984, formed Kentucky Bourbon Distillers, Ltd., DSP-KY-78 and began extensive renovations. Even & Martha's children Britt and Drew Kulsveen, joined the family business in the 2000's. After several years of refurbishment, the family began distilling again in 2012. Today Drew serves as Willett Master Distiller.

Johnny Drum Green Label

Proof:	80
Age:	NAS
Type:	Straight Bourbon
Style:	Traditional
Mash Bill:	Proprietary
Color:	Straw
Price:	$$

Mike

Nose: Fruit and spice – apricots and pepper. Very light.

Taste: Caramel and apricot with pepper spice and a little hint of oak.

Finish: Long. Starts sweet, but gets peppery and dry with oak tannins.

Susan

Nose: Caramel candy with a tiny bit of vanilla. Strongly reminiscent of Sugar Daddy candy.

Taste: Caramel dominates the palate as well. Not complex but flavorful at 80 proof.

Finish: Smooth with, you guessed, lots of caramel. Dries to a spicy end.

Notes

Caramel lovers will want this on their bar shelves. Enjoy with a chocolate dessert.

My Score

Notes: _____

_____

_____

Appearance (1-5) _____   Nose (1-25) _____

Taste (1-25) _____   Finish (1-25) _____

Complexity (1-10) _____   Overall Impression (1-10) _____

SCORE _____

Johnny Drum
Black Label

Proof:	86
Age:	8 years
Type:	Straight Bourbon
Style:	Traditional
Mash Bill:	Proprietary
Color:	Dark Amber
Price:	$$$$$

Mike

Nose: Light. Caramel and vanilla with a hint of oak.

Taste: Very lightly flavored. Caramel and vanilla with a hint of honey.

Finish: Very long and nice with a peppery ending and a bit of oak.

Susan

Nose: Vanilla, marzipan, bright herbal notes.

Taste: Peppery on the palate, with lots of vanilla with some nuts and pitted fruit.

Finish: Long finish with no burn.

Notes

Let this one open up in the glass for full flavor. Perhaps a drop of water would be useful, too. But no more than a drop.

My Score

Notes: _____

_____

_____

Appearance (1-5)	____	Nose (1-25)	____
Taste (1-25)	____	Finish (1-25)	____
Complexity (1-10)	____	Overall Impression (1-10)	____

SCORE ____

Johnny Drum Private Stock

Proof:	101
Age:	NAS
Type:	Straight Bourbon
Style:	Traditional
Mash Bill:	Proprietary
Color:	Amber
Price:	$$$

Mike

Nose: Smores. Caramel, marshmallow with a bit of chocolate, a little ripe apple and oak.

Taste: Caramel and milk chocolate with apples and pepper spice. Not hot, nice warmth in the throat.

Finish: Starts sweet and dries out with some oak and pepper spice.

Susan

Nose: Honeycomb, caramel, almonds, dried cherries.

Taste: Drier on the palate than on the nose. Oaky vanilla and nuts.

Finish: Medium long. Smooth. No burn.

Notes

Water brings out more fruit, especially cherries and some chocolate. Very nice with beef entrée or a cigar.

My Score

Notes: _____

_____

_____

Appearance (1-5) _____   Nose (1-25) _____

Taste (1-25) _____   Finish (1-25) _____

Complexity (1-10) _____   Overall Impression (1-10) _____

SCORE _____

Kentucky Vintage

Proof:	90
Age:	NAS
Type:	Straight
Style:	Small Batch
Mash Bill:	Proprietary
Color:	Dark Straw
Price:	$$$$

Mike

Nose: Vanilla and caramel with some dates and cherries. Small oak and floral notes.

Taste: Sweet vanilla and berries with some pepper spice.

Finish: Starts sweet and quickly becomes dry with spice and oak. last a long time.

Susan

Nose: Ripe apples and light spices with sweet oak.

Taste: Warm vanilla and walnuts. Not as much fruit as in the nose.

Finish: Long, warm, peppery.

Notes

Batch No. 13-30.

My Score

Notes: _____

_____

_____

Appearance (1-5) _____   Nose (1-25) _____

Taste (1-25) _____   Finish (1-25) _____

Complexity (1-10) _____   Overall Impression (1-10) _____

SCORE _____

Noah's Mill

Proof:	114.3
Age:	NAS
Type:	Straight
Style:	Small Batch
Mash Bill:	Proprietary
Color:	Light Amber
Price:	$$$$

Mike

Nose: Milk chocolate and caramel with some ripe peaches and tobacco. Some oak wood and very pleasant spice.

Taste: Caramel and apricots with oak and pepper spice. Water brings out the fruit and tames the pepper.

Finish: Long and dry. Water amplifies the oak.

Susan

Nose: Honey, caramel, cinnamon and nutmeg.

Taste: Add water to reveal sweet toffee, raisins, dates, and vanilla.

Finish: Long and smooth. No burn here.

Notes

Water brings out all the layers of flavor in this high proof sip. Batch QBC No. 14-61.

My Score

Notes: _____

_____

_____

Appearance (1-5) _____   Nose (1-25) _____

Taste (1-25) _____   Finish (1-25) _____

Complexity (1-10) _____   Overall Impression (1-10) _____

SCORE _____

Old Bardstown 80

Proof:	80
Age:	NAS
Type:	Straight Bourbon
Style:	Traditional
Mash Bill:	Not available
Color:	Straw
Price:	$$

Mike

Nose: Nice nose for 80 proof. Vanilla and honeysuckle with a hint of oak.

Taste: A little thin, but still sweet with caramel, apple fruit, and honey.

Finish: Starts a bit sweet and fades to some oak. Ends quickly.

Susan

Nose: Green apples and a little vanilla. Quite light.

Taste: Roasted, buttered corn. Light oak and a little honey.

Finish: Dries to black pepper and oak.

Notes
One of the first releases from Willett distilled on site. Quite nice for its low proof.

My Score

Notes: _____

_____

_____

Appearance (1-5) _____   Nose (1-25) _____

Taste (1-25) _____   Finish (1-25) _____

Complexity (1-10) _____   Overall Impression (1-10) _____

SCORE _____

Old Bardstown 90

Proof: 90
Age: NAS
Type: Straight
Style: Traditional

Mash Bill: Not available
Color: Light Amber
Price: $$

Mike
Nose: Orange blossoms, caramel, and baking spice.
Taste: Oranges, caramel, cinnamon, and spice.
Finish: Very nice! Starts spicy, but dries out with some sweet oak.

Susan
Nose: Corn, nutmeg, a little honey.
Taste: Caramel corn and sweet nuts. Some orange.
Finish: Warm and smooth with sweet oak.

Notes
One of the first releases from Willett distilled on site. Very attractive price, about $20 per bottle. Willett says they are using a low barrel entry proof.

My Score		
Notes: _____		
_____		
_____		
Appearance (1-5) ____	Nose (1-25)	____
Taste (1-25) ____	Finish (1-25)	____
Complexity (1-10) ____	Overall Impression (1-10)	____
SCORE ____		

Old Bardstown Bottled-in-Bond

Proof:	100
Age:	At least 4 years
Type:	Straight
Style:	Bonded
Mash Bill:	Not available
Color:	Dark Straw
Price:	$$

Mike

Nose: Vanilla, nutmeg, allspice. A bit of fruit and oak.

Taste: Nice mouthfeel, almost chewy. With caramel and apples leading into some oak pepper.

Finish: Long and interesting with oak spice. Ends quickly.

Susan

Nose: Caramel, vanilla, dark cherries.

Taste: Smooth sip with caramel, cocoa, some fruit and toasted oak.

Finish: Long, smooth, dry. very pleasant.

Notes

Water makes the bourbon sweeter, but one-dimensional. Made by Willett at its Bardstown distillery.

My Score

Notes: _____

_____

_____

Appearance (1-5) ____   Nose (1-25) ____

Taste (1-25) ____   Finish (1-25) ____

Complexity (1-10) ____   Overall Impression (1-10) ____

SCORE ____

Old Bardstown Estate Bottled

Proof:	101
Age:	NAS
Type:	Straight Bourbon
Style:	Traditional
Mash Bill:	Proprietary
Color:	Light Amber
Price:	$$$

Mike

Nose: Corn, vanilla, caramel with apples and pears and a hint of oak.

Taste: Corn, vanilla, caramel toffee with some apple, pepper spice and fine leather.

Finish: Starts peppery, but gets sweet before drying with some nice oak tannins.

Susan

Nose: Caramel, old leather, sweet oak, orange peel.

Taste: Caramel, toffee, citrusy spice with a touch of honey.

Finish: Sweet at the front and smooths to a long, dry ending.

Notes

Very smooth for the proof. Add a little, but very little, water to bring out more fruit. Limited availability outside of Kentucky.

My Score

Notes: _____

_____

_____

Appearance (1-5) ____   Nose (1-25) ____

Taste (1-25) ____   Finish (1-25) ____

Complexity (1-10) ____   Overall Impression (1-10) ____

SCORE ____

Pure Kentucky Extra Aged

Proof:	107
Age:	NAS
Type:	Straight
Style:	Small Batch
Mash Bill:	Proprietary
Color:	Light Amber
Price:	$$$$$

Mike

Nose: Sweet with caramel and oak, a hint of leather and sweet spices.

Taste: Fruity with berries and apricots. Vanilla, caramel and sweet spice – cinnamon, allspice. Some leather and oak.

Finish: Very nice. Starts sweet and gets spicy and dry with oak.

Susan

Nose: Caramel with perhaps a little leather. Dried fruit emerges after a couple of minutes.

Taste: Vanilla and nuts. Very like a candy bar, but not too sweet. Fruit blossoms with water.

Finish: Long and sweet with a spicy kick at the end.

Notes

Absolutely add a little water (or an ice cube) to bring out all the fruity/spicy character in this bourbon. The high proof can handle it.

My Score

Notes: _____

_____

_____

Appearance (1-5)	____	Nose (1-25)	____
Taste (1-25)	____	Finish (1-25)	____
Complexity (1-10)	____	Overall Impression (1-10)	____

SCORE ____

Rowan's Creek

Proof: 100.1
Age: NAS
Type: Straight Bourbon
Style: Small Batch

Mash Bill: Proprietary
Color: Straw
Price: $$$$

Mike

Nose: Vanilla and bread dough. Not overly complex. Hint of apples and hazelnuts.

Taste: Apricots and caramel with some some pepper spice and pipe tobacco.

Finish: Long and nice, starts sweet with fruit and dries to oak tannins.

Susan

Nose: Ripe apples and pears. Caramel. Fruit dominates, but a little yeasty, too.

Taste: Caramel with a touch of tobacco and new leather. Bright and peppery on the tongue.

Finish: Long and quite smooth for the proof. Dries to sweet oak.

Notes

Very good with a cigar.

My Score		
Notes: _____		
_____		
_____		
Appearance (1-5) ____	Nose (1-25)	____
Taste (1-25) ____	Finish (1-25)	____
Complexity (1-10) ____	Overall Impression (1-10)	____
SCORE ____		

Willett Pot Still Reserve

Proof: 94
Age: NAS "aged until fully mature."
Type: Straight Bourbon
Style: Traditional

Mash Bill: Proprietary
Color: Dark Straw
Price: $$$$

Mike

Nose: Corn, vanilla, caramel and sweet pipe tobacco.
Taste: Sweet corn, caramel and some pepper spice with a hint of tobacco. A bit chewy. Nice. No burn.
Finish: Starts peppery. Dries to nice oak.

Susan

Nose: Vanilla with some dark cherry and sprinkling of pumpkin pie spices.
Taste: Cherries, vanilla, toasted marshmallow. Rich mouthfeel.
Finish: Sweet to start and lingers to light peppery ending. Not at all hot.

Notes

Probably the most eye-catching bottle on the market. A bonus that the bourbon within is good, too.

My Score

Notes: _____

_____

_____

Appearance (1-5) _____   Nose (1-25) _____

Taste (1-25) _____   Finish (1-25) _____

Complexity (1-10) _____   Overall Impression (1-10) _____

SCORE _____

Additional KBD/Willett Releases

Name: _____

Distillery: _____

Proof: _____   **Mash Bill:** _____
Age: _____   _____
Type: _____   **Color:** _____
Style: _____   **Price:** _____

My Score

Notes: _____
_____
_____

Appearance (1-5) ____   Nose (1-25) ____
Taste (1-25) ____   Finish (1-25) ____
Complexity (1-10) ____   Overall Impression (1-10) ____
SCORE ____

Name: _____

Distillery: _____

Proof: _____   **Mash Bill:** _____
Age: _____   _____
Type: _____   **Color:** _____
Style: _____   **Price:** _____

My Score

Notes: _____
_____
_____

Appearance (1-5) ____   Nose (1-25) ____
Taste (1-25) ____   Finish (1-25) ____
Complexity (1-10) ____   Overall Impression (1-10) ____
SCORE ____

MICHTER'S

Chatham Imports rescued the Michter's brand from the dustpan of history in the 1990s. The brand was created in Pennsylvania in the 1950s and survived until the 1980s when the distillery went dark and the owners walked away from it, leaving the distillery and some inventory to the bank. The present owners saved the brand found old barrels for sale and contract distilled whiskies. Since 2015, Michter's has been distilling its own whiskies at its new distillery in Shively, Kentucky which happens to be right next door to Brown-Forman's distillery.

Michter's US*1 Barrel Strength

Proof: 110.6
Age: NAS
Type: Straight
Style: Barrel Strength

Mash Bill: Not available
Color: Amber
Price: $$$$$

Mike
Nose: Caramel apple or ripe pear with a little oak and spices.
Taste: Caramel and ripe apple, stone fruit and nutmeg.
Finish: Long and dry with oak and spice.

Susan
Nose: Toffee, vanilla, orange blossom. Whiff of cinnamon.
Taste: Sweet corn and lashings of caramel and vanilla with dried fruit.
Finish: Impressively smooth at this proof. Dries to sweet oak.

Notes
Water brings out fruit, cinnamon, and nutmeg and dries the finish. Excellent "book bourbon." Savor a sip after each chapter you read of your book of the evening. Released only in Kentucky.

My Score	
Notes: _____	
_____	
_____	
Appearance (1-5) ____	Nose (1-25) ____
Taste (1-25) ____	Finish (1-25) ____
Complexity (1-10) ____	Overall Impression (1-10) ____
SCORE ____	

Michter's US*1 Small Batch Bourbon

Proof:	91.4
Age:	NAS
Type:	Not Straight
Style:	Small Batch
Mash Bill:	Not available
Color:	Light Straw
Price:	$$$$

Mike

Nose: Caramel, toffee and fine leather. A bit of fruit – ripe pears.

Taste: Sweet caramel and apricots with pepper spice. Not overly complex. Nice mouthfeel with no burn.

Finish: Long. Starts sweet but gets dry with oak tannins and pepper spice.

Susan

Nose: Toffee, lots of pepper spice and vanilla with touch of ripe apple and honey.

Taste: Carmel corn and pepper spice with a tiny bit of green apple. Buttery mouthfeel.

Finish: Long and dry. Very peppery.

Notes

Try it in a Manhattan with a very good quality vermouth. Experiment with bitters to bring out the fruit notes. Michter's bourbons are currently sourced from other distilleries.

My Score

Notes: _____

_____

_____

Appearance (1-5) ____   Nose (1-25) ____

Taste (1-25) ____   Finish (1-25) ____

Complexity (1-10) ____   Overall Impression (1-10) ____

SCORE ____

Michter's US*1 Small Batch Toasted Barrel Finished

Proof: 91.4
Age: NAS
Type: Not Straight
Style: Small Batch #14I539

Mash Bill: Not available
Color: Dark Straw
Price: $$$$

Mike
Nose: Butterscotch and caramel. Sweet corn and butter. Fine leather and oak.
Taste: Butterscotch, vanilla, corn and oak with some sweet honey and apple.
Finish: Long. Starts sweet and the oak kicks in to dry it out. Very good.

Susan
Nose: Wood smoke, vanilla, leather, and peaches.
Taste: Vanilla ice cream with fruit and Small cocoa note and hint of mint. It's a sundae!
Finish: Long and sweet, with a fine smooth oak note a the end.

Notes
Great with a steak and a pipe afterwards.

My Score

Notes: _____

_____

_____

Appearance (1-5) ____   Nose (1-25) ____
Taste (1-25) ____   Finish (1-25) ____
Complexity (1-10) ____   Overall Impression (1-10) ____
SCORE ____

Michter's 10-Year-Old

Proof:	94.4
Age:	10
Type:	Straight
Style:	Small Batch, Extra Aged
Mash Bill:	Not available
Color:	Very Dark Straw
Price:	$$$$$

Mike

Nose: Caramel and milk chocolate with some apricot fruit. Just hint of spice.

Taste: Apricot and caramel with some sweet spice. Nutmeg and cinnamon with fine tobacco.

Finish: Long and dry with oak tannins and pepper. tannins and pepper spice.

Susan

Nose: Honeycomb, vanilla, touch of ripe cherries.

Taste: Honey, pitted fruit, sweet corn. Very mellow.

Finish: Long and dry with just a little pepper at the very end.

Notes

Addition of a little water makes the finish much sweeter. The fruit carries on longer.

My Score		
Notes: _____		
_____		
_____		
Appearance (1-5) _____	Nose (1-25)	_____
Taste (1-25) _____	Finish (1-25)	_____
Complexity (1-10) _____	Overall Impression (1-10)	_____
SCORE _____		

Michter's 20-Year-Old

Proof:	114.2
Age:	NAS
Type:	Straight
Style:	Single Barrel, #37/38, Extra Aged
Mash Bill:	Not available
Color:	Amber
Price:	$$$$$$

Mike

Nose: Crème brûlée, caramel and vanilla with some oak and sweet spice.

Taste: Caramel and apricot. Dates with oak wood and pepper spice.

Finish: Long and dry with oak tannins and pepper spice.

Susan

Nose: Vanilla, caramel, heavy honey with underlying spice and oak.

Taste: Serious sweet oak from the aging. But mellow with pitted fruit and honeycomb.

Finish: Long and dry, but very, very smooth.

Notes

Very smooth and elegant sip for its age and proof. A splash of water amplifies the sweet notes.

My Score

Notes: _____

_____

_____

Appearance (1-5) ____   Nose (1-25) ____

Taste (1-25) ____   Finish (1-25) ____

Complexity (1-10) ____   Overall Impression (1-10) ____

SCORE ____

Additional Michter's Releases

Name: _____

Distillery: _____

Proof: _____ **Mash Bill:** _____
Age: _____ _____
Type: _____ **Color:** _____
Style: _____ **Price:** _____

My Score		
Notes: _____		
_____		
_____		
Appearance (1-5) ____	Nose (1-25)	____
Taste (1-25) ____	Finish (1-25)	____
Complexity (1-10) ____	Overall Impression (1-10)	____
SCORE ____		

Name: _____

Distillery: _____

Proof: _____ **Mash Bill:** _____
Age: _____ _____
Type: _____ **Color:** _____
Style: _____ **Price:** _____

My Score		
Notes: _____		
_____		
_____		
Appearance (1-5) ____	Nose (1-25)	____
Taste (1-25) ____	Finish (1-25)	____
Complexity (1-10) ____	Overall Impression (1-10)	____
SCORE ____		

SAZERAC COMPANY

Bourbon Distilleries: Buffalo Trace Distillery, Frankfort, Ky., • Barton 1792 Distillery, Bardstown, Ky. • A. Smith Bowman Distillery, Fredericksburg, Va.

Thomas Handy purchased the Sazerac Coffee House in 1869 and eventually became the Sazerac Company. They purchased the Ancient Age distillery in 1992 and changed the name to Buffalo Trace in 1997. In 2003 Sazerac Company purchased the A. Smith Bowman Distillery and in 2009 they purchased Barton Brands and the Barton 1792 distillery.

Buffalo Trace started life as the OFC distillery founded by E. H. Taylor, Jr. in 1870. Taylor loses control of the distillery to the firm of Gregory and Stagg in 1879 and the distillery eventually becomes known as the Geo. T. Stagg distillery. During prohibition the distillery was tied to Schenley distilleries Corporation who purchase the distillery outright in 1933. It remains part of Schenley until 1984 when it becomes an independent distillery.

Tom Moore founded Barton 1792 in 1889. The distillery was closed during Prohibition but the Moore family re-opened it after Repeal. In 1944 Oscar Getz purchased the distillery and changed the name to the Barton Distillery. Getz retires in 1982 and the distillery was sold in 1983. It changed hands several times before it finally landed with Sazerac in 2009.

The A. Smith Bowman distillery was found in 1934 in Fairfax County, Va. In 1988 the distillery was relocated to its present site and retained only the pot still doubler, purchasing new make from other distilleries to double distill for their Bourbon brands. In 2003 the distillery was sold to Sazerac.

A. Smith Bowman

Smith Bowman Distillery opened after repeal of prohibition with Virginia Gentleman being introduced as a 2-year-old Bourbon in 1935. It was conceived as a distillery where the grains were grown on the property for the whiskey, but quickly outgrew that concept. It remained a family owned business until purchased by Sazerac in 2003.

Bowman Brothers

Proof:	90
Age:	NAS
Type:	Straight
Style:	Small Batch
Mash Bill:	Proprietary
Color:	Dark Straw
Price:	$$$$

Mike

Nose: Butter, caramel, and corn with a little pepper spice.

Taste: Candy corn and pepper spice with a bit of oak.

Finish: Long and dry with oak tannins and pepper spice.

Susan

Nose: Vanilla, honey, pleasant apple fruit and a tickling of pepper.

Taste: Surprisingly spicy after the sweet nose. Sweet corn and vanilla, too.

Finish: Sweet honey fades to pepper spice.

Notes

Comes from A. Smith Bowman Distillery, Fredericksburg, VA.

My Score

Notes: _____

_____

_____

Appearance (1-5) ____	Nose (1-25)	____
Taste (1-25) ____	Finish (1-25)	____
Complexity (1-10) ____	Overall Impression (1-10)	____

SCORE ____

John J. Bowman

Proof: 100
Age: NAS
Type: Straight
Style: Single Barrel

Mash Bill: Proprietary
Color: Dark Straw
Price: $$$$

Mike

Nose: Honey and vanilla with corn and oak.
Taste: Honey and corn, Candy corn with some oak and sweet spices.
Finish: Long and dry with spicy pepper and oak tannins.

Susan

Nose: Vanilla and apples, hint of sweet spice.
Taste: Buttery, yeasty, and toasty. Beautifully balanced.
Finish: Long and sweet. barely dries.

Notes

Comes from A. Smith Bowman Distillery, Fredericksburg, VA. Very smooth, elegant bourbon.

My Score

Notes: _____

_____

_____

Appearance (1-5) ____ Nose (1-25) ____
Taste (1-25) ____ Finish (1-25) ____
Complexity (1-10) ____ Overall Impression (1-10) ____
SCORE ____

Additional A. Smith Bowman Releases

Name: _____

Distillery: _____

Proof: _____   **Mash Bill:** _____
Age: _____   _____
Type: _____   **Color:** _____
Style: _____   **Price:** _____

My Score

Notes: _____
_____
_____

Appearance (1-5) ____   Nose (1-25) ____
Taste (1-25) ____   Finish (1-25) ____
Complexity (1-10) ____   Overall Impression (1-10) ____
SCORE ____

Name: _____

Distillery: _____

Proof: _____   **Mash Bill:** _____
Age: _____   _____
Type: _____   **Color:** _____
Style: _____   **Price:** _____

My Score

Notes: _____
_____
_____

Appearance (1-5) ____   Nose (1-25) ____
Taste (1-25) ____   Finish (1-25) ____
Complexity (1-10) ____   Overall Impression (1-10) ____
SCORE ____

BARTON 1792

Uses three different mash bills – BW 4, BW 6, BW 8 – including for bourbons contract distilled for independent bottlers. But no information released about grain proportions. That said Modern Thirst has published 75% corn, 15% rye, and 10 malted barley as the mash bill for the distillery's labels. Again, use this information advisedly.

1792 Full Proof

Proof: 125
Age: ~ 8 ½ years
Type: Straight
Style: Non-Chill Filtered

Mash Bill: Not available
Color: Dark Straw
Price: $$$$

Mike

Nose: Brown sugar and fruit.
Taste: Apples and pears. Cinnamon and cloves.
Finish: Dry oak and sweet fruit.

Susan

Nose: A caramel bomb with chocolate sprinkles.
Taste: Caramel, chocolate, fruit, and cloves.
Finish: Long, sweet, warm.

Notes

When the bourbon came out of the barrel it was 132-142 proof. Distilled water was used to return the bourbon to the proof at which it entered the barrel. Hence, "full proof."

My Score		
Notes: _____		
_____		
_____		
Appearance (1-5) ____	Nose (1-25) ____	
Taste (1-25) ____	Finish (1-25) ____	
Complexity (1-10) ____	Overall Impression (1-10) ____	
SCORE ____		

1792 High Rye

Proof: 94.3
Age: NAS
Type: Straight
Style: Small Batch

Mash Bill: Higher rye than usual expression
Color: Dark Straw
Price: $$$$

Mike
Nose: Candied fruit – cherries and dates.
Taste: Tobacco, cherries and dates, caramel, and sweet spice.
Finish: Long, dry, and spicy.

Susan
Nose: Caramel, spice, candy corn, sweet mint.
Taste: Surprisingly sweet for high rye content. Bing cherries and sweet mint.
Finish: Long with sweet oak and a whiff of honey.

Notes
The definition of "small batch" here is 80-120 barrels. A remarkably mellow sip for a robust rye mash bill.

My Score
Notes: _____
_____
_____

Appearance (1-5) ____   Nose (1-25) ____
Taste (1-25) ____   Finish (1-25) ____
Complexity (1-10) ____   Overall Impression (1-10) ____
SCORE ____

1792 Port Finish

Proof:	88.9
Age:	8 years
Type:	Straight
Style:	Special Finish
Mash Bill:	Not available
Color:	Light Amber
Price:	$$$$

Mike

Nose: Fruit and caramel. More port than bourbon.

Taste: Fruity with raisins and berries, some caramel and a hint of sweet spices.

Finish: Short and fruity with a hint of oak.

Susan

Nose: Port sweetness evident with some vanilla and honey.

Taste: Berries, caramel, sweet spices. Touch of licorice.

Finish: Long and fruity with sweet oak.

Notes

The bourbon spent six years in oak barrels and two more in port barrels. Water brings out the fruit.

My Score

Notes: _____

_____

_____

Appearance (1-5) _____   Nose (1-25) _____

Taste (1-25) _____   Finish (1-25) _____

Complexity (1-10) _____   Overall Impression (1-10) _____

SCORE _____

1792 Ridgemont Reserve

Proof: 93.7
Age: 8 years
Type: Straight Bourbon
Style: Small Batch

Mash Bill: BW 8
Color: Amber
Price: $$$$

Mike

Nose: Very complex. Vanilla/caramel, fine leather, sweet spice – nutmeg. Very ripe apple.

Taste: Nice mouthfeel. Apples and caramel with sweet spices that become a bit peppery. A little oak just before the finish.

Finish: Long and spicy with peppery spice and caramel. Very nice.

Susan

Nose: Vanilla, black pepper, new leather, cinnamon and light oak. Multilayered.

Taste: Vanilla and pepper. More sweet spices. Faint flavor of dark fruit mid-palate, but more spicy than fruity.

Finish: Long finish starts sweet and ends with black Pepper.

Notes

A good bourbon to accompany food. Enjoy with a variety of entrees. Fine with a fruity dessert. Good neat or mixed in cocktails, too.

My Score

Notes: _____

_____

_____

Appearance (1-5)	____	Nose (1-25)	____
Taste (1-25)	____	Finish (1-25)	____
Complexity (1-10)	____	Overall Impression (1-10)	____

SCORE ____

1792 Sweet Wheat

Proof:	91.2
Age:	NAS
Type:	Straight
Style:	Wheated
Mash Bill:	Not available
Color:	Straw
Price:	$$$

Mike

Nose: Caramel and apples with a little oak and pecans.

Taste: Caramel apple fruit with some vanilla and hazelnuts.

Finish: Starts sweet with some caramel, but slowly gets some oak.

Susan

Nose: Sweet corn, ripe apples, nutmeg.

Taste: Lots of vanilla, some pecans, sweet spices.

Finish: Smooth and drying to sweet oak.

Notes

Lovers of wheated bourbons will enjoy this. Limited release in 2015, but may still be on bourbon bar shelves.

My Score

Notes: _____

_____

_____

Appearance (1-5)	____	Nose (1-25)	____
Taste (1-25)	____	Finish (1-25)	____
Complexity (1-10)	____	Overall Impression (1-10)	____
	SCORE ____		

Colonel Lee

Proof:	80
Age:	NAS
Type:	Straight Bourbon
Style:	Traditional
Mash Bill:	BW 4
Color:	Light Straw
Price:	$

Mike

Nose: Vanilla and cherries/apricots, with a little leather and oak. Very light on the nose.

Taste: Sweet vanilla and corn with a bit of honey and pepper spice. A bit of oak and tobacco.

Finish: Starts sweet, but gets drier with the oak tannins and pepper.

Susan

Nose: Light caramel, faint nuttiness, oak notes.

Taste: Caramel corn, pecans, beeswax. Vanilla asserts itself in the middle of the mouth.

Finish: Medium finish with a peppery kick at the very end.

Notes

An inexpensive bourbon that is a natural to serve mixed with cola or ginger ale.

My Score

Notes: _____

_____

_____

Appearance (1-5) ____   Nose (1-25) ____

Taste (1-25) ____   Finish (1-25) ____

Complexity (1-10) ____   Overall Impression (1-10) ____

SCORE ____

Kentucky Gentleman

Proof: 80
Age: NAS
Type: Bourbon a Blend
Style: Traditional

Mash Bill: BW 8
Color: Light Straw
Price: $

Mike

Nose: Vanilla and corn with some leather, corn and toasted marshmallow.

Taste: Very light. Corn and vanilla with a little pepper spice.

Finish: Short and dry. Very disappointing on the finish.

Susan

Nose: Very simple – alcohol and wood with an undertone of vanilla.

Taste: Faint wood smoke and little vanilla and corn.

Finish: Flavors flash by. Very short and warm.

Notes

Drink this with mixers such as ginger ale or Coke.

My Score

Notes: _____

_____

_____

Appearance (1-5) ____   Nose (1-25) ____

Taste (1-25) ____   Finish (1-25) ____

Complexity (1-10) ____   Overall Impression (1-10) ____

SCORE ____

Kentucky Tavern

Proof:	80
Age:	NAS
Type:	Straight Bourbon
Style:	Traditional
Mash Bill:	BW 4
Color:	Very Light Straw
Price:	$

Mike

Nose: Caramel corn and oak with a hint of tobacco.
Taste: Very light with sweet corn and vanilla. A bit or fruit – apricot or peach – and pepper spice.
Finish: Starts sweet, but gets drier as the oak tannins kick in with some sweet spice.

Susan

Nose: Vanilla, sweet corn, dash of cinnamon.
Taste: Stone fruitiness (cherries?) with sweet caramel, vanilla and sweet spices.
Finish: Medium length finish that dries to the end. Smooth throughout; no burn.

Notes

Nice sip for the price. Louisville chef Kathy Cary, the owner of famed restaurant Lilly's, uses Kentucky Tavern to make her savory KT steak sauce served with the beef tenderloin sandwich.

My Score

Notes: _____

_____

_____

Appearance (1-5)	____	Nose (1-25)	____
Taste (1-25)	____	Finish (1-25)	____
Complexity (1-10)	____	Overall Impression (1-10)	____

SCORE ____

Ten High

Proof:	80
Age:	4 years
Type:	Bourbon a Blend
Style:	Traditional
Mash Bill:	BW 4
Color:	Pale Straw
Price:	$

Mike

Nose:	Alcohol, light vanilla. Very simple nose.
Taste:	Slightly musty. A little vanilla and corn.
Finish:	Short and sweet. A little mustiness.

Susan

Nose:	Very simple. Sweet corn and vanilla.
Taste:	Sweet vanilla and corn. A little hot mid-palate.
Finish:	Light, quick finish with touch of mustiness But no burn.

Notes

Because this is a blend, a high proportion is grain neutral spirits, which keeps the price bottom shelf. Inexpensive whiskey to use in your bourbon and Coke.

My Score		
Notes: _____		
_____		
_____		
Appearance (1-5) ____	Nose (1-25) ____	
Taste (1-25) ____	Finish (1-25) ____	
Complexity (1-10) ____	Overall Impression (1-10) ____	
SCORE ____		

Very Old Barton 80

Proof: 80
Age: NAS
Type: Straight Bourbon
Style: Traditional

Mash Bill: BW 4
Color: Amber
Price: $

Mike
Nose: Sweet caramel and fine leather. Apples and pears with some oak and tobacco.
Taste: A bit thin and watery. Sweet caramel and pears with oak tannins.
Finish: Very sweet at the start and gets peppery and dry. A bit short, but pleasant.

Susan
Nose: Caramel, apricot and sweet corn. A little spiced oak.
Taste: Oak up front followed by caramel and dried fruit.
Finish: Warm and smooth as it moves from sweet to spicy.

Notes
Good mixing bourbon for either cocktails or with carbonated sodas.

My Score

Notes: _____

_____

_____

Appearance (1-5) ____   Nose (1-25) ____
Taste (1-25) ____   Finish (1-25) ____
Complexity (1-10) ____   Overall Impression (1-10) ____
SCORE ____

Very Old Barton 86

Proof: 86
Age: 6 years
Type: Straight Bourbon
Style: Traditional

Mash Bill: BW 6
Color: Dark Straw
Price: $

Mike

Nose: Sweet caramel and leather. Corn and vanilla with a hint of oak. As it breathes, there is more caramel.
Taste: Caramel and oak. A bit thin, but spicy. A little fine leather, tobacco and fruit.
Finish: Short, but spicy with oak.

Susan

Nose: Caramel and marzipan with vanilla and cherries.
Taste: Vanilla and cherries with nuts and nutmeg.
Finish: Short, warm and spicy.

Notes

Priced to be a reliable everyday house bourbon.

My Score		
Notes: _____		
_____		
_____		
Appearance (1-5) ____	Nose (1-25)	____
Taste (1-25) ____	Finish (1-25)	____
Complexity (1-10) ____	Overall Impression (1-10)	____
SCORE ____		

Very Old Barton 90

Proof: 90
Age: 6 years
Type: Straight Bourbon
Style: Traditional

Mash Bill: BW 6
Color: Light Amber
Price: $

Mike

Nose: Apples and caramel with fine leather. Honey and sweet spices (nutmeg?). Hint of oak.

Taste: Honey and apples with some cinnamon spice, tobacco and oak.

Finish: Short and spicy. Starts sweet, but gets some peppery spice and oak.

Susan

Nose: Banana nut bread.

Taste: Vanilla, honey and sweet spices including cinnamon and allspice. Fruit on mid-palate.

Finish: Medium and smooth, pepper but no bite.

Notes

Excellent price point on this sipping bourbon that can be enjoyed with a little water. Would make a lovely Manhattan.

My Score

Notes: _____

_____

_____

Appearance (1-5) ____   Nose (1-25) ____

Taste (1-25) ____   Finish (1-25) ____

Complexity (1-10) ____   Overall Impression (1-10) ____

SCORE ____

Very Old Barton 100

Proof:	100
Age:	6 years
Type:	Straight Bourbon
Style:	Bonded
Mash Bill:	BW 6
Color:	Amber
Price:	$

Mike

Nose: Honey, apples, caramel and fine leather. Sweet spice and vanilla.

Taste: Very smooth with no burn, but a little warmth in the throat. Apples, caramel and tobacco. Sweet spice – cinnamon.

Finish: Long – starts fruity and sweet but gets dry and spicy. The oak really comes through at the end.

Susan

Nose: Black cherry, vanilla bean and cocoa.

Taste: Crème caramel, cherry pie, cinnamon and nuts.

Finish: Smooth, long, warm and sweet with a fine spicy oak ending.

Notes

A lot of complexity for the price. Good neat or with a splash of water. Mike's favorite bourbon to cook with "because its flavors really come through in cooking."

My Score

Notes: _____

_____

_____

Appearance (1-5)	____	Nose (1-25)	____
Taste (1-25)	____	Finish (1-25)	____
Complexity (1-10)	____	Overall Impression (1-10)	____

SCORE ____

Zackariah Harris

Proof:	80
Age:	NAS
Type:	Straight Bourbon
Style:	Traditional
Mash Bill:	BW 4
Color:	Light Straw
Price:	$

Mike

Nose: Vanilla and cherries with a little leather and oak.

Taste: Light and sweet – Corn, vanilla and a hint of pitted fruit; apricots or cherries

Finish: Surprisingly nice with sweet fruit and peppery on the end.

Susan

Nose: Banana, candy corn, and oak.

Taste: Sweet corn, touch of clove. Vanilla predominates on the mid-palate.

Finish: Unexpectedly long for its proof, with sweet spices at the end.

Notes

A rather more complex sip than might be expected from the proof and the price.

My Score

Notes: _____

_____

_____

Appearance (1-5) ____   Nose (1-25) ____

Taste (1-25) ____   Finish (1-25) ____

Complexity (1-10) ____   Overall Impression (1-10) ____

SCORE ____

Additional Barton Releases

Name: _____

Distillery: _____

Proof: _____   **Mash Bill:** _____
Age: _____   _____
Type: _____   **Color:** _____
Style: _____   **Price:** _____

My Score

Notes: _____
_____
_____

Appearance (1-5) _____   Nose (1-25) _____
Taste (1-25) _____   Finish (1-25) _____
Complexity (1-10) _____   Overall Impression (1-10) _____
SCORE _____

Name: _____

Distillery: _____

Proof: _____   **Mash Bill:** _____
Age: _____   _____
Type: _____   **Color:** _____
Style: _____   **Price:** _____

My Score

Notes: _____
_____
_____

Appearance (1-5) _____   Nose (1-25) _____
Taste (1-25) _____   Finish (1-25) _____
Complexity (1-10) _____   Overall Impression (1-10) _____
SCORE _____

BUFFALO TRACE

Limited Bottlings:

E.H. Taylor

Single Oak Project

Other Experimental Bottlings

Two mash bills – #1 and #2, which has higher rye content than #1. Exact recipes Not available. According to Modern Thirst, #1 is 75% corn, 10% rye, 15% malted barley. (We have also seen accounts claiming it is 80% corn.) Mash bill #2, again from Modern Thirst, may be 75% corn, 15% rye, and 10% malted barley. The Van Winkle bourbons may be 70% corn, 16% wheat, and 14% malted barley. In any event, Buffalo Trace is not telling.

Ancient Age

Proof:	80
Age:	NAS
Type:	Straight Bourbon
Style:	Traditional
Mash Bill:	#2
Color:	Straw
Price:	$

Mike

Nose: Candy corn and sweet spice. Nutmeg? But, simple overall.

Taste: Very thin on the palate. Corn and vanilla with a hint of oak.

Finish: Starts sweet but becomes dry with oak.

Susan

Nose: Sweet licorice and candy corn.

Taste: Orange note evolves into vanilla.

Finish: Medium. Warm without burn.

Notes

Balanced, inexpensive bourbon you may keep on hand for everyday uses.

My Score

Notes: _____

_____

_____

Appearance (1-5) ____   Nose (1-25) ____

Taste (1-25) ____   Finish (1-25) ____

Complexity (1-10) ____   Overall Impression (1-10) ____

SCORE ____

Ancient Age 10 Star

Proof:	90
Age:	NAS
Type:	Straight Bourbon
Style:	Traditional
Mash Bill:	#2
Color:	Dark Straw
Price:	$

Mike

Nose: Sweet caramel and cherries with a hint of sweet spices – cinnamon and a hint of oak.

Taste: Apricots and dates, caramel and spice – pepper and nutmeg.

Finish: Long and dry with oak tannins and spice.

Susan

Nose: Vanilla ice cream, ripe stone fruit, sweet spices.

Taste: Vanilla with sweet oak tannin, peach and Pear with sprinkling of spice.

Finish: Medium long. Rather hot and peppery on the tongue, but nutmeg revealed at the very end.

Notes

This is a more complex sip than you would expect from its price. Certainly there are more expensive bourbons that are not as interesting.

My Score

Notes: _____

_____

_____

Appearance (1-5)	____	Nose (1-25)	____
Taste (1-25)	____	Finish (1-25)	____
Complexity (1-10)	____	Overall Impression (1-10)	____
	SCORE ____		

Ancient Age 90

Proof:	90
Age:	36 months
Type:	Straight Bourbon
Style:	Traditional
Mash Bill:	#2
Color:	Straw
Price:	$

Mike

Nose: Sweet corn and vanilla, with a hint of oak wood and young ethanol.

Taste: Ethanol and corn; a little vanilla and pepper spice.

Finish: Short and sweet with nutmeg and a hint of oak.

Susan

Nose: Toffee/caramel with notes of sweet smoke, bright berries.

Taste: Sweet caramel and corn. A little clove heat, but no burn.

Finish: Fairly short. Spice smooths to corn and vanilla sweetness.

Notes

While still fairly uncomplicated, the 90 proof, as would be expected, has more heft than the 80 proof Ancient Age.

My Score

Notes: _____

_____

_____

Appearance (1-5)	____	Nose (1-25)	____
Taste (1-25)	____	Finish (1-25)	____
Complexity (1-10)	____	Overall Impression (1-10)	____

SCORE ____

Ancient Ancient Age

Proof:	86
Age:	10 years
Type:	Straight Bourbon
Style:	Extra Aged
Mash Bill:	#2
Color:	Light Amber
Price:	$$

Mike

Nose: Caramel and fruit – apples, pears, dates. Hint of oak wood and sweet spices.

Taste: Apples and caramel with hint of pecan. Almost chewy mouthfeel with some sweet spice – nutmeg and cinnamon.

Finish: Long. Starts sweet and spicy but gets drier as it progresses.

Susan

Nose: Loads of fruits and spices – peach, pear cinnamon and a little clove and vanilla.

Taste: Peaches and pears dusted in cinnamon. Rich vanilla on mid-palate with a bit of cocoa.

Finish: Long, sweet, and warm. Spice at the very end.

Notes

Beautifully balanced 10-year-old bourbon that tastes far more expensive than it is. Very suitable for sipping neat or with a splash.

My Score

Notes: _____

_____

_____

Appearance (1-5) ____   Nose (1-25) ____

Taste (1-25) ____   Finish (1-25) ____

Complexity (1-10) ____   Overall Impression (1-10) ____

SCORE ____

Blanton's Single Barrel

Proof:	93
Age:	NAS
Type:	Straight Bourbon
Style:	Single Barrel
Mash Bill:	Buffalo Trace #2 which is high in rye
Color:	Amber
Price:	$$$$

Mike

Nose: Apples and caramel with a bit of oak and leather. Opens after a minute to reveal cherries and dates.

Taste: Apples, vanilla, oak and leather with some sweet spice – nutmeg.

Finish: Long, dry and spicy, with oak tannins and sweet spices.

Susan

Nose: Honey vanilla, light spiciness with a touch of caramel. Fruit appears late.

Taste: Light, creamy mouthfeel, rich vanilla with prominent notes of apple and sweet spices.

Finish: Lingering and smooth with mellow beeswax at the end.

Notes

First commercially available, post-Prohibition, single barrel bourbon. It was the brainchild of Master Distiller Elmer T. Lee and named in honor of Col. Albert Blanton, distillery manager in the early 20th century.

My Score

Notes: _____

_____

_____

Appearance (1-5)	____	Nose (1-25)	____
Taste (1-25)	____	Finish (1-25)	____
Complexity (1-10)	____	Overall Impression (1-10)	____

SCORE ____

Blanton's Special Reserve

Proof:	80
Age:	NAS
Type:	Straight Bourbon, Export Only
Style:	Single Barrel, #124
Mash Bill:	Buffalo Trace #2 which is high in rye
Color:	Amber
Price:	$$$$

Mike

Nose: Caramel and fruit – apricots? – and a hint of oak. Very simple nose.

Taste: Very light taste. A hint of vanilla and caramel with some oak and leather. A bit thin, but some floral notes late.

Finish: Long – starts sweet and adds spiciness.

Susan

Nose: Very light, simple nose. Whiffs of vanilla and caramel.

Taste: Sweet corn, touch of honey, pleasantly oily mouthfeel. But light. No mistaking the low proof.

Finish: Smooth, long finish that retains sweetness to the end.

Notes

One of several expressions available overseas only. Given the low proof, interesting to have in order to compare to other expression.

My Score		
Notes: _____		
_____		
_____		
Appearance (1-5) ____	Nose (1-25)	____
Taste (1-25) ____	Finish (1-25)	____
Complexity (1-10) ____	Overall Impression (1-10)	____
SCORE ____		

Blanton's Export

Proof:	93.9
Age:	NAS
Type:	Straight Bourbon, Export Only
Style:	Single Barrel, #255
Mash Bill:	Buffalo Trace #2 which is high in rye
Color:	Amber
Price:	$$$$

Mike

Nose: Fruity. Apples and peaches with vanilla

Taste: Not overly complex. Apples and caramel with some peppery spice and fine leather.

Finish: Long and dry with oak tannins.

Susan

Nose: Sweet caramel apples, but light.

Taste: Creamy mouthfeel, saddle leather and vanilla.

Finish: Long, stays sweet most of the way But has a crisp ending.

Notes

One of several expressions available overseas only. Higher proof than the domestic expression.

My Score

Notes: _____

_____

_____

Appearance (1-5)	____	Nose (1-25)	____
Taste (1-25)	____	Finish (1-25)	____
Complexity (1-10)	____	Overall Impression (1-10)	____

SCORE ____

Blanton's Gold Edition

Proof:	103
Age:	NAS
Type:	Straight Bourbon, Export Only
Style:	Single Barrel, #157
Mash Bill:	Buffalo Trace #2 which is high in rye
Color:	Light Amber
Price:	$$$$

Mike

Nose: Surprisingly simple for its 103 proof. Apples and vanilla with a hint of oak. Drop of water opens it and reveals spice.

Taste: Oak and caramel with a hint of fruit-apple. No alcohol burn, but nice and warm in the throat. Water makes it a bit more fruity.

Finish: Dry with oak tannins and pepper spice, but quickly ends. Water makes it last longer.

Susan

Nose: Light spice, touch of vanilla. Drop of water brings out apple and caramel.

Taste: Vanilla, cherries, barest suggestion of cinnamon. Water reveals notes of chocolate.

Finish: Short and dry with a touch of pepper at the end.

Notes

Available overseas only. Notably higher proof than the domestic expression makes it worth seeking out.

My Score

Notes: _____

_____

_____

Appearance (1-5)	____	Nose (1-25)	____
Taste (1-25)	____	Finish (1-25)	____
Complexity (1-10)	____	Overall Impression (1-10)	____

SCORE ____

Buffalo Trace

Proof:	90
Age:	NAS
Type:	Straight Bourbon
Style:	Traditional
Mash Bill:	BT #1
Color:	Amber
Price:	$$

Mike
Nose: Apples and pears with sweet spices. Allspice, oak and honey with fine leather.

Taste: Honey and vanilla with some ripe pears. A hint of spice and oak wood. Nice Mouthfeel with no burn and little heat.

Finish: Short and sweet with spice and fruit. Second sip brings out the spice.

Susan
Nose: Strong caramel backed up with new leather, sweet spices and ripe apples.

Taste: Rich vanilla/caramel with dark fruit, honey, leather, tobacco and black pepper.

Finish: Medium. Warm and spicy.

Notes
Very versatile bourbon. Sip neat, on the rocks, or as the basis for a fine cocktail. (Susan loves this in a Manhattan.) Would good well at dinner with steak or even fish.

My Score

Notes: _____

_____

_____

Appearance (1-5) _____   Nose (1-25) _____

Taste (1-25) _____   Finish (1-25) _____

Complexity (1-10) _____   Overall Impression (1-10) _____

SCORE _____

Col. E.H. Taylor, Jr. Barrel Proof

Proof:	127.2
Age:	NAS
Type:	Straight
Style:	Barrel Proof, Small Batch

Mash Bill:	High Rye
Color:	Light Amber
Price:	$$$$$

Mike

Nose: Corn, ripe pear, and baking spices.
Taste: Caramel and pears with nutmeg.
Finish: Spicy and dry with oak.

Susan

Nose: Crème brulee and sweet spices. Water reveals ripe pears and almonds.
Taste: Spicy fruit cake. Add water for caramel, vanilla, fruit, nuts. Very layered.
Finish: Long and warm. Very smooth for the proof!

Notes

A very big bourbon. Uncut and unfiltered. This was Batch 8, Bottle 33.

My Score

Notes: _____

_____

_____

Appearance (1-5)	____	Nose (1-25)	____
Taste (1-25)	____	Finish (1-25)	____
Complexity (1-10)	____	Overall Impression (1-10)	____

SCORE ____

Col. E.H. Taylor, Jr. Bottled-in-Bond

Proof:	100
Age:	NAS
Type:	Straight Bourbon
Style:	Small Batch
Mash Bill:	Buffalo Trace #1
Color:	Light Amber
Price:	$$$$$

Mike

Nose: Caramel and honey with ripe apple and oak. Water intensifies the nose – more sweet honey.

Taste: Honey and molasses with apple fruit and pepper spice. A bit of tobacco and oak. Water brings out the fruit.

Finish: Very nice, with dry oak at the end, though water shortens it some.

Susan

Nose: Vanilla and roasted corn. Plus nutmeg and a little fruit and honey.

Taste: Rich mouthfeel. Hazelnuts, vanilla, dried apples. Water reveals honey, sweet spices, and some chocolate.

Finish: Long and spicy. Goes on and on. Touch of chocolate at the very end.

Notes

Col. E.H. Taylor, former owner of what is now the Buffalo Trace Distillery, promoted the Bottled-in-Bond Act of 1897 to guarantee bourbon quality. Annual releases of different expressions of Col. E.H. Taylor honor his legacy.

My Score

Notes: _____

_____

_____

Appearance (1-5) _____ Nose (1-25) _____

Taste (1-25) _____ Finish (1-25) _____

Complexity (1-10) _____ Overall Impression (1-10) _____

SCORE _____

Col. E.H. Taylor, Jr. Single Barrel

Proof: 100
Age: At least 4 years
Type: Straight
Style: Single Barrel, Bottled-in-Bond

Mash Bill: High Rye
Color: Light Amber
Price: $$$$$

Mike
Nose: Caramel corn, ripe apple, some floral notes.
Taste: Caramel, apple, baking spice, and oak pepper spice.
Finish: Dry oak tannins and pepper spice.

Susan
Nose: Caramel, ripe apples, walnuts, sweet mint.
Taste: Caramel/vanilla/chocolate sundae! Water brings out the fruit.
Finish: Sweet oak drying to spices.

Notes
Another big, layered sip from the Taylor series. Well worth seeking out.

My Score
Notes: _____
_____
_____

Appearance (1-5) ____   Nose (1-25) ____
Taste (1-25) ____   Finish (1-25) ____
Complexity (1-10) ____   Overall Impression (1-10) ____
SCORE ____

Eagle Rare
Single Barrel

Proof:	90
Age:	10 years
Type:	Straight Bourbon
Style:	Single Barrel, Extra Aged
Mash Bill:	Buffalo Trace #1
Color:	Amber
Price:	$$$$

Mike

Nose: Caramel and vanilla with a hint of citrus fruit. Some sweet spices and oak and fine leather.

Taste: Caramel and fruit – citrus and dates, with some honey and oak.

Finish: Long and dry with oak tannins with Some sweet spices and vanilla.

Susan

Nose: Vanilla, mint, new leather, and a trace of cocoa. Layers of sweet spice (cinnamon) and orange peel.

Taste: Caramel, toffee. Fine, chewy mouthfeel. Apple and stone fruit with dash of cinnamon.

Finish: Long and peppery with surprising sweet caramel at the very end.

Notes

A premium single barrel that is well worth its price. Its complexity merits multiple samplings. Sip neat or with a small splash or water.

My Score

Notes: _____

_____

_____

Appearance (1-5)	____	Nose (1-25)	____
Taste (1-25)	____	Finish (1-25)	____
Complexity (1-10)	____	Overall Impression (1-10)	____

SCORE ____

Eagle Rare 17-Year-Old

Proof:	90
Age:	17 years
Type:	Straight Bourbon
Style:	Single Barrel, Extra Aged
Mash Bill:	Buffalo Trace #1
Color:	Amber Red
Price:	$$$$$

Mike

Nose: Dominated by the barrel – oak, wood and leather. Caramel and dark fruit – berries, apricots, dates.

Taste: Cognac-like. Fruity with caramel. Apricots and apples with some fine fine tobacco and a hint of nutmeg.

Finish: Long and fruity sweet, but a bit of dry oak and tobacco.

Susan

Nose: Big vanilla and caramel with nuts and dark fruit. Lots of sweet oak.

Taste: Nutty caramel. A Snickers bar in a glass but with layers of dark fruit and dry oak.

Finish: Very long, lingering and peppery. Very dry at the end.

Notes

Deserving of utmost respect. A great bourbon to sip with a bite of cheese or fruit. Annual releases are produced in very limited quantities.

My Score

Notes: _____

_____

_____

Appearance (1-5)	____	Nose (1-25)	____
Taste (1-25)	____	Finish (1-25)	____
Complexity (1-10)	____	Overall Impression (1-10)	____

SCORE ____

Elmer T. Lee

Proof:	90
Age:	NAS
Type:	Straight Bourbon
Style:	Single Barrel
Mash Bill:	Buffalo Trace #2, which is high in rye
Color:	Light Amber
Price:	$$$

Mike

Nose: Apples and caramel with a bit of oak and leather. Opens after a minute to reveal cherries and dates.

Taste: Apples, vanilla, oak and leather with some sweet spice – nutmeg.

Finish: Long, dry and spicy, with oak tannins and sweet spices.

Susan

Nose: Honey vanilla, light spiciness with a touch of caramel. Fruit appears late.

Taste: Light, creamy mouthfeel, rich vanilla with prominent notes of apple and sweet spices.

Finish: Lingering and smooth with mellow beeswax at the end.

Notes

Elegant, medium-bodied bourbon that would please both new and experienced bourbon sippers. Each barrel for bottling was hand selected by the late Master Distiller Emeritus Elmer T. Lee.

My Score

Notes: _____

_____

_____

Appearance (1-5) ____   Nose (1-25) ____

Taste (1-25) ____   Finish (1-25) ____

Complexity (1-10) ____   Overall Impression (1-10) ____

SCORE ____

George T. Stagg

Proof:	142.6
Age:	NAS, but more than 10 years
Type:	Straight
Style:	Small Batch, Extra Aged, Unchilled, Unfiltered
Mash Bill:	Buffalo Trace #1
Color:	Bronze
Price:	$$$$$

Mike

Nose: Alcohol. Caramel and oak, fine leather and tobacco with pitted fruit – apricots and dates. A little spice – sweet cinnamon, nutmeg and allspice. Splash of water brings out oak and pecans.

Taste: Sweet fruit, almost brandy-like, with caramel and nutmeg. A splash of water brings out complexity with fruit, spice and oak.

Finish: Short and sweet. A splash of water makes the finish last longer and a bit drier.

Susan

Nose: Nutty, rich, and sweet. Lots of oak and spice and fruit layers. Strong note of beeswax.

Taste: Concentrated vanilla and oak work along the tongue revealing stone fruit, cinnamon and honey.

Finish: Dry, short and surprisingly light. Some pepper and spice.

Notes

A barrel-proof bourbon of great complexity when a few drops of water are added. Very limited annual release.

My Score

Notes: _____

_____

_____

Appearance (1-5)	____	Nose (1-25)	____
Taste (1-25)	____	Finish (1-25)	____
Complexity (1-10)	____	Overall Impression (1-10)	____

SCORE ____

Hancock's President's Reserve

Proof:	88.9
Age:	NAS
Type:	Straight Bourbon
Style:	Single Barrel
Mash Bill:	BT #2
Color:	Dark Straw
Price:	$$$$

Mike

Nose:	Vanilla and spice – nutmeg and allspice. Fine leather and oak. Light fruit could be pears or very ripe apples.
Taste:	Nice mouthfeel. Apples and vanilla with sweet spices – cinnamon and nutmeg.
Finish:	Long and fruity sweet. Almost brandy-like with some spicy oak tannins.

Susan

Nose:	Honeyed caramel, brown sugar, light oak and sweet spices.
Taste:	Vanilla, almonds and baked apples with a sprinkling of nutmeg and cinnamon.
Finish:	Long, warm and sweet with honey returning at the end.

Notes

For drinkers who favor the fruity, spicy style of bourbon, this will be one to have for special occasions. Sip it neat or with a single ice cube.

My Score

Notes: _____

_____

_____

Appearance (1-5)	____	Nose (1-25)	____
Taste (1-25)	____	Finish (1-25)	____
Complexity (1-10)	____	Overall Impression (1-10)	____

SCORE ____

McAfee's Benchmark Old No. 8

Proof:	80
Age:	NAS
Type:	Straight Bourbon
Style:	Traditional
Mash Bill:	BT #1
Color:	Straw
Price:	$

Mike

Nose:	Vanilla and corn, very light nose. Not complex.
Taste:	Very light. Corn and vanilla with some fruit – apples and peaches and sweet spices.
Finish:	Very short and sweet with a bit of honey and very little oak.

Susan

Nose:	Vanilla, candy corn, whiff of nutmeg and a faint citrus note. (Orange?)
Taste:	Vanilla and a little cocoa with new leather and nutty caramel. Surprisingly creamy mouthfeel.
Finish:	Medium and sweet. Very smooth.

Notes

A bargain-priced bourbon that would work very well in cocktails. You may even enjoy it neat.

My Score

Notes: _____

_____

_____

Appearance (1-5)	____	Nose (1-25)	____
Taste (1-25)	____	Finish (1-25)	____
Complexity (1-10)	____	Overall Impression (1-10)	____

SCORE ____

Old Charter 101

Proof:	101
Age:	NAS
Type:	Straight Bourbon
Style:	Traditional
Mash Bill:	Buffalo Trace #1
Color:	Light Straw
Price:	$$

Mike

Nose:	Sweet caramel and vanilla. Not overly complex. Just a hint of oak and leather
Taste:	Sweet corn and vanilla with some sweet spices and oak. A whisper of fruit – apples and cherries.
Finish:	Long and sweet with caramel and spice.

Susan

Nose:	Caramel, oranges and a note of honey. Pretty simple.
Taste:	Oak tannins, vanilla, spices. There is some orchard fruit lurking in the background.
Finish:	Medium long. Flash of sweetness before a smooth, dry ending.

Notes

A great bourbon to sip with chocolate. Relatively high proof means it will hold up well in a bourbon and soda.

My Score

Notes: _____

_____

_____

Appearance (1-5) ____		Nose (1-25)	____
Taste (1-25) ____		Finish (1-25)	____
Complexity (1-10) ____		Overall Impression (1-10)	____

SCORE ____

Old Charter 8-Year-Old

Proof:	80
Age:	8 years
Type:	Straight Bourbon
Style:	Traditional
Mash Bill:	Buffalo Trace #1
Color:	Dark Straw
Price:	$

Mike

Nose: Caramel corn and vanilla with a bit of oak. Very simple nose.

Taste: Sweet corn and vanilla with just a hint of Corn sweetness. Simple and straightforward. spice. A bit thin in the mouth.

Finish: Short and dry with oak tannins.

Susan

Nose: Light oak, vanilla, faint whiff of mint.

Taste: Oaky. Vanilla predominant with a bit of

Finish: Short and warm. Quite dry. No bite.

Notes

A good simple bourbon that goes well with food. You certainly can't beat the price.

My Score		
Notes: _____		
_____		
_____		
Appearance (1-5) ___	Nose (1-25)	___
Taste (1-25) ___	Finish (1-25)	___
Complexity (1-10) ___	Overall Impression (1-10)	___
SCORE ___		

Old Charter
10-Year-Old

Proof:	86
Age:	10 years
Type:	Straight Bourbon
Style:	Extra Aged
Mash Bill:	Buffalo Trace #1
Color:	Dark Straw
Price:	$$

Mike

Nose: Caramel corn and sweet spice with apple fruit and oak.

Taste: Corn and vanilla with sweet spices – cinnamon and nutmeg. Apples and pears with oak tannins. Great moth feel.

Finish: Long and spicy dry.

Susan

Nose: Sweet vanilla, with subtle touches of honey and caramel.

Taste: Vanilla and spiced pear. Not too sweet. Not very complex, but very enjoyable.

Finish: Medium long. Starts sweet, turns dry, but hen ends with a touch of corn sweetness.

Notes

Enjoyable on its own, but would also has the character to make an excellent bourbon cocktail ingredient.

My Score		
Notes: _____		
_____		
_____		
Appearance (1-5) ____	Nose (1-25)	____
Taste (1-25) ____	Finish (1-25)	____
Complexity (1-10) ____	Overall Impression (1-10)	____
SCORE ____		

Old Taylor

Proof: 80
Age: NAS
Type: Straight Bourbon
Style: Traditional

Mash Bill: Buffalo Trace #1
Color: Light Straw
Price: $

Mike

Nose: Very simple nose with corn and vanilla.
Taste: Very light taste. Corn and vanilla with a little pepper spice.
Finish: Longer than expected with wood tannins giving a dry finish.

Susan

Nose: Spice leaps out followed by vanilla and a drop of honey.
Taste: Warm vanilla with caramel and pleasant sweet spices. Light mouthfeel.
Finish: Medium finish ends with some heat.

Notes

Uncomplicated bourbon bottled a low proof. The price is such that a bourbon lover will want to have it on hand if, for no other reason, to honor the memory of its namesake, a giant of the bourbon industry who was instrumental in the Bottled in Bond Act.

My Score

Notes: _____

_____

_____

Appearance (1-5) ____   Nose (1-25) ____
Taste (1-25) ____   Finish (1-25) ____
Complexity (1-10) ____   Overall Impression (1-10) ____
SCORE ____

Old Rip Van Winkle 90°

Proof: 90
Age: 10 years
Type: Straight
Style: Wheated, Extra Aged

Mash Bill: Proprietary, but wheat in place of rye
Color: Pale Amber
Price: $$$$

Mike
Nose: Caramel and vanilla with some fine leather, apple/pear fruit and pecans. Not overly complex.
Taste: Rich caramel with apple fruit and pecans. Again, not overly complex.
Finish: Nice and long with dry oak and a hint of spice and nutmeg.

Susan
Nose: Light notes of vanilla, spice, and apple. Rather simple.
Taste: Sweet caramel with underlying soft nuttiness. Surprisingly simple.
Finish: Smooth with a spicy little kick at the end.

Notes
Pleasant, but uncomplicated bourbon. Would probably be lost in a cocktail, but would be very nice sipped neat or with a splash of water.

My Score	
Notes: _____	
_____	
_____	
Appearance (1-5) ____	Nose (1-25) ____
Taste (1-25) ____	Finish (1-25) ____
Complexity (1-10) ____	Overall Impression (1-10) ____
SCORE ____	

Old Rip Van Winkle 107°

Proof: 107
Age: 10 years
Type: Straight
Style: Wheated, Extra Aged

Mash Bill: Proprietary, but wheat in place of rye
Color: Dark Amber
Price: $$$$

Mike
Nose: Caramel and vanilla with some fine leather and tobacco. Ripe apple/pear with hazelnuts and oak.
Taste: Oak with caramel and apple. Also nutmeg and allspice.
Finish: Sweet with caramel apple and spice. The oak is hiding in the background, But not dry oakiness.

Susan
Nose: Vanilla, caramel apple, and light licorice.
Taste: Tobacco, dark cherry and light maple syrup. with faint spicy notes.
Finish: Vanilla and caramel corn, with touch of oak at the end, but the finish fades rather more quickly than one might want.

Notes
A very satisfying sip. The higher proof intensifies the flavors also present in the 10 year, 90 proof. Fascinating to compare the two side by side since aging and mash bill are the same, only the proof is different.

My Score
Notes: _____
_____
_____

Appearance (1-5) ____   Nose (1-25) ____
Taste (1-25) ____   Finish (1-25) ____
Complexity (1-10) ____   Overall Impression (1-10) ____
SCORE ____

Old Weller Antique

Proof:	107
Age:	NAS
Type:	Straight Bourbon
Style:	Wheated
Mash Bill:	Wheat in place of rye
Color:	Light Amber
Price:	$$

Mike

Nose: Apples, pears, vanilla and corn. A hint of oak and fine leather and pecans.

Taste: Nice mouthfeel. Almost chewy. Apples and caramel with hazelnuts and spice.

Finish: Long and spicy with cinnamon and pepper with oak. very good finish.

Susan

Nose: Caramel jumps right out, plus sweet corn and a suggestion of citrus. Quite oaky.

Taste: Begins with caramel sweetness and reveals vanilla and oak. More nutty than fruity with a touch of cinnamon.

Finish: Long, spicy, but not hot.

Notes

Fine example of the wheated bourbon style at a very reasonable (dare we say bargain?) price.

My Score

Notes: _____

_____

_____

Appearance (1-5)	____	Nose (1-25)	____
Taste (1-25)	____	Finish (1-25)	____
Complexity (1-10)	____	Overall Impression (1-10)	____

SCORE ____

Pappy Van Winkle's Family Reserve 15-Year-Old

Proof:	107
Age:	15 years
Type:	Straight
Style:	Wheated, Extra Aged
Mash Bill:	Proprietary, but wheat in place of rye
Color:	Deep Amber Red
Price:	$$$$$

Mike

Nose:	Green apple and vanilla with fine tobacco and oak.
Taste:	Caramel and fruit – pears! With oak tannins and pecans.
Finish:	Long and dry with oak tannins and anise.

Susan

Nose:	Big caramel right at the front bolstered by apple, pear and rich vanilla and underlying oak and dark honey.
Taste:	Very different from the nose showing more vanilla, hint of cherry and black pepper.
Finish:	Long smooth finish of polished oak.

Notes

Satisfyingly complex sip. A splash of water could bring out more complexity and tame the high proof a bit.

My Score

Notes: _____

_____

_____

Appearance (1-5)	____	Nose (1-25)	____
Taste (1-25)	____	Finish (1-25)	____
Complexity (1-10)	____	Overall Impression (1-10)	____

SCORE ____

Pappy Van Winkle's Family Reserve 20-Year-Old

Proof:	90.4
Age:	20 years
Type:	Straight
Style:	Wheated, Extra Aged
Mash Bill:	Proprietary, but wheat in place of rye
Color:	Red
Price:	$$$$$$

Mike

Nose: Sweet crème brûlée, with fine leather and oak wood. Background dates and cherries.

Taste: Sweet dark fruit and caramel with Tobacco and leathery oak tannins.

Finish: Long and dry with oak tannins and sweet vanilla.

Susan

Nose: Full of burnt sugar, dark fruit and oak.

Taste: Sweet saddle leather, light vanilla and underlying caramel.

Finish: Sweet, smooth vanilla finish. Wood fades to background.

Notes

A bourbon to savor neat. Cradle the glass to warm the whiskey. Pairs well with a cigar.

My Score

Notes: _____

_____

_____

Appearance (1-5)	____	Nose (1-25)	____
Taste (1-25)	____	Finish (1-25)	____
Complexity (1-10)	____	Overall Impression (1-10)	____

SCORE ____

Pappy Van Winkle's Family Reserve 23-Year-Old

Proof: 95.6
Age: 23 years
Type: Straight
Style: Wheated, Extra Aged

Mash Bill: Proprietary, but wheat in place of rye
Color: Deep Amber Red
Price: $$$$$$

Mike
Nose: Dark fruit, but dominated by oak making it very simple on the nose.
Taste: Dark fruit – plums – with lots of oak.
Finish: Dry oak tannins with some sweet caramel at the end.

Susan
Nose: Masses of oak and dry, dark fruit. (Prunes?)
Taste: Old leather and oak and dark fruit.
Finish: Long, dry finish with hint of sweetness at the end.

Notes
Considering this bourbon sells for $200, $300 and up (If you can find it.) it would not be unreasonable to expect more from it. Try a drop of water to help release the flavors.

My Score
Notes: _____
_____
_____

Appearance (1-5) ____   Nose (1-25) ____
Taste (1-25) ____   Finish (1-25) ____
Complexity (1-10) ____   Overall Impression (1-10) ____
SCORE ____

Rock Hill Farms

Proof: 100
Age: NAS
Type: Straight Bourbon
Style: Single Barrel

Mash Bill: BT #2
Color: Amber
Price: $$$$

Mike

Nose: Caramel and oak, a hint of milk chocolate. Apples, cherries and some sweet spices.
Taste: Spicy. Pepper and cinnamon with apple fruit and vanilla. Warmth, but no burn. Almost chewy. Water brings out strong vanilla flavor.
Finish: Long and spicy. Slightly dry with oak wood and pepper.

Susan

Nose: Chocolate (!) followed by vanilla and pear. Whiff of candied almonds.
Taste: Chocolate and vanilla with lots of cinnamon, nutmeg and vanilla bean. Notes of saddle leather and tobacco, especially with a little water.
Finish: Long and spicy, with a surprising note of candied orange peel at the very end.

Notes

Very elegant sip. Excellent with chocolate. Named in honor of Col. Albert Blanton's Farm that was next to the current Buffalo Trace distillery site.

My Score		
Notes: _____		
_____		
_____		
Appearance (1-5) _____	Nose (1-25)	_____
Taste (1-25) _____	Finish (1-25)	_____
Complexity (1-10) _____	Overall Impression (1-10)	_____
SCORE _____		

Stagg, Jr.

Proof:	134.4
Age:	NAS, but 8-9 years according to distiller
Type:	Straight Bourbon
Style:	Uncut, Unfiltered, Barrel Proof, Small Batch
Mash Bill:	BT #1
Color:	Dark Amber
Price:	$$$$$

Mike

Nose: Surprisingly light nose. Corn, vanilla, caramel and sweet spices. After 5 minutes, roasted marshmallow, caramel, oak.

Taste: Hot without water, but added water enhances caramel, apricot, nutmeg and cinnamon.

Finish: Pepper spice and oak tannins. Dilute to 50/50 water/bourbon and lingering finish is sweeter with spiced apricots.

Susan

Nose: Crème brûlée, dash of cocoa, and cinnamon. Opens up into complex spices with cherries.

Taste: Chocolate, dark cherry, honeycomb, cloves, cinnamon with vanilla oak.

Finish: Long, lingering. Dark fruit fades to black pepper and oak which lasts and lasts.

Notes

Let this barrel-proof, complex bourbon sit in the glass for a bit and add a little water to release all the layers of flavor. Very, very rewarding with that splash.

My Score		
Notes: _____		
_____		
_____		
Appearance (1-5) ____	Nose (1-25)	____
Taste (1-25) ____	Finish (1-25)	____
Complexity (1-10) ____	Overall Impression (1-10)	____
SCORE ____		

Van Winkle Special Reserve

Proof:	90.4
Age:	12 years
Type:	Straight
Style:	Wheated, Extra Aged
Mash Bill:	Proprietary, but wheat in place of rye
Color:	Amber
Price:	$$$$

Mike

Nose: Caramel and milk chocolate with hint of nuts and dark Cavendish pipe tobacco.

Taste: Caramel and apples with a hint of oak. Not overly complex. No burn at all.

Finish: Short finish. Sweet caramel, but then gone.

Susan

Nose: Baked apples, spicy vanilla, light caramel.

Taste: Honeyed flavor in the front moving to apple in the middle.

Finish: Very smooth finish but fades quickly.

Notes

Exhibits classic wheated bourbon attributes, especially mellowness and smoothness. Not a complex bourbon, but very enjoyable sipped neat. Short finish is disappointing.

My Score

Notes: _____

_____

_____

Appearance (1-5) ____   Nose (1-25) ____

Taste (1-25) ____   Finish (1-25) ____

Complexity (1-10) ____   Overall Impression (1-10) ____

SCORE ____

W.L. Weller
12-Year-Old

Proof:	90
Age:	12 years
Type:	Straight Bourbon
Style:	Wheated, Extra Aged
Mash Bill:	Wheat in place of rye
Color:	Straw
Price:	$$$

Mike

Nose: Oak and caramel with apple fruit. Very simple nose.

Taste: Sweet caramel and apples, pecans and oak. A nice warmth in the mouth

Finish: Nice and dry with oak, but a little sweet with ripe apples.

Susan

Nose: Vanilla, faint sweet nuttiness with underlying caramel.

Taste: Oak tannins predominate. Some apple but not a lot of depth.

Finish: Medium long with a sprinkle of pepper. Very smooth with no burn at all.

Notes

Extra aging has, not surprisingly, introduced more oak character to this Weller than to some of the other Weller expressions. Also hard to find, since the word is out that this is the bourbon from which Julian Van Winkle selects barrels to become Pappy Van Winkle.

My Score

Notes: _____

_____

_____

Appearance (1-5) ____   Nose (1-25) ____

Taste (1-25) ____   Finish (1-25) ____

Complexity (1-10) ____   Overall Impression (1-10) ____

SCORE ____

W.L. Weller Special Reserve

Proof:	90
Age:	NAS
Type:	Straight Bourbon
Style:	Wheated
Mash Bill:	Contains wheat, no rye
Color:	Dark Straw
Price:	$$

Mike

Nose: Candy – caramel corn and vanilla with some honey and nuts – hazelnuts.

Taste: Sweet corn, apples and pears with some caramel and nut flavor – pecans and hazelnuts. Very nice warmth and mouthfeel.

Finish: Long and dry with oak and spice.

Susan

Nose: Nutty caramel, light oak. a little apple and a whiff of honey.

Taste: More apple on the palate than in the nose. caramel and oak with some dried fruit and a flash of black pepper.

Finish: Short with a dry peppery finish.

Notes

A good bourbon with food or a cigar. Very nice sipped neat.

My Score

Notes: _____

_____

_____

Appearance (1-5)	____	Nose (1-25)	____
Taste (1-25)	____	Finish (1-25)	____
Complexity (1-10)	____	Overall Impression (1-10)	____

SCORE ____

William Larue Weller

Proof:	123.4
Age:	Minimum 10 years
Type:	Straight
Style:	Small Batch, Extra Aged, Unchilled, Unfiltered
Mash Bill:	Wheated
Color:	Amber Orange
Price:	$$$$$

Mike

Nose: Caramel and vanilla with apples and and pears. A little sweet spice with cinnamon and nutmeg. Oak wood. A little water opens the sweetness.

Taste: For such a high proof, not as much heat as expected. Rich caramel/maple syrup with apples and hazelnuts. Water takes the heat down a notch and sweetens the taste.

Finish: Not as long as expected, but of decent length with oak tannins and sweet fruit. Water makes the finish last longer.

Susan

Nose: Vanilla, candy corn, marzipan and pears. Faintly spicy.

Taste: Oak jumps out in front and settles into dry vanilla, apples, and almonds.

Finish: Medium long. Oak predominates. Dash of black pepper at the very end.

Notes

Part of the Antique Collection along with George T. Stagg, Eagle Rare 17-year-old and two ryes.

My Score	
Notes: _____	
_____	
_____	
Appearance (1-5) ____	Nose (1-25) ____
Taste (1-25) ____	Finish (1-25) ____
Complexity (1-10) ____	Overall Impression (1-10) ____
SCORE ____	

Additional Buffalo Trace Releases

Name: _____

Distillery: _____

Proof: _____   **Mash Bill:** _____

Age: _____   _____

Type: _____   **Color:** _____

Style: _____   **Price:** _____

My Score

Notes: _____

_____

_____

Appearance (1-5) ____   Nose (1-25) ____

Taste (1-25) ____   Finish (1-25) ____

Complexity (1-10) ____   Overall Impression (1-10) ____

SCORE ____

Name: _____

Distillery: _____

Proof: _____   **Mash Bill:** _____

Age: _____   _____

Type: _____   **Color:** _____

Style: _____   **Price:** _____

My Score

Notes: _____

_____

_____

Appearance (1-5) ____   Nose (1-25) ____

Taste (1-25) ____   Finish (1-25) ____

Complexity (1-10) ____   Overall Impression (1-10) ____

SCORE ____

WILD TURKEY

Bourbon Distilleries: Wild Turkey Distillery,
Lawrenceburg, Ky.

Austin, Nichols and Company was founded in 1855 as
a grocery in New York City where it became involved in the
food importing and distributing business. After the Repeal
of Prohibition the company entered the wine and liquor
business. By 1938 it has sold the food side of the business
to concentrate on spirits. In 1942 they introduce Wild
Turkey Bourbon at 101 proof and 8 years old. In 1969 the
tobacco firm of Liggett and Meyers purchases the company.
In 1971 they purchase the Ripy distillery in Lawrenceburg,
Kentucky. In 1980 Pernod Richard purchases the brand
and distillery. The Campari Group purchased the brand
and distillery in 2009.

A note on mash bill – Wild Turkey makes no secret
about the fact that every one of its bourbons is made with
the same mash bill. But they do not say what it is. Modern
Thirst claims it is 75% corn, 13% rye, 12% malted barley.

Special Release: Annual release of a single barrel, extra-
aged bourbon called Tradition. Age differs each year.

Bond & Lillard

Proof:	100
Age:	NAS
Type:	Straight Bourbon
Style:	Small Batch
Mash Bill:	Not available
Color:	Light Straw
Price:	$$$$$$

Mike

Nose: A little floral with light fruit – berries and vanilla.

Taste: Dries apricots and dates with a hint of baking spice and tobacco. Brandy-like.

Finish: Long and dry with oak and spice.

Susan

Nose: Sweet mint, ripe apples, vanilla custard.

Taste: Fruity with vanilla and sweet nuts. An elegant sip.

Finish: Stays sweet even through a peppery ending.

Notes

Price is about $50 for a 375ml bottle. Part of the Wild Turkey Whiskey Barons Collection reviving historic brands. Even though there is no age statement on the bottle, the distillery told us the whiskey used is between 6 and 8 years old. This was Batch No. 1.

My Score

Notes: _____

_____

_____

Appearance (1-5) _____   Nose (1-25) _____

Taste (1-25) _____   Finish (1-25) _____

Complexity (1-10) _____   Overall Impression (1-10) _____

SCORE _____

Old Ripy

Proof:	104
Age:	NAS
Type:	Straight
Style:	Non-Chill Filtered
Mash Bill:	Not available
Color:	Light Straw
Price:	$$$$$$

Mike

Nose: Corn, apples and pears with some caramel.

Taste: Creamy mouthfeel with apples and caramel and baking spices.

Finish: Dry with oak leading into a little pepper spice.

Susan

Nose: Vanilla, sweet corn, almonds.

Taste: Caramel, vanilla. Very smooth at 104 proof. Dash of cinnamon. Splash of water reveals apples and pears.

Finish: Sweet oak. Some spice.

Notes

Price is about $50 for a 375ml bottle. Part of the Wild Turkey Whiskey Barons Collection reviving historic brands. Even though there is no age statement on the bottle, the distillery told us the whiskey used is between 8 and 12 years old.

My Score

Notes: _____

_____

_____

Appearance (1-5) ____	Nose (1-25) ____
Taste (1-25) ____	Finish (1-25) ____
Complexity (1-10) ____	Overall Impression (1-10) ____

SCORE ____

Russell's Reserve

Proof:	90
Age:	10 years
Type:	Straight
Style:	Small Batch
Mash Bill:	Not available
Color:	Amber
Price:	$$$

Mike

Nose: Vanilla and honeysuckle with a bit of oak. Very complex – leather and tobacco and sweet spices. Water brings out some very long time.

Taste: Very nice thick and chewy mouthfeel with caramel, oak and sweet spice. A hint of apples and apricots.

Finish: Long. Starts sweet and spicy, but gets a nice oak dryness. Water makes the finish even more intense.

Susan

Nose: Sweet almond (marzipan), vanilla, cocoa, with sweet spices and cherry. Complex. This is a bourbon you can just nose for a nice caramel.

Taste: Sweet caramel with lots of orchard fruits, nuts, and sweet spices. Flash of cocoa, too.

Finish: Long and smooth. The fruit dries to pleasant nuttiness at the end.

Notes

Beautiful, snifter-worthy bourbon to be savored after a fine meal. Just a few drops of water help bring out the many flavor layers.

My Score

Notes: _____

_____

_____

Appearance (1-5)	____	Nose (1-25)	____
Taste (1-25)	____	Finish (1-25)	____
Complexity (1-10)	____	Overall Impression (1-10)	____

SCORE ____

Russell's Reserve Single Barrel

Proof: 110
Age: NAS
Type: Straight
Style: Single Barrel, Non-Chill Filtered

Mash Bill: Not available
Color: Amber
Price: $$$$

Mike
Nose: Very intense. Caramel and sweet spices with hint of chocolate and oak. Water opens up the caramel and fruit.
Taste: Oak tannins and caramel with some fruit – apples and pears.
Finish: Long and spicy with oak tannins.

Susan
Nose: Dark honey, maple syrup, intense caramel, pecans, beeswax, oak and touch of leather.
Taste: Honey, almonds, cocoa, with dried cherries layered throughout the rich caramel.
Finish: Long and smooth starting with fruit and honey and ending with peppery spice.

Notes
Worth every penny of the sticker price. Beautifully complex and balanced.

My Score

Notes: _____

_____

_____

Appearance (1-5) ____   Nose (1-25) ____

Taste (1-25) ____   Finish (1-25) ____

Complexity (1-10) ____   Overall Impression (1-10) ____

SCORE ____

Wild Turkey 81

Proof:	81
Age:	NAS
Type:	Straight
Style:	Traditional
Mash Bill:	Not available
Color:	Pale Straw
Price:	$$

Mike

Nose: Very light nose. Vanilla and oak with some light fruit and spice. Hard to distinguish the types.

Taste: Nice mouthfeel. Almost chewy. Nice apple fruit and caramel with some tobacco. Better than expected from the nose.

Finish: Short but sweet with vanilla and spices.

Susan

Nose: Light caramel and light citrus with a little vanilla.

Taste: Very smooth. Light caramel corn and a bit of honeyed nuts. Much more interesting than the nose would have indicated.

Finish: Fairly short and sweet with no burn.

Notes

Good introductory bourbon for someone who thinks bourbon is "hot" or "harsh." It would change his/her mind. Refreshing in bourbon and soda and very nice as the base for an Old Fashioned.

My Score

Notes: _____

_____

_____

Appearance (1-5)	____	Nose (1-25)	____
Taste (1-25)	____	Finish (1-25)	____
Complexity (1-10)	____	Overall Impression (1-10)	____

SCORE ____

Wild Turkey 101

Proof:	101
Age:	NAS
Type:	Straight
Style:	Traditional
Mash Bill:	Not available
Color:	Light Amber
Price:	$$

Mike

Nose: Caramel and fine leather. A bit of fruit – cherries and dates – and oak wood.

Taste: Fruit – cherries and berries with caramel and peppery spices. Very full-bodied and flavorful.

Finish: Long and spicy turning to nice, dry oak.

Susan

Nose: Vanilla and pitted fruit with a hint of honey and a whiff of tobacco leaf.

Taste: Lovely creamy mouthfeel. Remarkably smooth for the high proof. Vanilla, honey, caramel corn, citrusy fruit and spices.

Finish: Long smooth, spicy finish ends with flavor of honeycomb.

Notes

An absolute classic. Great sipping bourbon which also goes well with steak or a cigar. Splendid for a hot toddy on a cold winter evening.

My Score

Notes: _____

_____

_____

Appearance (1-5)	____	Nose (1-25)	____
Taste (1-25)	____	Finish (1-25)	____
Complexity (1-10)	____	Overall Impression (1-10)	____

SCORE ____

Wild Turkey Kentucky Spirit

Proof: 101
Age: NAS
Type: Straight
Style: Single Barrel

Mash Bill: Not available
Color: Amber
Price: $$$$

Mike

Nose: Rich caramel and milk chocolate. Fine tobacco and oak with apple/pear fruit. A little water brings out the caramel.

Taste: Apples and sweet spice – nutmeg and cinnamon. With oak tannins and caramel.

Finish: Long and dry with oak tannins and spice. Water tames the dryness, but makes it less interesting.

Susan

Nose: Caramel, green apple, pecans, beeswax, oak and a touch of leather.

Taste: Nuts, apples and honey supplement strong vanilla/caramel flavor. Dashes of cinnamon and sweet chocolate.

Finish: Long and smooth. Absolutely no burn. Dries to a spicy oak ending.

Notes

Enjoy neat. Our particular sample was bottled in May, 2012 from Barrel #41 which had been stored in Warehouse M, Rick 3.

My Score		
Notes: _____		
_____		
_____		
Appearance (1-5) ____	Nose (1-25) ____	
Taste (1-25) ____	Finish (1-25) ____	
Complexity (1-10) ____	Overall Impression (1-10) ____	
SCORE ____		

Wild Turkey Master's Keep

Proof: 86.8
Age: 17 years
Type: Straight
Style: Small Batch, Extra Aged

Mash Bill: Not available
Color: Amber
Price: $$$$$$

Mike
Nose: Berries, caramel, crème brulee, and tobacco.
Taste: Berries and pears with caramel and oak. Nice mouthfeel with chewy texture and no burn.
Finish: Surprisingly sweet for the age. Just a hint of tannins, a little chocolate and oak.

Susan
Nose: Vanilla, honey ripe apples, oak.
Taste: Vanilla and apples with pepper. Substantial mouthfeel.
Finish: Long and warm with a little cocoa and a peppery ending.

Notes
This was small batch number 1. Was moved during aging from a wood warehouse to a stone warehouse, and back to wood. Creation of Eddie Russell.

My Score		
Notes: _____		
_____		
_____		
Appearance (1-5) ____	Nose (1-25)	____
Taste (1-25) ____	Finish (1-25)	____
Complexity (1-10) ____	Overall Impression (1-10)	____
SCORE ____		

Wild Turkey Rare Breed

Proof: 108.2
Age: NAS
Type: Straight
Style: Barrel Proof, Small Batch

Mash Bill: Not available
Color: Amber
Price: $$$$

Mike

Nose: Dark fruit (cherries/dates) with vanilla and caramel, oak and fine leather. A few drops of water brings out the caramel and fruit.

Taste: Fruit and spice. Apricots and nutmeg/allspice with oak tannins and vanilla.

Finish: Long and dry oak. Just a hint of spice. Water makes the finish longer and spicier.

Susan

Nose: Strong honey on the nose, then vanilla, caramel, ripe peach, almonds and chocolate.

Taste: Rich, chewy, creamy mouthfeel. Vanilla, stone fruits, honey, brown sugar, caramel.

Finish: Long and lingering. Fruit gives way to tannins with a touch of sweet tobacco at the very end.

Notes

Sip neat or with a few drops of water. Perfect after dinner treat with a rich chocolate dessert. Would pair well with a mild cigar.

My Score

Notes: _____

_____

_____

Appearance (1-5) ____   Nose (1-25) ____

Taste (1-25) ____   Finish (1-25) ____

Complexity (1-10) ____   Overall Impression (1-10) ____

SCORE ____

Wild Turkey Tradition

Proof:	101
Age:	14 years
Type:	Straight
Style:	Extra Aged, Limited Release
Mash Bill:	Not available
Color:	Amber
Price:	$$$$$$

Mike

Nose: Apples, pears, caramel, tobacco and a bit of oak and spice. Opens nicely over time with more fruit and spice.

Taste: Berries and pears, maybe some dates, with vanilla and caramel, tobacco and nutmeg.

Finish: Long. Starts with very sweet vanilla and spice and gets oak as it lasts. Brandy-like.

Susan

Nose: Oak, vanilla, apple with cinnamon and spiced, roasted nuts, old book leather.

Taste: Caramel, honey, vanilla, and lots of figs. Seems a bit closed at first.

Finish: Long. Sweet at beginning and dries slowly. Very, very smooth.

Notes

Sweet fruit and spices emerge that are not apparent at first. There will be nutmeg, cinnamon, and chocolate. Drop of water turns this to milk chocolate. Mike calls this a "book bourbon." Pour a glass, settle in with a good book, and take a sip every 15 minutes or so for emerging flavors.

My Score	
Notes: _____	
_____	
_____	
Appearance (1-5) ____	Nose (1-25) ____
Taste (1-25) ____	Finish (1-25) ____
Complexity (1-10) ____	Overall Impression (1-10) ____
SCORE ____	

Additional Wild Turkey Releases

Name: _____

Distillery: _____

Proof: _____   **Mash Bill:** _____
Age: _____   _____
Type: _____   **Color:** _____
Style: _____   **Price:** _____

My Score		
Notes: _____		
_____		
_____		
Appearance (1-5) ____	Nose (1-25)	____
Taste (1-25) ____	Finish (1-25)	____
Complexity (1-10) ____	Overall Impression (1-10)	____
SCORE ____		

Name: _____

Distillery: _____

Proof: _____   **Mash Bill:** _____
Age: _____   _____
Type: _____   **Color:** _____
Style: _____   **Price:** _____

My Score		
Notes: _____		
_____		
_____		
Appearance (1-5) ____	Nose (1-25)	____
Taste (1-25) ____	Finish (1-25)	____
Complexity (1-10) ____	Overall Impression (1-10)	____
SCORE ____		

CRAFT DISTILLERS

Independent distilleries making relatively small amounts of whiskey, and in many cases, other spirits as well. Bourbons are listed alphabetically by name.

11 Wells Minnesota 13 Barrel Aged

Proof:	84
Age:	12 months
Type:	Not Straight
Style:	Wheated
Mash Bill:	51% corn, 39% wheat, 10% malted barley
Color:	Straw
Price:	$$$$$

Mike

Nose: Bread dough and vanilla dominate.

Taste: Vanilla and cereal –Wheat Chex – with a hint of oak.

Finish: Short and dry with oak.

Susan

Nose: Corn and new leather.

Taste: Corn flakes, vanilla, some sweet spice.

Finish: Starts sweet and dries to resinous oak.

Notes

From 11 Wells Spirits Company of St. Paul, Minnesota. Sold in 375ml bottles.

My Score

Notes: _____

_____

_____

Appearance (1-5) ____   Nose (1-25) ____

Taste (1-25) ____   Finish (1-25) ____

Complexity (1-10) ____   Overall Impression (1-10) ____

SCORE ____

Andy's Old No. 5

Proof: 90
Age: NAS
Type: Not Straight
Style: Small Batch

Mash Bill: Not available
Color: Very Light Straw
Price: $$$$

Mike

Nose: Bread dough and corn, a hint of vanilla.
Taste: Corn and vanilla with a hint of bread dough.
Finish: Dry with oak and pepper.

Susan

Nose: Corn and oak.
Taste: Dry cereal with a dash of cinnamon.
Finish: Oaky with a dash of pepper.

Notes

From Indian Creek Distillery, Staley Mill Farm and Distillery of New Carlisle, Ohio. This was Bottle 50 from Batch Number 2.

My Score

Notes: _____

_____

_____

Appearance (1-5) ____   Nose (1-25) ____

Taste (1-25) ____   Finish (1-25) ____

Complexity (1-10) ____   Overall Impression (1-10) ____

SCORE ____

Balcones Texas Blue Corn Bourbon

Proof:	129.8
Age:	24 months
Type:	Straight
Style:	Non-Chill Filtered, Barrel Strength
Mash Bill:	100% blue corn
Color:	Amber
Price:	$$$$$

Mike
Nose: Corn, vanilla, and some ginger. Water opens it up with more corn.

Taste: Caramel corn and baking spices. Water brings out tannins.

Finish: Long and sweet with a hint of pepper.

Susan
Nose: Sweet caramel corn, milk chocolate, berry fruit.

Taste: Licorice, baking spices, apples.

Finish: Long, sweet, with apricot notes.

Notes
Made by Balcones Distilling, Waco, Texas. Add one ice cube to open it up and reveal fruit. Any more water or ice flattens it and removes complexity.

My Score

Notes: _____

_____

_____

Appearance (1-5)	____	Nose (1-25)	____
Taste (1-25)	____	Finish (1-25)	____
Complexity (1-10)	____	Overall Impression (1-10)	____

SCORE ____

Belle Meade Madeira Finish

Proof:	90.4
Age:	NAS
Type:	Finished
Style:	Small Batch, Special Finish
Mash Bill:	Not available
Color:	Light Amber
Price:	$$$$$

Mike
Nose: Raisins and cherries with caramel and baking spices.

Taste: Fruity with raisins and dates, a bit of caramel, baking spice and oak.

Finish: Long and dry. Starts fruity, but turns to nice oak.

Susan
Nose: Sweet wood smoke, fruit, light caramel.

Taste: Fruity caramel. Madeira note accounts for sweetness.

Finish: Dry and peppery.

Notes
From Nelson's Green Brier Distillery, Nashville, Tennessee. This was Batch 1, Bottle Number 1432.

My Score

Notes: _____

_____

_____

Appearance (1-5) ____ Nose (1-25) ____

Taste (1-25) ____ Finish (1-25) ____

Complexity (1-10) ____ Overall Impression (1-10) ____

SCORE ____

Belle Meade Sherry Cask

Proof:	90.4
Age:	9 years
Type:	Finished
Style:	Small Batch, Special Finish
Mash Bill:	Not available
Color:	Light Amber
Price:	$$$$$

Mike

Nose: Berries and chocolate with a hint of oak.
Taste: Berries, caramel, vanilla. Hint of baking spice.
Finish: Fruity start which dries out to oak and spice.

Susan

Nose: Sweetly nutty, with vanilla and caramel.
Taste: Berries, caramel, almonds, sweet spice.
Finish: Dry with figs at the end.

Notes

From Nelson's Green Brier Distillery, Nashville, Tennessee. Finished in Oloroso sherry casks. Small Batch Number 1 and Bottle 492.

My Score

Notes: _____

_____

_____

Appearance (1-5) _____   Nose (1-25) _____

Taste (1-25) _____   Finish (1-25) _____

Complexity (1-10) _____   Overall Impression (1-10) _____

SCORE _____

Benjamin Prichard's Double Barrel

Proof:	90
Age:	9 years
Type:	Not Straight
Style:	Special Finish
Mash Bill:	Not available
Color:	Light Amber
Price:	$$$

Mike

Nose: Vanilla and toffee with a hint of pear.
Taste: Pears and caramel with some pepper and oak.
Finish: Starts fruity and dries to oak.

Susan

Nose: Caramel, light pear, sweet nuts.
Taste: Caramel and nuts with a little pear.
Finish: Warm and smooth with oak note at the end.

Notes

Prichard's Distillery, Kelso, TN. Uses copper pot stills. Aged for several years in one barrel and then for a few more in another new, charred oak barrel.

My Score

Notes: _____

_____

_____

Appearance (1-5)	____	Nose (1-25)	____
Taste (1-25)	____	Finish (1-25)	____
Complexity (1-10)	____	Overall Impression (1-10)	____

SCORE ____

Berkshire Bourbon

Proof:	86
Age:	NAS
Type:	Not Straight
Style:	Pot Stilled, Small Batch, Craft
Mash Bill:	Not available
Color:	Light Straw
Price:	$$$$

Mike
Nose: A little butter toffee and leather.
Taste: A little cherry/berry fruit and vanilla with sweet spices. A bit creamy.
Finish: Starts sweet but gets sine oak toward the end. Fairly short.

Susan
Nose: Very light. Grain – rye as well as complex. Faint tobacco.
Taste: Light oak with a little corn sweetness some and sweet spices.
Finish: Medium. Dries to black pepper.

Notes
Berkshire Mountain Distillers, Sheffield, MA. Would be interesting to see what more age could do for this bourbon. Grains are locally sourced.

My Score
Notes: _____

Appearance (1-5) ____ Nose (1-25) ____
Taste (1-25) ____ Finish (1-25) ____
Complexity (1-10) ____ Overall Impression (1-10) ____
SCORE ____

Big Bottom Small Batch

Proof: 91
Age: NAS
Type: Straight
Style: Small Batch, Craft

Mash Bill: 36% rye
Color: Dark Straw
Price: $

Mike

Nose: Vanilla with corn and sweet spice – nutmeg and cinnamon.
Taste: Sweet vanilla with some cherries. Nutmeg and cinnamon here, too.
Finish: Long and spicy with oak tannins.

Susan

Nose: Caramel, apple, nutmeg. Very appealing.
Taste: Vanilla and fruit. Almost a sundae.
Finish: Spicy oak and sweet vanilla.

Notes

Made by Big Bottom Distilling, Hillsboro Oregon. Distiller Ted Pappas also makes bourbons finished in port, zinfandel, and cabernet barrels, as well as a 111 proof bourbon. Named for an Oregon nature preserve. Certainly worth seeking out.

My Score

Notes: _____

_____

_____

Appearance (1-5) ____   Nose (1-25) ____
Taste (1-25) ____   Finish (1-25) ____
Complexity (1-10) ____   Overall Impression (1-10) ____
SCORE ____

Blind Tiger

Proof: 90
Age: NAS
Type: Not Straight
Style: Small Batch

Mash Bill: Not available
Color: Dark Straw
Price: $$$$

Mike

Nose: Corn and vanilla. Hint of fruit.
Taste: Corn and vanilla, Very young. A bit thin.
Finish: Sweet corn and vanilla. Very sweet and long.

Susan

Nose: Corn predominates. Whiff of vanilla and some underlying sweetness.
Taste: Corn dominates the palate. A little candy corn sweetness.
Finish: Vanilla shows up here and lingers after a sprinkling of pepper. Very nice finish.

Notes

Chicago Distilling Company, Chicago, Illinois. Quite nice for a young bourbon. We hope future batches will be allowed to age longer. This was Batch Number 1.

My Score

Notes: _____

_____

_____

Appearance (1-5) ____   Nose (1-25) ____
Taste (1-25) ____   Finish (1-25) ____
Complexity (1-10) ____   Overall Impression (1-10) ____
SCORE ____

Bluegrass Distillers Bourbon

Proof:	109
Age:	NAS, but less than 2 years
Type:	Not Straight
Style:	Small Batch
Mash Bill:	80% corn, 20% rye
Color:	Dark Straw
Price:	$$$$$

Mike

Nose:	Bread dough and vanilla. Very light for the proof.
Taste:	Bread dough, vanilla and a hint of fruit and oak.
Finish:	Oaky and astringent.

Susan

Nose:	Oak. Like sniffing an old log.
Taste:	Oak and some corn and pepper.
Finish:	Short and woody, but a sweet note a emerges at the end.

Notes

Bluegrass Distillers. Lexington, Kentucky. Aged in 25-gallon barrels with #4 char. Planned release of a straight, 2-year-old bourbon in 2017.

My Score

Notes: _____

_____

_____

Appearance (1-5)	____	Nose (1-25)	____
Taste (1-25)	____	Finish (1-25)	____
Complexity (1-10)	____	Overall Impression (1-10)	____

SCORE ____

Bootlegger 21

Proof:	92
Age:	18 months
Type:	Not Straight
Style:	Small Batch
Mash Bill:	Not available
Color:	Straw
Price:	$$$$$

Mike

Nose: Bread dough, yeast, hint of corn and vanilla.
Taste: Bread dough, vanilla, hint of pepper.
Finish: Short and peppery.

Susan

Nose: Corn and bread dough. Nut shells.
Taste: Like chewing on pistachios shells with some vanilla.
Finish: Short and warm.

Notes

Prohibition Distillery, Roscoe, New York. Batch #2, Bottle 453. Sold in 375ml bottles.

My Score

Notes: _____

_____

_____

Appearance (1-5)	____	Nose (1-25)	____
Taste (1-25)	____	Finish (1-25)	____
Complexity (1-10)	____	Overall Impression (1-10)	____

SCORE ____

Bourbon 30
Barrel Crafted

Proof:	90
Age:	6 months
Type:	Not Straight
Style:	Small Batch
Mash Bill:	Not available
Color:	Straw
Price:	$$$$

Mike

Nose: Young, but citrus notes and vanilla. Corn and a hint of oak.

Taste: Thin in the mouth. Caramel and corn with a hint of oak.

Finish: Thin and short with just a hint of oak.

Susan

Nose: Maple syrup, caramel, dash of cinnamon.

Taste: Corn, some honey. White pepper.

Finish: Short. Dry oak ending.

Notes

Distilled and bottled by Three Boys Farm Distillery, Graefenburg, KY.

My Score

Notes: _____

_____

_____

Appearance (1-5)	____	Nose (1-25)	____
Taste (1-25)	____	Finish (1-25)	____
Complexity (1-10)	____	Overall Impression (1-10)	____

SCORE ____

Bourbon 30
Single Barrel

Proof: 119
Age: 4 months
Type: Not Straight
Style: Special Finish, Barrel
Strength, Single Barrel

Mash Bill: Not available
Color: Straw
Price: $$$$

Mike
Nose: Corn, pears and berries, vanilla and oak.
Taste: Fruity with berries and vanilla, oak, an spice.
Finish: Starts fruity, then dries to oak and spice.

Susan
Nose: Bacon and wood smoke.
Taste: Pears, vanilla, some sweet spices.
Finish: Short, peppery.

Notes
From Three Boys Farm Distillery, Graefenburg, KY.
Finished with toasted barrel staves. Barrel #14, bottle 195.

My Score

Notes: _____

_____

_____

Appearance (1-5) _____   Nose (1-25) _____

Taste (1-25) _____   Finish (1-25) _____

Complexity (1-10) _____   Overall Impression (1-10) _____

SCORE _____

Bourbon 30 Small Batch

Proof:	118.5
Age:	4 months
Type:	Not Straight
Style:	Small Batch, Barrel Strength
Mash Bill:	Not available
Color:	Straw
Price:	$$$$$

Mike

Nose: Pears and citrus with corn and vanilla.
Taste: Corn, pears and vanilla. Hint of oak.
Finish: Dry with oak and pepper.

Susan

Nose: Light. Some corn and citrus.
Taste: Corn with some pear. Water releases some sweet spice.
Finish: Very peppery.

Notes

Bottle #524, batch #11. Made by Three Boys Farm Distillery, Frankfort, KY.

My Score

Notes: _____

_____

_____

Appearance (1-5)	____	Nose (1-25)	____
Taste (1-25)	____	Finish (1-25)	____
Complexity (1-10)	____	Overall Impression (1-10)	____

SCORE ____

Breckenridge

Proof:	86
Age:	2-3 years
Type:	Straight
Style:	Small Batch, Craft
Mash Bill:	56% corn, 38% rye, 6% malted barley
Color:	Dark Straw
Price:	$$$$$

Mike

Nose:	Corn and oak with a hint of spice. A little fruit in the background
Taste:	Corn and vanilla with a hint of spice. A bit thin and watery. Not complex.
Finish:	Short and sweet.

Susan

Nose:	Orange peel, vanilla, cinnamon.
Taste:	Pepper on the palate overwhelms any other flavors.
Finish:	Short, but not hot.

Notes

From Breckenridge Distillery, Breckenridge, CO. Earlier expressions of the bourbon were sourced from Kentucky. Own expression released in 2014. Bourbon is proofed using snowmelt.

My Score

Notes: _____

_____

_____

Appearance (1-5)	____	Nose (1-25)	____
Taste (1-25)	____	Finish (1-25)	____
Complexity (1-10)	____	Overall Impression (1-10)	____

SCORE ____

Cedar Ridge

Proof:	80
Age:	NAS
Type:	Not Straight
Style:	Small Batch
Mash Bill:	~ 75% corn
Color:	Very Light Straw
Price:	$$$$

Mike

Nose: Corn and vanilla. very light.
Taste: Thin and watery. Corn and vanilla
Finish: Short and sweet with vanilla.

Susan

Nose: Corn and cellulose.
Taste: Vanilla and sweet corn. Not complex, but pleasant.
Finish: Very warm for 80 proof. Lingers.

Notes

Cedar Ridge Distillery, Swisher, Iowa. Made in copper pot stills.

My Score

Notes: _____

_____

_____

Appearance (1-5)	____	Nose (1-25)	____
Taste (1-25)	____	Finish (1-25)	____
Complexity (1-10)	____	Overall Impression (1-10)	____

SCORE ____

Cody Road

Proof:	90
Age:	Less than 4 years
Type:	Not Straight
Style:	Small Batch
Mash Bill:	Not available
Color:	Very Pale Straw
Price:	$$$

Mike

Nose: Very light. Sweet vanilla and peaches.

Taste: Very light, but pleasant. Peaches and vanilla with a hint of spice.

Finish: Short and simple. Just a hint of oak.

Susan

Nose: Corn and a little sweet spice.

Taste: Rich mouthfeel, but not complex. Some sweet corn and a little sweet oak.

Finish: Smooth and sweet. Not hot.

Notes

Mississippi River Distilling Co., LeClaire, IA. This was Batch 7, Bottle 273. Would be interesting to see what some more aging would do for this.

My Score

Notes: _____

_____

_____

Appearance (1-5) _____   Nose (1-25) _____

Taste (1-25) _____   Finish (1-25) _____

Complexity (1-10) _____   Overall Impression (1-10) _____

SCORE _____

Copper Fiddle

Proof:	92
Age:	NAS
Type:	Not Straight
Style:	Traditional
Mash Bill:	Not available
Color:	Straw
Price:	$$$$$

Mike

Nose: Fruity. Berries and honey with some spice.
Taste: Very fruity with butterscotch. Peaches, spice, a hint of oak.
Finish: Sweet caramel and oak.

Susan

Nose: Caramel and pecans. Dates.
Taste: Wood smoke, caramel, vanilla, apples.
Finish: Sweet, drying to oak and smoke.

Notes

Copper Fiddle Distillery, Lake Zurich, Illinois. Unusual, but enjoyable. Could be a fine fireside sip given the smokiness.

My Score

Notes: _____

_____

_____

Appearance (1-5) ____   Nose (1-25) ____
Taste (1-25) ____   Finish (1-25) ____
Complexity (1-10) ____   Overall Impression (1-10) ____
SCORE ____

C.W. Irwin

Proof:	80
Age:	NAS
Type:	Straight
Style:	Four Grain, Craft
Mash Bill:	65% corn, 18% rye, 9% barley, 8% wheat*
Color:	Very Pale Straw
Price:	$$$

Mike
Nose: Very light – vanilla and bread dough.
Taste: Brown vodka, Very light. Some vanilla and corn.
Finish: Long and dry with oak.

Susan
Nose: Light, some fruit and yeasty dough.
Taste: Light. Butterscotch, but little else.
Finish: Begins smoothly, but a light woody aftertaste.

Notes
From Oregon Spirit Distiller, Bend, OR. The mash bill recipe* from information received from the purchaser of the bourbon. Named in honor of Craig Weber Irwin, brother of Brad Irwin. Brad and his wife Kathy are the distillers and made the first two barrels in their garage. Craig bought the barrels, thus funding their new distilling enterprise.

My Score

Notes: _____

_____

_____

Appearance (1-5)	____	Nose (1-25)	____
Taste (1-25)	____	Finish (1-25)	____
Complexity (1-10)	____	Overall Impression (1-10)	____

SCORE ____

Dancing Pines
Bourbon

Proof:	88
Age:	Less than 4 years
Type:	Not Straight
Style:	Small Batch
Mash Bill:	Not available
Color:	Light Straw
Price:	$$$$$

Mike

Nose: Corn and vanilla with a hint of apricots.

Taste: Corn and vanilla with apricots and oak.

Finish: Starts fruity and dries to oak.

Susan

Nose: Light caramel, white pepper, cinnamon.

Taste: Caramel, some vanilla, oak, sweet fruit.

Finish: Short and dry.

Notes

Made by Dancing Pines Distillery, Loveland, Colorado. This was small batch #17.

My Score

Notes: _____

_____

_____

Appearance (1-5) _____   Nose (1-25) _____

Taste (1-25) _____   Finish (1-25) _____

Complexity (1-10) _____   Overall Impression (1-10) _____

SCORE _____

Delaware Phoenix

Proof: 100
Age: Under 12 months
Type: Not Straight
Style: Craft

Mash Bill: ~ 69% corn, 18% rye, 13% malted barley
Color: Amber
Price: $$$

Mike

Nose: Honey and vanilla with corn and a bit of yeasty bread dough.
Taste: Corn and vanilla with some pepper spice. Fine tobacco and oak.
Finish: Long. Starts spicy but gets drier with oak tannins.

Susan

Nose: Corn! No mistaking that this is a corn-based whiskey. Caramel emerges with time in the glass.
Taste: Vanilla wafers, nutmeg, cinnamon. Creamy mouthfeel.
Finish: Long and dry. Very smooth.

Notes

Pot-stilled, craft bourbon from Walton, New York distiller Cheryl Lin is aged in small oak casks for less than a year. Impressive character for such a young bourbon. Note that the pricing is for 375ml bottles. It is not bottled in fifths.

My Score

Notes: _____

_____

_____

Appearance (1-5) _____   Nose (1-25) _____
Taste (1-25) _____   Finish (1-25) _____
Complexity (1-10) _____   Overall Impression (1-10) _____
SCORE _____

Dry Fly Bourbon 101

Proof: 101
Age: NAS
Type: Straight
Style: Small Batch

Mash Bill: Not available
Color: Straw
Price: $$$$$

Mike

Nose: Corn, bread dough, and vanilla.
Taste: Corn and vanilla with a hint of pepper.
Finish: Dry oak and corn. Gets sweet with some honey and oak.

Susan
Nose: Grilled corn and herbs. Succotash!
Taste: Very vegetative. Some vanilla sweetness.
Finish: Dry and oaky. A hint of vanilla at the end.

Notes
From Dry Fly Distilling, Spokane, Washington. Sold in 375ml bottles. This was small batch #2.

My Score
Notes: _____
_____
_____

Appearance (1-5) ____ Nose (1-25) ____
Taste (1-25) ____ Finish (1-25) ____
Complexity (1-10) ____ Overall Impression (1-10) ____
SCORE ____

Featherbone Bourbon

Proof:	90
Age:	NAS
Type:	Not Straight
Style:	Small Batch
Mash Bill:	Not available
Color:	Dark Straw
Price:	$$$$

Mike
Nose: Bread dough and vanilla with a hint of nutmeg.
Taste: Corn, vanilla and lots of oak.
Finish: Dry with lots of oak.

Susan
Nose: Pine resin, pears, underlying oak.
Taste: Sweet oak, some roasted corn, new leather.
Finish: Oaky, peppery.

Notes
Made by Journeyman Distillery, Three Oaks, Michigan. This was from small batch PB3, Bottle 17.

My Score

Notes: _____

_____

_____

Appearance (1-5)	____	Nose (1-25)	____
Taste (1-25)	____	Finish (1-25)	____
Complexity (1-10)	____	Overall Impression (1-10)	____

SCORE ____

F.E.W.

Proof: 93
Age: Less than 4 years
Type: Not Straight
Style: Small Batch

Mash Bill: Proprietary
Color: Straw
Price: $$$$

Mike

Nose: Corn and bread dough. Yeast with a hint of vanilla and oak.

Taste: Citrus fruit and vanilla. Just a hint of oak and spice. Water brings out vanilla.

Finish: Starts spicy but then gets a bit sweet. Water lessens the spice.

Susan

Nose: Cornfield. Faint vanilla. Smells young.

Taste: More sweetness on the palate than the nose. Still, corn predominates.

Finish: Highlight of the bourbon. Sweet spices and a whiff of cocoa linger in the smooth finish.

Notes

Simple, but pleasant, sip. Made by F.E.W. Spirits of Evanston, Illinois. The company name is a tongue-in-cheek nod to Evanston/Chicago prohibitionist Frances Elizabeth Willard. Handsome label depicts the World's Fair: Columbian Exposition, held in Chicago in 1893.

My Score

Notes: _____

_____

_____

Appearance (1-5) ____   Nose (1-25) ____

Taste (1-25) ____   Finish (1-25) ____

Complexity (1-10) ____   Overall Impression (1-10) ____

SCORE ____

Garrison Brothers

Proof: 94
Age: 4 years
Type: Straight
Style: Craft, Wheated

Mash Bill: Not available
Color: Light Amber
Price: $$$$$

Mike

Nose: Sweet corn and yeast. Cornbread dough. Not complex. Just a hint of oak.
Taste: Sweet corn and spice. Bit of pepper but rotten peach as well.
Finish: Long and sickly sweet – rotten peaches. Dries to oak.

Susan

Nose: Caramel, spiced pecans. Ripe apples emerge as it sits.
Taste: Caramel apples evolving into hot has some pepper.
Finish: Long and peppery hot.

Notes

Garrison Brothers, Hye, TX. Aged in small casks rather than 53 gallon barrels. Uses locally sourced white corn and winter wheat. This was bottle No. 14882.

My Score

Notes: _____

_____

_____

Appearance (1-5) ____   Nose (1-25) ____
Taste (1-25) ____   Finish (1-25) ____
Complexity (1-10) ____   Overall Impression (1-10) ____
SCORE ____

Grand River Baby Bourbon

Proof:	80.9
Age:	6 months or less
Type:	Not Straight
Style:	Small Batch, Single Barrell
Mash Bill:	Not available
Color:	Very, Very Light Straw
Price:	$$$$

Mike

Nose: Honey and citrus with a hint of yeast.
Taste: Citrus and vanilla with some spice.
Finish: Short with a little spice.

Susan

Nose: Sweet corn, a little new leather.
Taste: Frosted corn flakes. Buttery mouthfeel.
Finish: Very sweet with a dash of pepper at the end.

Notes

Made by Grand River Spirits, Carbondale, Illinois. This was from small batch #8, single barrel #23. Aged in 15 or 30 gallon white oak barrels.

My Score

Notes: _____

_____

_____

Appearance (1-5) ____   Nose (1-25) ____
Taste (1-25) ____   Finish (1-25) ____
Complexity (1-10) ____   Overall Impression (1-10) ____
SCORE ____

Hartfield & Co.

Proof:	100
Age:	NAS
Type:	Not Straight
Style:	Small Batch
Mash Bill:	62% corn, 19% rye, 19% malted barley
Color:	Straw
Price:	$$$$

Mike

Nose: Berries and corn with vanilla, honey, and tobacco.

Taste: Berries, corn, vanilla and pepper.

Finish: Dry oak and pepper with a hint of fruit.

Susan

Nose: Corn and rye. Whiff of honey.

Taste: Roasted corn, leather, dried apples.

Finish: Dry new oak. Touch of woodsmoke.

Notes

Made by Hartfield Distillery, Paris, Kentucky. This was from small batch #10, bottle 208 of 296. Hartfield is the first distillery to open in Bourbon County, Kentucky since Prohibition.

My Score

Notes: _____

_____

_____

Appearance (1-5)	____	Nose (1-25)	____
Taste (1-25)	____	Finish (1-25)	____
Complexity (1-10)	____	Overall Impression (1-10)	____

SCORE ____

Henry DuYore's

Proof:	91.3
Age:	NAS
Type:	Straight
Style:	Small Batch
Mash Bill:	56% corn, 31% rye, 13% malted barley
Color:	Dark Straw
Price:	$$$$

Mike

Nose: Caramel with a hint of turpentine and ripe fruit.

Taste: Caramel and apples with oak. Better than the nose would indicate.

Finish: Sweet with caramel, hint of chocolate and oak.

Susan

Nose: Vanilla, ripe apples, new leather.

Taste: Caramel, sweet oak, raisins.

Finish: Long and dry with peppery ending and a little cocoa powder.

Notes

Made by Ransom Spirits, Sheridan, Oregon. This was from small batch #13, bottle #1354. Label depicts a bootlegger. "Henry DuYore is not my real name."

My Score		
Notes: _____		
_____		
_____		
Appearance (1-5) ____	Nose (1-25)	____
Taste (1-25) ____	Finish (1-25)	____
Complexity (1-10) ____	Overall Impression (1-10)	____
SCORE ____		

High West Whiskey

Proof: 92
Age: NAS
Type: Straight Bourbon
Style: Small Batch, Non-Chill Filtered

Mash Bill: Not available
Color: Dark Straw
Price: $$$$

Mike
Nose: Honey and vanilla with corn. A little sweet spice.
Taste: A bit thin in the mouth. Vanilla and corn with some sweet clove.
Finish: Long and sweet with the spices – clove and nutmeg.

Susan
Nose: Prominent vanilla with touch of sweet spices faint floral note.
Taste: Vanilla and spices with a very faint note of green apple.
Finish: Medium long, warm and spicy.

Notes
Made by High West Distillery, Park City, UT. Boasts it is the only ski-in gastro-distillery and we believe them.

My Score
Notes: _____
_____
_____

Appearance (1-5) ____   Nose (1-25) ____
Taste (1-25) ____   Finish (1-25) ____
Complexity (1-10) ____   Overall Impression (1-10) ____
SCORE ____

High West Whiskey American Prairie

Proof: 92
Age: 2 years
Type: Straight
Style: Small Batch

Mash Bill: Not available
Color: Straw
Price: $$$$

Mike

Nose: Apricots and honey with a hint of spice.
Taste: Fruity with apricots and apples. Some corn vanilla and spice.
Finish: Very nice with oak and spice. A hint of fruit sweetness.

Susan

Nose: Corn, fresh evergreens.
Taste: Brown sugar, apples, sweet spices.
Finish: Dry and peppery with touch of sweetness.

Notes

This is a mingling of straight bourbons. High West Distillery is in Park City, Utah. This bottle was from batch #16C15. The distillery donates 10% of profits to prairie preservation.

My Score		
Notes: _____		
_____		
_____		
Appearance (1-5) ____	Nose (1-25)	____
Taste (1-25) ____	Finish (1-25)	____
Complexity (1-10) ____	Overall Impression (1-10)	____
SCORE ____		

Hillrock Estate

Proof:	90.6
Age:	NAS
Type:	Not Straight
Style:	Special Finish
Mash Bill:	Not available
Color:	Straw
Price:	$$$$$$

Mike

Nose:	Honey, vanilla, graham crackers.
Taste:	Berries with caramel and oak. A bit thin sweet in the mouth.
Finish:	Short and thin – caramel and oak.

Susan

Nose:	Caramel apple with some pear, baking spice, touch of anise.
Taste:	Caramel candy bar with some sweet spice.
Finish:	Long and peppery. Water tames the pepper.

Notes

Aged using the Solara method. From Hillrock Estate Distillery, Hudson Halley, New York. According to the label, the distillery floor malts its grains.

My Score	
Notes: _____	
_____	
_____	
Appearance (1-5) _____	Nose (1-25) _____
Taste (1-25) _____	Finish (1-25) _____
Complexity (1-10) _____	Overall Impression (1-10) _____
SCORE _____	

Hudson Baby Bourbon

Proof:	90.7
Age:	Under 4 years
Type:	Not Straight
Style:	Small Batch, Craft
Mash Bill:	Not available
Color:	Dark Straw
Price:	$$$$$

Mike

Nose: Very light. Oak and corn with some yeast dough. Very light floral note.

Taste: Oak tannins and corn. Hint of pepper spice. Not complex.

Finish: Long and dry with oak tannins and spice. Water tames the dryness, but makes it less interesting.

Susan

Nose: Corn and oak. A little vanilla as it sits in the glass.

Taste: Cinnamon, some corn. Spice dominates. Not complex.

Finish: Long and hot. Ouch.

Notes

Batch 11 of 2013, Bottle 3230. Tuthilltown Spirits, Gardiner, NY. Sold in 375ml bottles. Uses corn grown in New York state.

My Score

Notes: _____

_____

_____

Appearance (1-5) _____   Nose (1-25) _____

Taste (1-25) _____   Finish (1-25) _____

Complexity (1-10) _____   Overall Impression (1-10) _____

SCORE _____

Hunter's Select Barrel

Proof: 95
Age: 9 years
Type: Straight
Style: Tennessee, Small Batch

Mash Bill: 72% corn, 20% rye, 8% malted barley
Color: Straw
Price: $$$$$

Mike
Nose: Corn and vanilla with a hint of leather.
Taste: Corn, caramel/vanilla with peach or apricot and oak.
Finish: Very nice dry oak and fruit.

Susan
Nose: Candy corn, sweet mint, light spice, a little vanilla.
Taste: Matches the nose note for note. Water tames some surprising heat.
Finish: Dry oak, but rather short.

Notes
From Leiper's Fork Distillery, Franklin, Tennessee. This was bottle 77 of 800 from Batch. No. 1.

My Score
Notes: _____

_____

_____

Appearance (1-5) ____   Nose (1-25) ____
Taste (1-25) ____   Finish (1-25) ____
Complexity (1-10) ____   Overall Impression (1-10) ____
SCORE ____

J. Henry & Sons
Bellefontaine Reserve

Proof: 105
Age: 5 years
Type: Straight Bourbon
Style: Special Finish, Four Grain

Mash Bill: 60% corn, 14% wheat, 14% rye, 12% malted barley
Color: Light Amber
Price: $$$$$

Mike
Nose: Vanilla and cotton candy, raisins and a hint of oak.
Taste: Fruit – raisins and berries – with caramel and spice.
Finish: Very peppery and dry with oak tannins.

Susan
Nose: Honeyed fruit with sweet mint and caramel corn.
Taste: Rich mouthfeel with ripe apples, marzipan, and sweet spices.
Finish: Pepper drying to sweet oak.

Notes
Family farm distillery in Dane, Wisconsin. Red heirloom corn, rye, and wheat grown on the farm are used in the bourbon. Finished for 4-6 months in cognac casks. Available in WI, MN, and Chicago area. Bottle tasted was no. 78 of batch no. 2. Water softens and sweetens without diminishing.

My Score

Notes: _____

_____

_____

Appearance (1-5) ____   Nose (1-25) ____

Taste (1-25) ____   Finish (1-25) ____

Complexity (1-10) ____   Overall Impression (1-10) ____

SCORE ____

J. Henry & Sons Cask Strength

Proof: 125.2
Age: 5 years
Type: Straight Bourbon
Style: Barrel Strength, Four Grain, Small Batch

Mash Bill: 60% corn, 14% wheat, 14% rye, 12% malted barley
Color: Straw
Price: $$$$$

Mike

Nose: Vanilla and corn with some leather and oak.
Taste: Citrus, vanilla, and pepper.
Finish: Long, citrus notes and spice. Water makes it very peppery.

Susan

Nose: Fruit, hard candy, crème brulee.
Taste: Sweet on the tongue. Bananas and vanilla.
Finish: Long and fruity with a lingering warmth.

Notes

Water brings out vanilla on the nose and pepper on the palate. Strangely, does not amplify fruit as is often the case with cask strength bourbons. Small Batch No. 2, Bottle 629.

My Score

Notes: _____

_____

_____

Appearance (1-5) ____   Nose (1-25) ____

Taste (1-25) ____   Finish (1-25) ____

Complexity (1-10) ____   Overall Impression (1-10) ____

SCORE ____

J. Henry & Sons Straight Bourbon

Proof: 92
Age: 5 years
Type: Straight Bourbon
Style: Small Batch, Four Grain

Mash Bill: 60% corn, 14% wheat, 14% rye, 12% malted barley
Color: Straw
Price: $$$$$

Mike
Nose: Vanilla and cotton candy with a hint of oak.
Taste: Vanilla and corn, some baking spices and oak.
Finish: Starts sweet but dries out with oak.

Susan
Nose: Sweet mint, roasted corn, sweet spices.
Taste: Fresh cereal, anise, bit of apple.
Finish: Both sweet and peppery. Nicely balanced.

Notes
From Henry Farms Prairie Spirits in Dane, Wisconsin. Bourbons from this distillery are available in WI, MN, and Chicago area. Corn is an heirloom red.

My Score

Notes: _____

_____

_____

Appearance (1-5) ____   Nose (1-25) ____

Taste (1-25) ____   Finish (1-25) ____

Complexity (1-10) ____   Overall Impression (1-10) ____

SCORE ____

Kings County

Proof: 90
Age: 1-2 years
Type: Not Straight
Style: Peated, Craft

Mash Bill: 70% corn, 30% peated malt
Color: Light Straw
Price: $$$$$

Mike

Nose: Peat, vanilla, and corn. Dominated by peat.
Taste: Peak, sweet corn, and vanilla. Peat dominates.
Finish: Long and peaty. Not complicated. Too much like Scotch. Not enough like bourbon.

Susan

Nose: Grass clippings, oak, a whiff of corn.
Taste: Smoke and more smoke. Some sweet.
Finish: Long and smoky. One-dimensional.

Notes

Made by Kings County Distillery, Brooklyn, NY. Located in the Brooklyn Navy Yard. Sold in 200ml bottles for $25 or so. Price works out to over $90/fifth.

Koval

Proof: 94
Age: Less than 4 years
Type: Not Straight
Style: Single Barrel

Mash Bill: Not available
Color: Light Straw
Price: $$$$

Mike
Nose: Chemical – wormwood and herbs.
Taste: Sweet honey and fruit. Raisins and berries.
Finish: Very dry. Almost astringent.

Susan
Nose: Herbal and slightly resinous.
Taste: Pepper dominates vanilla and orchard fruit.
Finish: Long and peppery with a little mint at the end.

Notes
The taste is better than the nose. This could make a very interesting Manhattan. From Koval Distillery, Chicago, Illinois.

My Score

Notes: _____

_____

_____

Appearance (1-5) ____   Nose (1-25) ____

Taste (1-25) ____   Finish (1-25) ____

Complexity (1-10) ____   Overall Impression (1-10) ____

SCORE ____

Leadslingers

Proof:	80
Age:	NAS
Type:	Not Straight
Style:	Small Batch

Mash Bill:	Not available
Color:	Very Faint Straw
Price:	$$$$

Mike

Nose:	Corn and not much else. Hint of faint vanilla.
Taste:	Thin but sweet, with vanilla and corn.
Finish:	Short and sweet.

Susan

Nose:	Light leather, corn, alcohol.
Taste:	A little caramel and butterscotch.
Finish:	Short, oaky.

Notes

From Scissortail Distillery, Moore, Oklahoma.

My Score

Notes: _____

_____

_____

Appearance (1-5)	____	Nose (1-25)	____
Taste (1-25)	____	Finish (1-25)	____
Complexity (1-10)	____	Overall Impression (1-10)	____

SCORE ____

McKenzie

Proof:	91
Age:	NAS (website says it is 2 years old)
Type:	Not Straight
Style:	Craft, Non-Chill Filtered
Mash Bill:	Not available
Color:	Dark Straw
Price:	$$$

Mike

Nose: Very yeasty – bread dough – with corn and vanilla. Some floral notes (roses?) and sweet spices.

Taste: Sweet corn and caramel with some spices – nutmeg and allspice – leather tobacco, pecans.

Finish: Starts sweet, but gets dry with oak tannins. Lasts a long time.

Susan

Nose: Dried corn, ethanol, tobacco opening into yeasty bread dough.

Taste: Sweet corn and caramel. Some sweet spices – cinnamon, allspice.

Finish: Medium long, sweet and smooth a little pepper on the tongue.

Notes

Made at the Finger Lakes Distilling of Burdett, NY. Whiskey is made from locally grown grains.

My Score		
Notes: _____		
_____		
_____		
Appearance (1-5) ____	Nose (1-25)	____
Taste (1-25) ____	Finish (1-25)	____
Complexity (1-10) ____	Overall Impression (1-10)	____
SCORE ____		

Metze's Select

Proof:	93
Age:	7-9 years
Type:	Straight
Style:	Small Batch
Mash Bill:	See notes
Color:	Straw
Price:	$$$$$

Mike

Nose: Caramel and sweet spices with hint of raisins and anise.

Taste: Sweet caramel, berries and dates, some baking spice.

Finish: Starts sweet with fruit. Dries to spicy oak tannins.

Susan

Nose: Caramel, wood smoke, dried apples.

Taste: Baked toffee, sweet mint, baked pears.

Finish: Starts sweet, but jarring bitter note at the end.

Notes

Distilled and released by MGP, Lawrenceburg, Indiana, which otherwise contract distills liquor for independent bottlers. Mingling of 2006 bourbon (21% rye), 3% 2006 bourbon (36% rye), and 59% 2008 bourbon (21% rye). Bottled and released in 2015. Limited to 6000 bottles.

My Score

Notes: _____

_____

_____

Appearance (1-5)	____	Nose (1-25)	____
Taste (1-25)	____	Finish (1-25)	____
Complexity (1-10)	____	Overall Impression (1-10)	____

SCORE ____

Neversweat

Proof:	80
Age:	NAS
Type:	Straight
Style:	Craft
Mash Bill:	Not available
Color:	Light Straw
Price:	$$$

Mike

Nose: Corn and vanilla with a hint of oak. Very light and simple.

Taste: Very young with sweet vanilla and corn. Some fruit. Peaches? Apricots? Pepper spice.

Finish: Very good. Starts sweet but dries out with some oak tannins and peppery spice.

Susan

Nose: Spicy – anise and clove.

Taste: Sweet spices with caramel and vanilla arriving next with some fruit. Tannins arrive last.

Finish: Quite smooth for a bourbon with such a spicy start. Bit of cinnamon aftertaste.

Notes

Made by Headframe Spirits of Butte, Montana, which also makes craft gin and vodka. Beverage names, as well as the distillery name, come from mining terms.

My Score

Notes: _____

_____

_____

Appearance (1-5)	____	Nose (1-25)	____
Taste (1-25)	____	Finish (1-25)	____
Complexity (1-10)	____	Overall Impression (1-10)	____
	SCORE ____		

New Southern Revival Four Grain

Proof:	94
Age:	NAS
Type:	Not Straight
Style:	Wheated
Mash Bill:	See notes
Color:	Light Straw
Price:	$$$$

Mike

Nose: Young. Corn with hint of honey.
Taste: Young with honey and spice. Hint of peaches.
Finish: Short and sweet.

Susan

Nose: Sweet corn. Simple.
Taste: Lots of grain. Some vanilla.
Finish: Short. Oaky at the end.

Notes

Made by High Wire Distilling Co., Charleston, South Carolina. Mash bill uses heirloom white corn, red winter wheat, Carolina Gold rice, and malted barely. This was bottle 187 of batch 3.

My Score

Notes: _____

_____

_____

Appearance (1-5)	____	Nose (1-25)	____
Taste (1-25)	____	Finish (1-25)	____
Complexity (1-10)	____	Overall Impression (1-10)	____

SCORE ____

OCD #5

Proof: 105
Age: At least 6 months
Type: Not Straight
Style: Single Barrel, Barrel Proof

Mash Bill: Not available
Color: Dark Straw
Price: $$$$$

Mike
Nose: Caramel candy and a hint of leather.
Taste: Thin. Caramel and tobacco.
Finish: Starts sweet with caramel and moves towards milk chocolate.

Susan
Nose: Molasses, caramel, roasted corn.
Taste: Roasted corn. Pleasant oak, but not complex.
Finish: Long, warm. Some chocolate.

Notes
Made by Glenns Creek Distillery, Frankfort, Kentucky. This was bottle 202 from barrel 4. Described on the label as "triple oaked."

My Score
Notes: _____

_____

_____

Appearance (1-5) ____   Nose (1-25) ____

Taste (1-25) ____   Finish (1-25) ____

Complexity (1-10) ____   Overall Impression (1-10) ____

SCORE ____

Old 55 Bourbon

Proof:	80
Age:	NAS
Type:	Not Straight
Style:	Single Barrel
Mash Bill:	100% sweet corn
Color:	Very Light Straw
Price:	$$$$$$

Mike

Nose: Sweet and floral with banana and vanilla. Banana pudding.

Taste: Corn and vanilla with banana and a hint of oak and spice.

Finish: Very sweet with a hint of oak and spice.

Susan

Nose: Cornbread with a whiff of sweet mint and very ripe apples.

Taste: Sweet corn, ripe apples and light caramel.

Finish: Sweet, with a bit of pepper and a distinct floral note at the end.

Notes

From Old 55 Distillery, Newtown, IN. Produces "estate whiskeys" by growing, milling, and mashing their own grains. Aged in 30 gallon barrels.

My Score

Notes: _____

_____

_____

Appearance (1-5)	____	Nose (1-25)	____
Taste (1-25)	____	Finish (1-25)	____
Complexity (1-10)	____	Overall Impression (1-10)	____

SCORE ____

Old 55 Single Barrel

Proof: 80
Age: NAS
Type: Not Straight
Style: Single Barrel

Mash Bill: Not available
Color: Very Light Straw
Price: $$$$$$

Mike
Nose: Corn and vanilla with some leather.
Taste: Buttered corn and pepper spice with some oak.
Finish: Dry with oak and pepper. A little creamy.

Susan
Nose: Corn husk, tobacco leaf and tobacco smoke.
Taste: Smoky, like a mouthful of pipe tobacco smoke. Some nuttiness.
Finish: Lingering and dry with oak tannins.

Notes
From Old 55 Distillery, Newtown, IN. Produces "estate whiskeys" by growing, milling, and mashing their own grains. Aged in 30 gallon barrels. Batch 15H5, bottle 108.

My Score		
Notes: _____		
_____		
_____		
Appearance (1-5) ____	Nose (1-25)	____
Taste (1-25) ____	Finish (1-25)	____
Complexity (1-10) ____	Overall Impression (1-10)	____
SCORE ____		

Old Log Cabin

Proof:	86
Age:	At least 18 months
Type:	Not Straight
Style:	Two Grain
Mash Bill:	51% corn, 49% malted barley
Color:	Light Straw
Price:	$$$$$

Mike

Nose:	Corn and malt, not surprisingly with a hint of vanilla.
Taste:	Corn and vanilla with some malty notes.
Finish:	Corn and a hint of pepper and wood.

Susan

Nose:	Breakfast cereal. Some honey sweetness.
Taste:	Barley malt with some corn sweetness. Very like a Scotch. perhaps a pear note.
Finish:	Short and dry.

Notes

We loved the cabin-shaped bottle. Very interesting to taste what happens when there is not rye or wheat. Comes from Batch 206 Distillery, Seattle, WA.

My Score

Notes: _____

_____

_____

Appearance (1-5)	____	Nose (1-25)	____
Taste (1-25)	____	Finish (1-25)	____
Complexity (1-10)	____	Overall Impression (1-10)	____

SCORE ____

Old Pogue

Proof:	91
Age:	NAS
Type:	Straight
Style:	Craft
Mash Bill:	Not available
Color:	Dark Straw
Price:	$$$$

Mike

Nose: Caramel corn and oak. very simple nose. Bit fruit (pears?) and sweet spice.

Taste: Corn and vanilla with a bit of spice and tobacco.

Finish: Starts sweet, then gets spicy and dry. Lasts fairly long and gets drier and more oaky as it lasts.

Susan

Nose: Sweet buttered corn, caramel, dark fruit (plum? black cherry?)

Taste: Light caramel, buttered popcorn, hint of sweet maple syrup.

Finish: Long and smooth. Stays sweet until it dries to an oaky ending.

Notes

A fine sipping bourbon with enough presence and proof to make excellent cocktails, such as a classic Manhattan. Use top shelf vermouth.

My Score

Notes: _____

_____

_____

Appearance (1-5)	____	Nose (1-25)	____
Taste (1-25)	____	Finish (1-25)	____
Complexity (1-10)	____	Overall Impression (1-10)	____

SCORE ____

Oppidan

Proof: 92
Age: NAS
Type: Not Straight
Style: Special Finish

Mash Bill: See notes
Color: Light Amber
Price: $$$$$

Mike

Nose: Bread dough and caramel apple.
Taste: Caramel and apple with some leather and spice.
Finish: Dry with oak and pepper spice.

Susan

Nose: Corn, oak, then caramel.
Taste: Sweet corn, some fig, baking spices.
Finish: Herbal at first. Finishes with sweet corn.

Notes

From Oppidan Spirits, Wheeling, Illinois. Not complex, but nicely made. Distillers use the Solara process. The 5-grain mash bill contains corn, malted rye, chocolate malted rye, special B and 2-row barley.

My Score		
Notes: _____		
_____		
_____		
Appearance (1-5) ____	Nose (1-25) ____	
Taste (1-25) ____	Finish (1-25) ____	
Complexity (1-10) ____	Overall Impression (1-10) ____	
SCORE ____		

O.Z. Tyler Small Batch Reserve

Proof: 90
Age: 4 months
Type: Not Straight
Style: Small Batch

Mash Bill: Not available
Color: Light Straw
Price: $$

Mike
Nose: Cornbread and honey.
Taste: Corn and honey with some pepper spice.
Finish: Sweet with a hint of oak and spice.

Susan
Nose: Cherries, light vanilla.
Taste: Floral, almost perfume. Very sweet.
Finish: Short and sweet.

Notes
Made by TerrePURE Spirits, North Charleston, SC. A second distillery with the same owners started producing at the former Charles Medley facility in Owensboro, KY in 2016. Both use a special process involving ultrasonic waves, heat, and oxygen to accelerate aging.

My Score
Notes: _____

Appearance (1-5) ____ Nose (1-25) ____
Taste (1-25) ____ Finish (1-25) ____
Complexity (1-10) ____ Overall Impression (1-10) ____
SCORE ____

Rock Town Arkansas Bourbon Whiskey

Proof:	92
Age:	Under 4 years
Type:	Not Straight
Style:	Small Batch, Wheated
Mash Bill:	Not available
Color:	Very Light Amber
Price:	$$$$$

Mike

Nose:	Corn bread dough. Very yeasty with a hint of honey.
Taste:	Corn bread and honey with a hint of oak.
Finish:	Oaky and dry.

Susan

Nose:	Cereal grain, dried corn. Touch of sugar.
Taste:	Sweet oak. Some faint vanilla and peach.
Finish:	Short and oaky.

Notes

From Rock Town Distillery, Little Rock, AR. Not complex, but nicely made. Corn and wheat sourced from Arkansas.

My Score

Notes: _____

_____

_____

Appearance (1-5)	____	Nose (1-25)	____
Taste (1-25)	____	Finish (1-25)	____
Complexity (1-10)	____	Overall Impression (1-10)	____

SCORE ____

Six & Twenty 5 Grain

Proof:	90
Age:	NAS
Type:	Not Straight
Style:	Small Batch
Mash Bill:	See notes
Color:	Dark Straw
Price:	$$$$

Mike
Nose:	Sweet honey and peached. Water makes candied fruit come forward.
Taste:	Honey and fruit. Some baking spices. Water dilutes the flavor.
Finish:	Sweet and spicy with some oak.

Susan
Nose:	Sweet. Candy corn and whiff of mint.
Taste:	Light vanilla, whisper of orchard fruit. Some toasted marshmallow.
Finish:	Mellow with a touch of black pepper at the end.

Notes
From Six & Twenty Distillery, Piedmont, South Carolina. Very enjoyable sip. Why not straight? Website says it is aged 2 years. Mashbill: Corn, soft red winter wheat, rye, barley, rice. Bottle #33 from a small batch of 8 barrels.

My Score

Notes: _____

_____

_____

Appearance (1-5)	____	Nose (1-25)	____
Taste (1-25)	____	Finish (1-25)	____
Complexity (1-10)	____	Overall Impression (1-10)	____

SCORE ____

Smooth Ambler

Proof:	92
Age:	2 years, 11 months
Type:	Not Straight
Style:	Small Batch, Craft, Wheated
Mash Bill:	Not available
Color:	Light Amber
Price:	$$$

Mike

Nose: Corn and vanilla with some floral and sweet oak. Water weakens the nose.

Taste: Corn and vanilla with some pepper and oak. Nice mouthfeel with very little burn. Water brings out sweet corn but lessens spice.

Finish: Long and spicy, leading into oak. Very nice. Still nice when water added.

Susan

Nose: Corn, light apple, vanilla.

Taste: Sweet corn, cinnamon red hots. Water tames heat and reveals more sweet apple and vanilla.

Finish: Medium long, spicy.

Notes

Smooth Ambler, Maxwelton, WV. Pot still used in distillation. Batch No. 15, bottled 7/10/2014.

My Score

Notes: _____

_____

_____

Appearance (1-5) ____   Nose (1-25) ____

Taste (1-25) ____   Finish (1-25) ____

Complexity (1-10) ____   Overall Impression (1-10) ____

SCORE ____

Smooth Ambler Contradiction

Proof:	100
Age:	2 years
Type:	Mingling of Straight Bourbons
Style:	Traditional
Mash Bill:	Not available
Color:	Light Amber
Price:	$$$$$

Mike

Nose: Fruit and caramel. Ripe apples, baking spices and oak.

Taste: Apples, caramel. pepper spice and oak.

Finish: Long and dry with oak and pepper.

Susan

Nose: Caramel, vanilla, baking spices, nuts, apples.

Taste: Fruity, nutty caramel candy bar.

Finish: Smooth with peppery oak at the end.

Notes

Best 2-year-old ever! Smooth Ambler Spirits, Maxwelton, WV. Bourbons produced both here and at MGP in Indiana were used. Majority share of this small distillery was purchased by liquor giant Pernod Richard in 2016.

My Score

Notes: _____

_____

_____

Appearance (1-5) _____   Nose (1-25) _____

Taste (1-25) _____   Finish (1-25) _____

Complexity (1-10) _____   Overall Impression (1-10) _____

SCORE _____

Smooth Ambler Old Scout

Proof: 99
Age: 6 years
Type: Straight
Style: Traditional

Mash Bill: Not available
Color: Dark Straw
Price: $$$$

Mike

Nose: Fruit and caramel with a hint of tobacco.
Taste: Ripe apples and pear with vanilla and oak.
Finish: Starts sweet with some pepper and dries out nicely.

Susan

Nose: Sweet mint, anise, baking spice, vanilla.
Taste: Crème brulee, cinnamon, peaches and cherries.
Finish: Starts sweet with a dash of pepper at the end.

Notes

This was actually produced at MGP in Indiana. Smooth Ambler describes it as "fine curated whiskey scouted," hence the company name. But they are making and releasing more of their own whiskies as they have aged.

My Score		
Notes: _____		
_____		
_____		
Appearance (1-5) ____	Nose (1-25) ____	
Taste (1-25) ____	Finish (1-25) ____	
Complexity (1-10) ____	Overall Impression (1-10) ____	
SCORE ____		

Smooth Ambler Old Scout Single Barrel

Proof: 112.2
Age: 11 years
Type: Straight
Style: Single Barrel, Barrel Strength, Extra Aged

Mash Bill: Not available
Color: Light Amber
Price: $$$$$

Mike

Nose: Berries and pitted fruit. Vanilla with a hint of chocolate.
Taste: Fruit and caramel. Hint of baking spice and chocolate.
Finish: Caramel and chocolate leading into oak.

Susan

Nose: Caramel, sweet spices, dark cherries.
Taste: Toffee, meringue, cocoa, sweet spices.
Finish: Long and sweet. pleasantly warm.

Notes

Distilled at MGP in Indiana. Single barrel #811. The proof and age can vary.

My Score

Notes: _____

_____

_____

Appearance (1-5) ____   Nose (1-25) ____
Taste (1-25) ____   Finish (1-25) ____
Complexity (1-10) ____   Overall Impression (1-10) ____
SCORE ____

Smooth Ambler Old Scout - The Lion's Share Collection

Proof: 93
Age: 10 years
Type: Straight
Style: Single Barrel

Mash Bill: Not available
Color: Dark Straw
Price: $$$$$

Mike
Nose: Caramel, fruit and baking spice.
Taste: Caramel and milk chocolate with some berries and nutmeg.
Finish: Starts sweet and dries with some pepper and spices.

Susan
Nose: Rich candy corn and honey.
Taste: Sweet orchard fruit, nutmeg, sweet leather.
Finish: Very smooth and sweet. Touch of spice.

Notes
Distilled at MGP in Indiana. This was barrel #939. Excellent sip.

My Score	
Notes: _____	
_____	
_____	
Appearance (1-5) ____	Nose (1-25) ____
Taste (1-25) ____	Finish (1-25) ____
Complexity (1-10) ____	Overall Impression (1-10) ____
SCORE ____	

Stillwrights Bourbon

Proof:	90
Age:	2 years
Type:	Straight
Style:	Small Batch, Craft
Mash Bill:	Not available
Color:	Dark Straw
Price:	$$$

Mike
Nose: Vanilla and corn bread. Very light caramel.
Taste: Young – vanilla and cornbread dough and a hint of pepper spice.
Finish: Long with a bit of oak and pepper.

Susan
Nose: Corn, fusel oils, hayloft, faint with a hint of spice and oak.
Taste: Toffee and a little mint, hazelnuts.
Finish: Long with lots of black pepper at the end.

Notes
Overall quite young. Flat Rock Spirits of Fairborn, OH (near Dayton) is the distiller. They like to use locally sourced ingredients.

My Score

Notes: _____

_____

_____

Appearance (1-5)	____	Nose (1-25)	____
Taste (1-25)	____	Finish (1-25)	____
Complexity (1-10)	____	Overall Impression (1-10)	____

SCORE ____

Thirteenth Colony Bourbon

Proof:	95
Age:	NAS
Type:	Not Straight
Style:	Small Batch, Craft

Mash Bill:	Not available
Color:	Light Straw
Price:	$$$

Mike

Nose: Sweet corn and vanilla. A little honey, sweet spice.

Taste: A bit thin on the mouth. More pepper spice, then vanilla. Very astringent.

Finish: Very astringent and peppery finish. Not complex. Not good.

Susan

Nose: Very light. Some vanilla, corn, and touch of honey.

Taste: Corn and some pepper. Very simple.

Finish: Long, painfully hot, peppery.

Notes

Thirteenth Colony Distilleries, Americus, GA. Batch No. 2014. Bottle No. 3149.

My Score

Notes: _____

_____

_____

Appearance (1-5)	____	Nose (1-25)	____
Taste (1-25)	____	Finish (1-25)	____
Complexity (1-10)	____	Overall Impression (1-10)	____

SCORE ____

Tom's Foolery Barrel 11

Proof:	112
Age:	~ 3 years
Type:	Straight
Style:	Single Barrel, Craft
Mash Bill:	57% corn, 7% rye, 36% vienna malt
Color:	Dark Straw
Price:	$$$$

Mike

Nose: Corn, vanilla, and apricots.

Taste: Corn and anise with vanilla and spice. Very sweet, with nice mouthfeel. No burn at 112 proof!!!

Finish: Short and sweet.

Susan

Nose: Lightly toasted oak and touch of leather.

Taste: Sweeter on palate with ripe fruit, almonds and honey notes.

Finish: Short and sweet with mild pepper spice. Soft, oaky ending.

Notes

Tom's Foolery Distillery, Chagin Falls, OH. (Near Cleveland.) The owners bought some used equipment from the decommissioned Michter's Distiller in Schaeffertown, PA.

My Score

Notes: _____

_____

_____

Appearance (1-5)	____	Nose (1-25)	____
Taste (1-25)	____	Finish (1-25)	____
Complexity (1-10)	____	Overall Impression (1-10)	____

SCORE ____

Tom's Foolery Barrel 19

Proof:	120
Age:	~ 3 ½ years
Type:	Straight
Style:	Single Barrel, Craft
Mash Bill:	73% corn, 13% rye, 12% malted barley
Color:	Dark Straw
Price:	$$$$

Mike

Nose: Corn and honey with a hint of only a little oak. Water complex, but pleasant. Softens the nose and brings out candy corn.

Taste: Corn and yeasty bread dough. Vanilla and pepper spice. Surprisingly not hot at barrel proof. Water brings out more vanilla.

Finish: Sweet and long with honey and pecans.

Susan

Nose: Corn! And a little pitted fruit. Not vanilla.

Taste: Candies nuts, new saddle leather, peppery spice. Water amplifies the leather.

Finish: Very long. Add a little water to tame the proof heat.

Notes

Single Barrel bottling from Tom's Foolery Distillery near Cleveland. Nice layers for a young bourbon.

My Score

Notes: _____

_____

_____

Appearance (1-5)	____	Nose (1-25)	____
Taste (1-25)	____	Finish (1-25)	____
Complexity (1-10)	____	Overall Impression (1-10)	____
	SCORE ____		

Tom's Foolery Barrel 118

Proof: 108
Age: 3 years
Type: Straight
Style: Single Barrel, Craft

Mash Bill: 52% white corn, 10% rye, 32% barley*
Color: Light Straw
Price: $$$$

Mike
Nose: Very light. Vanilla and corn with some peaches.
Taste: Corn and spice – anise and vanilla. peach or apricot and just a hint of oak.
Finish: Medium length. Sweet and spicy.

Susan
Nose: Soft oak, like woodshop shavings.
Taste: Quite sweet with vanilla, sweet Some ripe spices and a hint dash of candied nuts.
Finish: Medium long and smooth. No burn. Perhaps its outstanding feature.

Notes
Each single barrel from Tom's Foolery is different. This one employs a trio of barleys* – 29% barley malt, 6% crystal malt, 3% roasted barley.

My Score		
Notes: _____		
_____		
_____		
Appearance (1-5) ____	Nose (1-25) ____	
Taste (1-25) ____	Finish (1-25) ____	
Complexity (1-10) ____	Overall Impression (1-10) ____	
SCORE ____		

Tom's Foolery
Small Batch 2015.1

Proof:	90
Age:	2 ½ years
Type:	Straight
Style:	Small Batch
Mash Bill:	Not available
Color:	Light Straw
Price:	$$$$

Mike

Nose:	Very young. Corn and vanilla. Hint of peaches.
Taste:	Very nice. Corn and peaches with some cinnamon.
Finish:	Slightly oaky with spices and vanilla.

Susan

Nose:	Corn predominates. Yeasty.
Taste:	Sweet corn at first. Then caramel and vanilla.
Finish:	Short, sweet, warm, and smooth.

Notes

From Tom's Foolery Distillery, Cleveland, OH. Not complex, but a very pleasant sip. Bottle #1185.

My Score

Notes: _____

_____

_____

Appearance (1-5)	____	Nose (1-25)	____
Taste (1-25)	____	Finish (1-25)	____
Complexity (1-10)	____	Overall Impression (1-10)	____

SCORE ____

Town Branch

Proof: 80
Age: NAS
Type: Straight
Style: Craft

Mash Bill: 72% corn, 15% rye,
13% malted barley
Color: Pale Straw
Price: $$$

Mike

Nose: Corn and vanilla with a hint of spice. Very simple nose.
Taste: Candy corn and pepper spice with a bit of oak. A bit thin in the mouth.
Finish: Starts peppery and fades quickly.

Susan

Nose: Simple. Corn, light caramel.
Taste: Corn predominates, followed by caramel, a little vanilla and faint nuttiness.
Finish: Short and slightly bitter with tannins at the end.

Notes

An all-around rather light-bodied whiskey for a bourbon. Produced at Town Branch Distillery in Lexington, KY. It is owned by All-Tech.

My Score

Notes: _____

_____

_____

Appearance (1-5) ____   Nose (1-25) ____

Taste (1-25) ____   Finish (1-25) ____

Complexity (1-10) ____   Overall Impression (1-10) ____

SCORE ____

Waitsburg Bourbon Whiskey

Proof:	80
Age:	NAS
Type:	Straight
Style:	Small Batch, Craft
Mash Bill:	Not available
Color:	Light Straw
Price:	$

Mike

Nose:	Vanilla and sweet corn. Very light with just a hint of oak.
Taste:	Sweet spice and vanilla. Not complex. Some corn and oak.
Finish:	Moderately long. A bit spicy with oak tannins.

Susan

Nose:	Minty, light, with a whiff of spice.
Taste:	Light oak with some spice and a little vanilla.
Finish:	Short and quite peppery for 80 proof.

Notes

From the Oola Distillery in Seattle, WA. Craft distiller makes other spirits, as well, including gin, vodka, and infused vodkas.

My Score

Notes: _____

_____

_____

Appearance (1-5)	____	Nose (1-25)	____
Taste (1-25)	____	Finish (1-25)	____
Complexity (1-10)	____	Overall Impression (1-10)	____

SCORE ____

Watershed

Proof: 94
Age: NAS
Type: Not Straight
Style: Small Batch

Mash Bill: Corn, wheat, rye, spelt
Color: Straw
Price: $$$$

Mike
Nose: Candied corn with a hint of spice.
Taste: Corn and vanilla with some pepper.
Finish: Long and dry with oak. A bit astringent.

Susan
Nose: Candied apples and some burnt vanilla.
Taste: Buttered popcorn, green apples.
Finish: Short. Not complex.

Notes
From Watershed Distillery, Columbus, OH. Small batch #013.

My Score
Notes: _____

Appearance (1-5) ____   Nose (1-25) ____
Taste (1-25) ____   Finish (1-25) ____
Complexity (1-10) ____   Overall Impression (1-10) ____
SCORE ____

West of Kentucky No. 2

Proof:	95
Age:	1 year
Type:	Unfiltered
Style:	Small Batch, Wheated
Mash Bill:	Not available
Color:	Straw
Price:	$$$$

Mike
Nose: Very light. Bread dough and vanilla.
Taste: Corn and citrus with some vanilla and spice.
Finish: Dry oak and spice.

Susan
Nose: Cellulose. Some caramel and vanilla.
Taste: Corn, oak, vanilla.
Finish: Short and peppery.

Notes
Made by Sonoma County Distilling Co., Rohnert Park, CA. Bottle #1243 from batch #3.

My Score

Notes: _____

_____

_____

Appearance (1-5) ____	Nose (1-25) ____
Taste (1-25) ____	Finish (1-25) ____
Complexity (1-10) ____	Overall Impression (1-10) ____

SCORE ____

West of Kentucky No. 2 Cask Strength

Proof: 107
Age: 1 year
Type: Not Straight
Style: Wheated, Small Batch, Barrel Strength

Mash Bill: Not available
Color: Straw
Price: $$$$$

Mike
Nose: Bread dough and vanilla. Hint of oak.
Taste: Corn and citrus. Some pecans and oak.
Finish: Dry with oak and spice.

Susan
Nose: Corn husk. Nut shells.
Taste: Oak and roasted corn. Some dates.
Finish: Very oaky.

Notes
Made by Sonoma County Distilling Co., Rohnert Park, CA. Bottle #248 from batch #3.

My Score

Notes: _____

_____

_____

Appearance (1-5) ____   Nose (1-25) ____
Taste (1-25) ____   Finish (1-25) ____
Complexity (1-10) ____   Overall Impression (1-10) ____
SCORE ____

Whiskey Acres

Proof: 87
Age: 1 year
Type: Not Straight
Style: Farm Distilled

Mash Bill: Not available
Color: Straw
Price: $$$$$

Mike
Nose: Very young. Bread dough and candied fruit.
Taste: Corn bread dough and vanilla with some pepper.
Finish: Short and sweet with vanilla and spice.

Susan
Nose: Corn and oak with some leather and honey.
Taste: Jalapeno cornbread with some fruit.
Finish: Short and sweet with warmth at the end.

Notes
Made by Whiskey Acres Distilling Co., DeKalb, IL. Farm distillery that produces spirits from its own grain. They are experimenting with different corn varieties.

My Score

Notes: _____

_____

_____

Appearance (1-5) ____   Nose (1-25) ____
Taste (1-25) ____   Finish (1-25) ____
Complexity (1-10) ____   Overall Impression (1-10) ____
SCORE ____

Widow Jane

Proof: 91
Age: 8 years
Type: Straight
Style: Single Barrel, Craft

Mash Bill: Not available
Color: Straw
Price: $$$$$

Mike

Nose: Blackstrap molasses, cherries, oak.
Taste: Sweet caramel and pitted fruit – cherries and apricots.
Finish: Long and sweet with a hint of oak as it lingers.

Susan

Nose: Spicy corn, cherries. oak.
Taste: Spicy caramel with vanilla, pecan, ripe cherries.
Finish: Long, warm, ending in mild pepper spice.

Notes

Cacao Prieto Distillery, Brooklyn, NY. Also produces chocolate from the beans. Water comes from the limestone caves of the Widow Jane Mine in Rosendale, NY.

My Score		
Notes: _____		
_____		
_____		
Appearance (1-5) ____	Nose (1-25)	____
Taste (1-25) ____	Finish (1-25)	____
Complexity (1-10) ____	Overall Impression (1-10)	____
SCORE ____		

Winchester

Proof: 90
Age: At least 2 years
Type: Straight
Style: Small Batch

Mash Bill: Not available
Color: Straw
Price: $$

Mike
Nose: Vanilla, oak, and corn in that order.
Taste: Very light. Vanilla and peaches with corn and oak.
Finish: Short and sweet. Just a hint of oak.

Susan
Nose: Honeyed vanilla and caramel.
Taste: Sweet corn, light caramel, faint fruit.
Finish: Medium long. Dry, but no burn.

Notes
Made by TerrePURE Spirits, North Charleston, SC. A second distillery with the same owners started producing at the former Charles Medley facility in Owensboro, KY in 2016. Both use a special process involving ultrasonic waves, heat, and oxygen to accelerate aging.

My Score

Notes: _____

_____

_____

Appearance (1-5) ____   Nose (1-25) ____

Taste (1-25) ____   Finish (1-25) ____

Complexity (1-10) ____   Overall Impression (1-10) ____

SCORE ____

Woodstone Creek

Proof:	94
Age:	NAS*
Type:	Straight
Style:	Single Barrel, Craft
Mash Bill:	Five grains**
Color:	Dark Straw
Price:	$$$$$

Mike

Nose: Very malty – corn and barley malt. Caramel and vanilla with hint of sweet spices and tobacco.

Taste: Sweet with malt and corn. A bit of pepper spice and oak. Touch of hickory nuts and hazelnuts.

Finish: Long and spicy turning to nice, dry oak.

Susan

Nose: Light caramel, popcorn, light pepper, tobacco.

Taste: Vanilla and caramel. Not-quite-ripe apricots and toasted pecans.

Finish: Long and dry. Ends with black pepper.

Notes

Woodstone Creek Distillery, Cincinnati, OH. Distiller told us it is 5 years old.* No proportions given, but made with white corn, yellow corn, malted rye, malted wheat, and malted barley.** Made in a pot still. Only 2-3 barrels made per year and price weighs in at about $100/bottle.

My Score

Notes: _____

_____

_____

Appearance (1-5)	____	Nose (1-25)	____
Taste (1-25)	____	Finish (1-25)	____
Complexity (1-10)	____	Overall Impression (1-10)	____
	SCORE ____		

Wyoming Whiskey

Proof:	88
Age:	3 years
Type:	Straight
Style:	Small Batch, Craft, Wheated
Mash Bill:	Includes wheat
Color:	Straw
Price:	$$$$

Mike

Nose: Sweet honey and ripe apple. Vanilla and corn.

Taste: Sweet honey and corn with some spice. Allspice and apples.

Finish: Long and sweet with a bit of spice.

Susan

Nose: Corn an oak and a little clove.

Taste: Vanilla and apples.

Finish: Long and warm. Some spice.

Notes

Wyoming Whiskey, Kirby, WY. Batch 14, Bottled June 13, 2013. This would be an even better bourbon at 4 years old. Gets better as it breathes.

My Score

Notes: _____

_____

_____

Appearance (1-5) _____   Nose (1-25) _____

Taste (1-25) _____   Finish (1-25) _____

Complexity (1-10) _____   Overall Impression (1-10) _____

SCORE _____

Yellow Rose Double Barrel

Proof:	86
Age:	NAS
Type:	Straight
Style:	Special Finish
Mash Bill:	Not available
Color:	Dark Straw
Price:	$$$

Mike

Nose:	Caramel and figs. Hint of spice.
Taste:	Caramel and fruit. Hint of butterscotch.
Finish:	Long and fruity with butterscotch and oak.

Susan

Nose:	Light caramel, dark fruit, oak.
Taste:	Caramel and oak with touch of black pepper and tobacco.
Finish:	Short and warm. No burn.

Notes

Wine barrel finished. This was bottle #618 from Batch #1. From Yellow Rose Distilling, Houston, TX.

My Score

Notes: _____
_____
_____

Appearance (1-5)	____	Nose (1-25)	____
Taste (1-25)	____	Finish (1-25)	____
Complexity (1-10)	____	Overall Impression (1-10)	____
	SCORE ____		

Yellow Rose Outlaw

Proof:	92
Age:	6 months
Type:	Not Straight
Style:	Small Batch
Mash Bill:	Not available
Color:	Light Amber
Price:	$$$$$

Mike

Nose:	Corn and vanilla. Hint of oak and pecans.
Taste:	Corn and vanilla with some pecans and oak.
Finish:	Dry with pecans and oak.

Susan

Nose:	Oak, nuts, some sweet spice.
Taste:	Oak and corn, plus pecans.
Finish:	Very dry/woody.

Notes

From Yellow Rose Distilling, Houston, TX. Bottle #467 from batch #27. Aged in 25-gallon casks.

My Score

Notes: _____

_____

_____

Appearance (1-5) ____   Nose (1-25) ____

Taste (1-25) ____   Finish (1-25) ____

Complexity (1-10) ____   Overall Impression (1-10) ____

SCORE ____

Additional Craft Distiller Releases

Name: _____

Distillery: _____

Proof: _____   **Mash Bill:** _____
Age: _____   _____
Type: _____   **Color:** _____
Style: _____   **Price:** _____

My Score

Notes: _____
_____
_____

Appearance (1-5) _____   Nose (1-25) _____
Taste (1-25) _____   Finish (1-25) _____
Complexity (1-10) _____   Overall Impression (1-10) _____
SCORE _____

Name: _____

Distillery: _____

Proof: _____   **Mash Bill:** _____
Age: _____   _____
Type: _____   **Color:** _____
Style: _____   **Price:** _____

My Score

Notes: _____
_____
_____

Appearance (1-5) _____   Nose (1-25) _____
Taste (1-25) _____   Finish (1-25) _____
Complexity (1-10) _____   Overall Impression (1-10) _____
SCORE _____

INDEPENDENT BOTTLERS

Many of these brands may have a Kentucky address and even be bottled in Kentucky, but the bourbon is sourced from elsewhere, including from MGP (Midwest Grain Products) in Lawrenceburg, Indiana. (Not to be confused with Lawrenceburg, Kentucky, home to both Four Roses and Wild Turkey.) This facility was formerly known as LDI (Lawrenceburg Distillers Indiana) and was, before that, a Seagrams distillery.

The bourbons are listed alphabetically. Many of these bottlers are going to begin distilling, but the bourbons we sampled were still being sourced.

Amador Double Barrel

Proof:	86.8
Age:	NAS
Type:	Not Straight
Style:	Special Finish
Mash Bill:	Not available
Color:	Straw
Price:	$$$$

Mike
Nose: Raisins and dates. Vanilla and sweet spice.
Taste: Thin and watery with some fruit and vanilla.
Finish: Dry and oaky.

Susan
Nose: Very light. Corn and some cherries.
Taste: Fruit note, probably from wine barrel.
Finish: Short and hot.

Notes
Sourced from undisclosed Kentucky distillery and finished in Napa Valley wine barrels by Amador Whiskey Co., St. Helena, CA.

My Score

Notes: _____

_____

_____

Appearance (1-5) _____   Nose (1-25) _____

Taste (1-25) _____   Finish (1-25) _____

Complexity (1-10) _____   Overall Impression (1-10) _____

SCORE _____

Angel's Envy

Proof:	86.6
Age:	NAS
Type:	Straight
Style:	Special Finish, Small Batch
Mash Bill:	72% corn, 18% rye, 10% malted barley
Color:	Straw
Price:	$$$

Mike

Nose: Vanilla and fruit with some caramel and corn and hint of fine tobacco.

Taste: Sweet fruit and caramel with tobacco and oak.

Finish: Long and sweet with the port wine coming out at the end. Some oak adds balance.

Susan

Nose: Very fruity, with good vanilla and caramel notes.

Taste: Lovely vanilla on the tongue with dark fruit and light spices and a wine-like note.

Finish: Long and warm.

Notes

Batch No. FA14, Bottle No. 1. Finished by aging in used port wine casks. Sourced from Kentucky distilleries and selected by the late Lincoln Henderson, retired Master Distiller from Brown-Forman who created Woodford Reserve Distributed by Louisville Distilling Company, Crestwood, KY. The company opened its own distillery on Main Street in Louisville in 2016 and is now producing whiskey there.

My Score

Notes: _____

_____

_____

Appearance (1-5)	____	Nose (1-25)	____
Taste (1-25)	____	Finish (1-25)	____
Complexity (1-10)	____	Overall Impression (1-10)	____

SCORE ____

Angel's Envy Cask Strength Bottled 2012

Proof:	123.7
Age:	NAS
Type:	Straight
Style:	Special Finish, Small Batch
Mash Bill:	72% corn, 18% rye, 10% malted barley
Color:	Amber
Price:	$$$$$$

Mike

Nose: Rich caramel – almost molasses – with berries and grapes and a hint of tobacco. Water. weakens the nose, but brings out the fruit.

Taste: Rich fruit and caramel, a bit if tobacco and oak. Water sweetens it (more fruit than caramel) and amplifies the tobacco.

Finish: Long and dry with oak tannins. Water does not change the finish.

Susan

Nose: Rich caramel, pecans, cocoa.

Taste: Lots of oak at barrel proof. Water brings out licorice, pecan, toffee, and dried fruit.

Finish: Long, warm, and nutty. Elegant.

Notes

Save this for a snifter in an armchair by the fireplace. There is a limited release of this expression each year. Cask strength varies. For example, the 2014 for 119.3 proof.

My Score

Notes: _____

_____

_____

Appearance (1-5)	____	Nose (1-25)	____
Taste (1-25)	____	Finish (1-25)	____
Complexity (1-10)	____	Overall Impression (1-10)	____

SCORE ____

Backbone Bourbon

Proof:	115.4
Age:	NAS
Type:	Straight
Style:	Uncut, Barrel Strength, Small Batch
Mash Bill:	Not available
Color:	Dark Straw
Price:	$$$$

Mike

Nose: Sweet caramel, ginger and nutmeg. Water softens the spices.

Taste: Sweet and spice with molasses and spice. Water makes it sweeter.

Finish: Long, sweet, spicy. Water makes it peppery.

Susan

Nose: Crème brulee, ripe apple/pear. Faint note of cocoa.

Taste: Sweet vanilla, sweet spices, baked apples.

Finish: Warm with black pepper and oak at the end.

Notes

Bottled by Bardstown Backbone Bourbon Co. This was small batch #10. Distilled at MGP in Lawrenceburg, IN.

My Score

Notes: _____

_____

_____

Appearance (1-5) _____   Nose (1-25) _____

Taste (1-25) _____   Finish (1-25) _____

Complexity (1-10) _____   Overall Impression (1-10) _____

SCORE _____

Banker's Club

Proof:	80
Age:	NAS
Type:	Straight
Style:	Traditional

Mash Bill:	Not available
Color:	Light Straw
Price:	$

Mike

Nose: Vanilla and sweet corn. Very light with just a hint of oak.

Taste: Sweet spice and vanilla. Not complex. Some corn and oak.

Finish: Moderately long. A bit spicy with oak tannins.

Susan

Nose: Minty, light, with a whiff of spice.

Taste: Light oak with some spice and a little vanilla.

Finish: Short and oddly hot for 80 proof.

Notes

Not bad for the price. Use it to make cocktails for a crowd. Distributed by Regent Distillers Products Company, Scobeyville, NJ. Made in Kentucky.

My Score

Notes: _____

_____

_____

Appearance (1-5)	____	Nose (1-25)	____
Taste (1-25)	____	Finish (1-25)	____
Complexity (1-10)	____	Overall Impression (1-10)	____

SCORE ____

Barrel Bourbon

Proof:	124.7
Age:	8 years, 3 months
Type:	Straight
Style:	Small Batch, Barrel Proof
Mash Bill:	70% corn, 26% rye, 4% malted barley
Color:	Dark Straw
Price:	$$$$$

Mike

Nose: Maple smoke and apples with a hint of vanilla.
Taste: Sweet caramel with smoky wood and apples. Hint of pepper spice.
Finish: Dry and smoky with oak.

Susan

Nose: Caramel corn. Apples.
Taste: Very sweet entry – candy corn, maple syrup, cinnamon.
Finish: Cinnamon grows at the end.

Notes

Distilled in Tennessee (George Dickel?). Bottled by Barrel Craft Spirits, Crestwood, KY. This was batch 005. Tasted a lot like juice from George Dickel Distillery. Each batch sourced differently. A very pleasant sip. Water amplifies the apples. Barrel announced plans in 2017 to built its own distillery in Louisville.

My Score

Notes: _____

_____

_____

Appearance (1-5) _____   Nose (1-25) _____

Taste (1-25) _____   Finish (1-25) _____

Complexity (1-10) _____   Overall Impression (1-10) _____

SCORE _____

Battlefield Bourbon

Proof:	91.2
Age:	NAS
Type:	Not Straight
Style:	Small Batch
Mash Bill:	Not available
Color:	Very Light Straw
Price:	$$$$$

Mike
Nose: Corn and vanilla with a hint of pecans.
Taste: Corn, vanilla, honey with some citrus notes.
Finish: Short and sweet with a hint of oak.

Susan
Nose: Sweet corn, nuts, nutmeg, orange zest.
Taste: Sweet spices, citrus, vanilla.
Finish: Sweet, drying to oak and cornmeal.

Notes
Speakeasy Spirits LLC, Nashville. Distilled, aged and bottled in Tennessee. This was bottle #882 of 1863. Proceeds help preserve and restore Civil War battlefield sites.

My Score

Notes: _____

_____

_____

Appearance (1-5)	_____	Nose (1-25)	_____
Taste (1-25)	_____	Finish (1-25)	_____
Complexity (1-10)	_____	Overall Impression (1-10)	_____

SCORE _____

Beanball Bourbon

Proof:	90
Age:	NAS
Type:	Not Straight
Style:	Small Batch
Mash Bill:	Not available
Color:	Light Straw
Price:	$$$$

Mike

Nose:	Corn bread and vanilla/honey.
Taste:	Peaches and vanilla with a hint of spice.
Finish:	Not much. A little sweet and gone.

Susan

Nose:	Sweet oak and Bit O'Honey.
Taste:	Ripe peaches and some vanilla.
Finish:	Short and light.

Notes

Bottle number 6-8-15. Made in Indiana at MGP and bottled by Cooperstown Distillery, Cooperstown, NY.

My Score

Notes: _____

_____

_____

Appearance (1-5) _____   Nose (1-25) _____

Taste (1-25) _____   Finish (1-25) _____

Complexity (1-10) _____   Overall Impression (1-10) _____

SCORE _____

Beer Barrel Bourbon

Proof:	80
Age:	NAS
Type:	Not Straight
Style:	Special Finish
Mash Bill:	Not available
Color:	Straw
Price:	$$$$

Mike
Nose: Very malty. Not complex. Had a hard time getting anything else. A little vanilla

Taste: Very light. Some malt and chocolate notes with some caramel and corn.

Finish: Very short and light A little sweet with a hint of oak.

Susan
Nose: Light and malty. Some oak and faint vanilla. Not complex.

Taste: Caramel and sweet spices.

Finish: Short and peppery. Oddly hot for 80 proof.

Notes
New Holland Artisan Spirits, Holland, MI. New Holland is known for its craft beers. This bourbon is sourced from Kentucky and aged for an additional three months in used beer barrels. Might make an interesting Manhattan.

My Score

Notes: _____

_____

_____

Appearance (1-5)	____	Nose (1-25)	____
Taste (1-25)	____	Finish (1-25)	____
Complexity (1-10)	____	Overall Impression (1-10)	____

SCORE ____

Belle Meade

Proof:	90.4
Age:	5 ½ - 7 ½ years
Type:	Straight
Style:	Small Batch
Mash Bill:	30% rye
Color:	Light Amber
Price:	$$$$

Mike

Nose: Corn and vanilla with a hint of caramel and oak.

Taste: Corn, nutmeg, clove, with some vanilla oak.

Finish: Dry with oak tannins and a bit astringent.

Susan

Nose: Maple syrup, cinnamon, and vanilla.

Taste: Caramel corn, very dry stone fruit and new oak.

Finish: Short and dry.

Notes

Bottled by Nelson's Green Brier Distillery, Nashville, TN. Sourced from MGP in Lawrenceburg, IN. Belle Meade Bourbon distilled at Green Brier to be released in 2015.

My Score

Notes: _____

_____

_____

Appearance (1-5) _____   Nose (1-25) _____

Taste (1-25) _____   Finish (1-25) _____

Complexity (1-10) _____   Overall Impression (1-10) _____

SCORE _____

Bib & Tucker

Proof: 92
Age: 6 years
Type: Straight
Style: Small Batch

Mash Bill: Not available
Color: Light Amber
Price: $$$$$

Mike
Nose: Peaches and vanilla with some cinnamon oak and leather. Nuttiness.
Taste: Caramel and apricots. Some allspice. Oak, too.
Finish: Nice finish. Medium long with caramel and oak. Dries out nicely.

Susan
Nose: Corn and rye. Warm cereal. Some spice.
Taste: Caramel, vanilla, nutmeg and cinnamon.
Finish: Long and sweet, ending in sweet oak.

Notes
Bottled by 35 Maple Street Spirits, Crestwood, KY. Very handsome, flask-style bottle.

My Score
Notes: _____
_____
_____

Appearance (1-5) _____   Nose (1-25) _____
Taste (1-25) _____   Finish (1-25) _____
Complexity (1-10) _____   Overall Impression (1-10) _____
SCORE _____

Big Ass Bourbon Barrel Strength

Proof: 119.5
Age: 4 months
Type: Not Straight
Style: Barrel Strength

Mash Bill: Not available
Color: Very Light Straw
Price: $$$$

Mike

Nose: Young. Bread dough and vanilla.
Taste: Corn and vanilla. Very light.
Finish: Pepper and little else.

Susan

Nose: Oak and alcohol. Whiff of vanilla.
Taste: Vanilla. Almost flavorless.
Finish: Oaky and hot.

Notes

Probably an MGP product. Owned by Diversa Brands, Louisville, KY.

My Score		
Notes: _____		
_____		
_____		
Appearance (1-5) ____	Nose (1-25)	____
Taste (1-25) ____	Finish (1-25)	____
Complexity (1-10) ____	Overall Impression (1-10)	____
SCORE ____		

Big House

Proof: 90
Age: 6 years
Type: Straight Bourbon
Style: Small Batch

Mash Bill: 60% corn, 35% rye, 5% malted barley
Color: Dark Straw
Price: $$

Mike

Nose: Caramel and citrus fruit with hint of honeysuckle. Some sweet spice – allspice – in the background.

Taste: A bit of corn and vanilla with some citrus fruit and oak.

Finish: Starts sweet with caramel, but dries with oak tannins and spice.

Susan

Nose: Vanilla, light caramel, sweet licorice and a little new leather.

Taste: Crème brulee, citrus, and faint nuttiness. Creamy mouthfeel.

Finish: Weakest aspect. Rather short and hot.

Notes

Underdog Wine and Spirits, Livermore, CA. Sourced from MGP in Indiana. Limited distribution.

My Score

Notes: _____

_____

_____

Appearance (1-5) ____   Nose (1-25) ____

Taste (1-25) ____   Finish (1-25) ____

Complexity (1-10) ____   Overall Impression (1-10) ____

SCORE ____

Bird Dog

Proof: 80
Age: NAS
Type: Not Straight
Style: Traditional

Mash Bill: Not available
Color: Light Straw
Price: $$

Mike
Nose: Very light – vanilla and honey.
Taste: Very simple. A little vanilla and corn. Hint of pepper spice.
Finish: Short and sweet with vanilla.

Susan
Nose: Light. Corn and alcohol. Vanilla.
Taste: Corn and vanilla. That's it. Hot for 80 proof.
Finish: Short. Heat subsides at the end.

Notes
Three Springs Bottling Company, Bowling Green, KY. Says "Kentucky" on the label, but no distiller identified.

My Score

Notes: _____

_____

_____

Appearance (1-5) ____   Nose (1-25) ____

Taste (1-25) ____   Finish (1-25) ____

Complexity (1-10) ____   Overall Impression (1-10) ____

SCORE ____

Bird Dog Small Batch

Proof:	86
Age:	NAS
Type:	Not Straight
Style:	Small Batch
Mash Bill:	Not available
Color:	Straw
Price:	$$$

Mike
Nose: Corn and honeysuckle with hint of vanilla.
Taste: Corn and vanilla with pepper spice.
Finish: Short, dry and peppery.

Susan
Nose: Vanilla, pitted fruit, flowers.
Taste: Sweet buttered corn, apples, faint spice.
Finish: Medium long, drying to oak.

Notes
Western Spirits and 3 Springs Bottling Co., Bowling Green, KY.

My Score

Notes: _____

_____

_____

Appearance (1-5) ____   Nose (1-25) ____

Taste (1-25) ____   Finish (1-25) ____

Complexity (1-10) ____   Overall Impression (1-10) ____

SCORE ____

Black Ridge Small Batch

Proof: 90
Age: NAS
Type: Straight
Style: Small Batch

Mash Bill: Not available
Color: Dark Straw
Price: $$$$

Mike
Nose: Ripe fruit, leather, caramel.
Taste: Ripe apples, pears and caramel with baking spice and tobacco.
Finish: Starts fruity, but gets some nice oak and spice as it lingers. Very nice.

Susan
Nose: Sweet corn, light cinnamon, pitted fruit.
Taste: Vanilla, caramel, wood smoke.
Finish: Sweet, drying to oak and smoke.

Notes
Brand from Clear Springs Distilling Company, Louisville, KY, which is owned by Sazarac.

My Score		
Notes: _____		
_____		
_____		
Appearance (1-5) ____	Nose (1-25) ____	
Taste (1-25) ____	Finish (1-25) ____	
Complexity (1-10) ____	Overall Impression (1-10) ____	
SCORE ____		

Black Saddle

Proof: 90
Age: 12 years
Type: Does not say "Straight" on label
Style: Traditional

Mash Bill: Not available
Color: Straw
Price: $$$$

Mike

Nose: Caramel and apple with a hint of nutmeg and oak.
Taste: Caramel and ripe apples with some pepper spice.
Finish: Long and dry with oak and pepper.

Susan

Nose: Appealing vanilla character.
Taste: Cherry and a little wood smoke. Caramel, some pitted fruit and nuts.
Finish: Dries to pleasant oak spiciness.

Notes

From Frank-Lin Distillers Products Ltd. Fairfield, CA. Distributors of several Kentucky-sourced bourbons of indeterminate origin.

My Score

Notes: _____

_____

_____

Appearance (1-5) _____   Nose (1-25) _____
Taste (1-25) _____   Finish (1-25) _____
Complexity (1-10) _____   Overall Impression (1-10) _____
SCORE _____

Blood Oath

Proof:	98.6
Age:	NAS
Type:	Straight
Style:	Small Batch
Mash Bill:	Four Grain, "favoring rye," includes wheat
Color:	Straw
Price:	$$$$$

Mike

Nose: Caramel and leather with a hint of honeysuckle.
Taste: Caramel and apricots with some pepper spice.
Finish: Woody and a bit astringent.

Susan

Nose: Banana, apricot, vanilla, sweet spice.
Taste: Light caramel, fruit and sweet spices.
Finish: Warm with dash of black pepper.

Notes

Very smooth sip, especially give the proof, which is a play on blood temperature. This was from "Pact No. 1" (a mingling of three different mash bills) and batch number 1. Bottled 2-20-15. Distributed by Luxco of St. Louis from sourced bourbons, including a wheated. A Pact No. 2 was released in 2016 featuring a different combination of mashbills.

My Score

Notes: _____

_____

_____

Appearance (1-5)	_____	Nose (1-25)	_____
Taste (1-25)	_____	Finish (1-25)	_____
Complexity (1-10)	_____	Overall Impression (1-10)	_____
	SCORE _____		

Bower Hill Barrel Reserve

Proof:	86
Age:	NAS
Type:	Straight
Style:	Small Batch
Mash Bill:	Not available
Color:	Straw
Price:	$$$$

Mike
Nose: Bread dough and yeast. Some corn and vanilla.
Taste: Corn bread and vanilla. Hint of pepper.
Finish: Short and sweet with hint of oak.

Susan
Nose: Caramel corn, honey, sweet spices.
Taste: More caramel corn, some ripe peach.
Finish: Pepper and oak.

Notes
Distilled and aged in Louisville, KY. Bottles by Bower Hill Distillery, Silverton, OH. Bower Hill was the deadliest battle of the Whiskey Rebellion of 1794. There is also a very limited barrel strength release.

My Score
Notes: _____

_____

_____

Appearance (1-5) ____   Nose (1-25) ____

Taste (1-25) ____   Finish (1-25) ____

Complexity (1-10) ____   Overall Impression (1-10) ____

SCORE ____

Breaker

Proof:	90
Age:	5 years
Type:	Straight
Style:	Small Batch
Mash Bill:	Not available
Color:	Straw
Price:	$$$$

Mike

Nose: Corn, vanilla, sweet spices. Hint of peaches.
Taste: Corn and vanilla with some peaches and oak.
Finish: Starts sweet and dries with some oak.

Susan

Nose: Light caramel, apples and pears.
Taste: Caramel and a bit of chocolate with some apples.
Finish: Dry and oaky.

Notes

Distilled by MGP. Bottled by Ascendant Spirits, Santa Barbara Co., CA. Batch a mingling of 8 barrels. This was bottle 774 from batch 13. More recent releases *may* be distilled in CA.

My Score

Notes: _____
_____
_____

Appearance (1-5)	____	Nose (1-25)	____
Taste (1-25)	____	Finish (1-25)	____
Complexity (1-10)	____	Overall Impression (1-10)	____
	SCORE ____		

Breaking & Entering

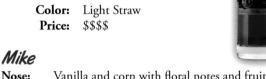

Proof:	86
Age:	NAS
Type:	Not Straight
Style:	Small Batch
Mash Bill:	Not available
Color:	Light Straw
Price:	$$$$

Mike

Nose: Vanilla and corn with floral notes and fruit – apricots and berries.

Taste: Sweet caramel, light apricot, and some leather. Bit of spice.

Finish: Very long and dry with oak and pepper.

Susan

Nose: Vanilla, pitted fruit, a little honey and light spice.

Taste: Vanilla, oak, a little nutmeg.

Finish: Medium long and oaky. Dash of pepper.

Notes

St. George Spirits. Alameda, CA. Craft distillery, but this is a batching of some 80 barrels of different bourbons sourced from Kentucky. Distilleries unknown.

My Score

Notes: _____

_____

_____

Appearance (1-5)	____	Nose (1-25)	____
Taste (1-25)	____	Finish (1-25)	____
Complexity (1-10)	____	Overall Impression (1-10)	____

SCORE ____

Broken Bell

Proof:	90
Age:	NAS
Type:	Not Straight
Style:	Small Batch
Mash Bill:	Not available
Color:	Light Straw
Price:	$$$

Mike
Nose: Very light. A hint of vanilla and corn.

Taste: Very light on the tongue with a hint of candy corn and spice.

Finish: Gets peppery with time and lasts longer than taste would indicate.

Susan
Nose: Vanilla, but very light. Perhaps a bit of cinnamon or nutmeg.

Taste: Mirrors the nose. Some vanilla and fairly full mouthfeel. Not complex.

Finish: Medium long and dry.

Notes
Broken Bell Whiskey Co., Princeton, MN. Sourced from an unidentified distillery. Does not say "Kentucky" on the label.

My Score

Notes: _____

_____

_____

Appearance (1-5)	____	Nose (1-25)	____
Taste (1-25)	____	Finish (1-25)	____
Complexity (1-10)	____	Overall Impression (1-10)	____

SCORE ____

Buck

Proof:	90
Age:	8 years
Type:	Straight
Style:	Small Batch
Mash Bill:	Not available
Color:	Dark Straw
Price:	$$$

Mike
Nose: Very light. Some vanilla and saddle leather.
Taste: Very light. Some apple and caramel leading to a spicy finish.
Finish: Fairly short and peppery.

Susan
Nose: Cinnamon, oak, nuts.
Taste: Ripe pears, vanilla and caramel. A dash of black pepper.
Finish: Medium long and tannic.

Notes
Frank-Lin Distillers, Fairfield, CA. This facility sources bourbon from undisclosed distilleries in Kentucky and bottles it under several labels. This is curiously simple bourbon for 8 years old.

My Score
Notes: _____

_____

_____

Appearance (1-5)	____	Nose (1-25)	____
Taste (1-25)	____	Finish (1-25)	____
Complexity (1-10)	____	Overall Impression (1-10)	____

SCORE ____

Burnside Double Barrel

Proof: 96
Age: NAS
Type: Straight
Style: Special Finish

Mash Bill: 75% corn, 10% rye, 15% malted barley
Color: Straw
Price: $$$$

Mike
Nose: Sweet vanilla and berries with some ginger.
Taste: Sweet vanilla and ginger with some citrus and tobacco.
Finish: Starts sweet and dries to oak tannins.

Susan
Nose: Toasted marshmallow and light fruit.
Taste: Vanilla, ginger, and orange rind.
Finish: Sweet vanilla ending in spicy oak.

Notes
From Eastside Distilling, Portland, OR. The company sources its mashed grain (No word from where.) and ferments, distills, and bottles. After initial aging, this is aged an extra 60 days in heavily charred, Oregon oak barrels. This was Batch No. 6, Bottle No. 325.

My Score		
Notes: _____		
_____		
_____		
Appearance (1-5) ____	Nose (1-25)	____
Taste (1-25) ____	Finish (1-25)	____
Complexity (1-10) ____	Overall Impression (1-10)	____
SCORE ____		

Calumet Farm

Proof:	86
Age:	NAS
Type:	Does not say "Straight" on label
Style:	Traditional
Mash Bill:	Not available
Color:	Light Straw
Price:	$$$$

Mike

Nose: Very floral – honeysuckle and vanilla sweet corn and some oak.

Taste: Sweet corn and vanilla up front with pepper spice coming afterwards.

Finish: Long and dry with oak.

Susan

Nose: Very light. Some caramel and dried fruit.

Taste: Light maple syrup. Some caramel.

Finish: Long and dry. Best aspect of this bourbon.

Notes

Kentucky-sourced bourbon of indeterminate origin. Bottled by Three Springs Bottling Co. of Bowling Green and owned by Western Spirits of the same city. Pretty packaging and the famed Calumet Farm name (producer of eight Kentucky Derby winners) are the rationales for the high price tag. Contents not unpleasant, but should be much better for the money.

My Score

Notes: _____

_____

_____

Appearance (1-5) ____	Nose (1-25)	____
Taste (1-25) ____	Finish (1-25)	____
Complexity (1-10) ____	Overall Impression (1-10)	____
	SCORE ____	

Cassius Clay

Proof:	100
Age:	NAS
Type:	Straight
Style:	Traditional
Mash Bill:	Not available
Color:	Light Straw
Price:	$$$$

Mike

Nose:	Corn and orange blossom. Honey.
Taste:	Corn and honey with some peaches and oak.
Finish:	Long. Starts with sweet peaches and vanilla. Dries to oak.

Susan

Nose:	Caramel corn, raisins.
Taste:	Sweet vanilla and some berries.
Finish:	Warm and sweet with oak at the end.

Notes

Not complex, but smooth and enjoyable. Distilled in Tennessee and bottled in Bardstown, KY by Cary King Bottling Co.

My Score

Notes: _____

_____

_____

Appearance (1-5)	____	Nose (1-25)	____
Taste (1-25)	____	Finish (1-25)	____
Complexity (1-10)	____	Overall Impression (1-10)	____

SCORE ____

CH Bourbon

Proof:	105
Age:	NAS
Type:	Not Straight
Style:	Traditional
Mash Bill:	Not available
Color:	Straw
Price:	$$$$

Mike

Nose: Corn, caramel and a hint of spice.

Taste: Corn and vanilla with some ripe pear and baking spice.

Finish: Starts sweet and dries nicely.

Susan

Nose: Corn and sweet alcohol.

Taste: Light vanilla, light cornbread, some apples.

Finish: Warm with pepper notes.

Notes

Sourced by CH Distillery, Chicago, IL, which distills gin, vodka and rum.

My Score

Notes: _____

_____

_____

Appearance (1-5)	____	Nose (1-25)	____
Taste (1-25)	____	Finish (1-25)	____
Complexity (1-10)	____	Overall Impression (1-10)	____

SCORE ____

Charles Goodnight

Proof: 100
Age: NAS
Type: Straight
Style: Small Batch

Mash Bill: Not available
Color: Straw
Price: $$$$

Mike
Nose: Vanilla and corn. Very light.
Taste: Rotten corn and vanilla with hint of oak.
Finish: Dry with spoiled corn.

Susan
Nose: Corn with some vanilla sweetness.
Taste: Overripe corn. Some berries and vanilla.
Finish: Short and dry. Funky aftertaste.

Notes
Small batch #0012. Named after a famous Texas Ranger and cattleman. Sourced from Kentucky and bottled by Goodnight Distilling, Parlier, CA.

My Score	
Notes: _____	
_____	
_____	
Appearance (1-5) ____	Nose (1-25) ____
Taste (1-25) ____	Finish (1-25) ____
Complexity (1-10) ____	Overall Impression (1-10) ____
SCORE ____	

Charred Oak

Proof: 100
Age: NAS
Type: Not Straight
Style: Traditional

Mash Bill: Not available
Color: Light Straw
Price: $$$

Mike

Nose: Vanilla and corn. Very light.
Taste: Corn and pepper spice. Hint of corn silk.
Finish: Spicy with hint of oak and corn silk.

Susan

Nose: Alcohol with some corn and vanilla.
Taste: Nail polish.
Finish: Hot, dry.

Notes

No indication on the label of the origin of this bourbon. Website states "blend of Kentucky and Wisconsin bourbons." Blended and bottled by Off-the-Clock Spirits, Madison, WI.

My Score

Notes: _____

_____

_____

Appearance (1-5) _____   Nose (1-25) _____

Taste (1-25) _____   Finish (1-25) _____

Complexity (1-10) _____   Overall Impression (1-10) _____

SCORE _____

Chestnut Farms

Proof:	90
Age:	NAS
Type:	Straight
Style:	Traditional
Mash Bill:	Not available
Color:	Light Amber
Price:	$$$$

Mike

Nose: Caramel and vanilla, corn and leather.
Taste: Corn, vanilla and pepper with hint of tobacco.
Finish: Short and dry with oak and pepper.

Susan

Nose: Spicy with vanilla, caramel and baked apples.
Taste: Some orange peel, baking spices, caramel.
Finish: Warm and oaky with pepper at the end.

Notes

From Clear Springs Distilling Co., Louisville, KY.

My Score

Notes: _____

_____

_____

Appearance (1-5) _____   Nose (1-25) _____

Taste (1-25) _____   Finish (1-25) _____

Complexity (1-10) _____   Overall Impression (1-10) _____

SCORE _____

Chicken Cock Heritage Reserve

Proof: 90
Age: 6 months
Type: Not Straight
Style: Small Batch

Mash Bill: Not available
Color: Straw
Price: $$$$

Mike
Nose: Yeast, corn and hint of peaches and vanilla.
Taste: Brown vodka. Not much flavor – corn and a little oak.
Finish: Dry with alcohol and faintest hint of oak.

Susan
Nose: Ripe apples, berries with vanilla.
Taste: Faint, but apples, vanilla and some banana.
Finish: Short with pepper.

Notes
This brand originated in the 1850s, but went extinct. Grain and Barrel of North Charleston, SC, acquired the name and is sourcing and bottling

---

My Score

Notes: _____

_____

_____

Appearance (1-5) ____   Nose (1-25) ____
Taste (1-25) ____   Finish (1-25) ____
Complexity (1-10) ____   Overall Impression (1-10) ____
SCORE ____

Cleveland Bourbon

Proof: 87
Age: Less than 2 years
Type: Not Straight
Style: Age Accelerated

Mash Bill: Not available
Color: Very Light Straw
Price: $$$$

Mike
Nose: Corn and oak.
Taste: Corn and oak and not much else.
Finish: Oak and lots of it.

Susan
Nose: Corn and wood.
Taste: Sweet corn and alcohol.
Finish: Sweet oak.

Notes
Distilled in Indiana, but pressure aged and bottled by Cleveland Whiskey, LLC., Ohio. So something of a hybrid rather than true craft distiller. Slogan: "Drink what you like. Age is irrelevant."

My Score

Notes: _____

_____

_____

Appearance (1-5) _____   Nose (1-25) _____

Taste (1-25) _____   Finish (1-25) _____

Complexity (1-10) _____   Overall Impression (1-10) _____

SCORE _____

Corner Creek

Proof:	88
Age:	NAS
Type:	Reserve Bourbon Whiskey
Style:	Single Barrel
Mash Bill:	Proprietary
Color:	Light Amber
Price:	$$$

Mike

Nose:	Caramel and vanilla with sweet corn and spice. A little oak in the background.
Taste:	Very light. Vanilla and pepper spice. Not complicated. No burn. But not much flavor.
Finish:	This is the saving grace. Nice peppery finish with oak tannins lasting a long time.

Susan

Nose:	Candied fruit, candied almonds, a little caramel and vanilla.
Taste:	Buttered popcorn, crème brûlée, and fruit cocktail. Luscious mouthfeel.
Finish:	Long and smooth. Sweet finish dries to a little oaky spice.

Notes

Water helps bring out the caramel notes in Corner Creek.

My Score

Notes: _____

_____

_____

Appearance (1-5)	____	Nose (1-25)	____
Taste (1-25)	____	Finish (1-25)	____
Complexity (1-10)	____	Overall Impression (1-10)	____

SCORE ____

Cyrus Noble

Proof:	90
Age:	NAS
Type:	Straight
Style:	Small Batch
Mash Bill:	Not available
Color:	Straw
Price:	$$$

Mike

Nose: Corn and vanilla. Hint of chocolate.

Taste: Sweet vanilla and berries. Hint of oak.

Finish: Short and sweet. Hint of oak.

Susan

Nose: Very light caramel. Not complex.

Taste: Corn and black pepper with underlying caramel and fruit.

Finish: Short.

Notes

Sourced from an unnamed Kentucky distillery and bottled by Haas Brothers, San Francisco, California.

My Score		
Notes: _____		
_____		
_____		
Appearance (1-5) ____	Nose (1-25) ____	
Taste (1-25) ____	Finish (1-25) ____	
Complexity (1-10) ____	Overall Impression (1-10) ____	
SCORE ____		

David Nicholson 1843

Proof: 100
Age: NAS
Type: Straight
Style: Traditional

Mash Bill: Not available
Color: Light Straw
Price: $$

Mike

Nose: Corn and vanilla with a hint of banana.
Taste: Corn husk and vanilla. Thin for 100 proof.
Finish: Short and dry. Corn husk lingers.

Susan

Nose: Toffee and orange zest.
Taste: Some caramel and corn with black pepper.
Finish: Herbal, peppery.

Notes

Brand originated with Stitzel-Weller. Sourced from Kentucky. Distributed by Luxco of St. Louis.

My Score

Notes: _____

_____

_____

Appearance (1-5) ____   Nose (1-25) ____

Taste (1-25) ____   Finish (1-25) ____

Complexity (1-10) ____   Overall Impression (1-10) ____

SCORE ____

Duke

Proof:	88
Age:	Batched election of 5-10 year old barrels
Type:	Straight
Style:	Traditional
Mash Bill:	High Rye
Color:	Dark Straw
Price:	$$$$

Mike
Nose: Corn and saddle leather. Hint of vanilla oak. Not complex.

Taste: Thin and watery mouthfeel – caramel and some pepper spice.

Finish: Dry and peppery. Not bad, but a bit hot.

Susan
Nose: Caramel, spiced pecans. Ripe apples and emerge as it sits.

Taste: Caramel apples evolving into hot Corn with pepper.

Finish: Long and peppery hot.

Notes
Could make a good Manhattan with a strong, sweet vermouth. Bottle says "Monument Valley Distillers" and "Duke Spirits, Lawrenceburg, KY." It is sourced from Wild Turkey.

My Score		
Notes: _____		
_____		
_____		
Appearance (1-5) ____	Nose (1-25)	____
Taste (1-25) ____	Finish (1-25)	____
Complexity (1-10) ____	Overall Impression (1-10)	____
SCORE ____		

Eighteen 33

Proof: 80.8
Age: 10 years
Type: Straight
Style: Extra Aged

Mash Bill: Not available
Color: Straw
Price: $$$$$

Mike
Nose: Very light. Vanilla with a hint of fruit.
Taste: Better than the nose indicates. Fruit and spice with caramel.
Finish: Starts sweet with caramel and nicely dries to oak.

Susan
Nose: Caramel corn, orange blossom, vanilla sugar.
Taste: Cinnamon, some chocolate, lots of caramel.
Finish: Warm and spicy.

Notes
Very nice sip bottled by Boone County Distillery, Boone, County, KY. Sourced from MGP in Lawrenceburg, IN.

My Score		
Notes: _____		
_____		
_____		
Appearance (1-5) ____	Nose (1-25) ____	
Taste (1-25) ____	Finish (1-25) ____	
Complexity (1-10) ____	Overall Impression (1-10) ____	
SCORE ____		

Ezra B

Proof:	99
Age:	12 years
Type:	Straight
Style:	Single Barrel, Extra Aged
Mash Bill:	Not available
Color:	Light Amber
Price:	$$$$

Mike

Nose: Old leather and caramel. Apricot with pepper spice. Caramel gets stronger as it breathes.

Taste: Nice caramel and fruit – apricot, apple – apples with pepper spice and fine leather and tobacco.

Finish: Long and dry with oak and pepper. A hint of fruit sweetness.

Susan

Nose: Caramel corn, vanilla, sweet oak, and some dried stone fruit.

Taste: Caramel, cherries, ripe apple, vanilla. Whiff of tobacco leaf.

Finish: Long and warm with pleasant amounts of spice and fruit.

Notes

Let this bourbon open up in the glass for a few minutes to reveal its full complexity. Made by Heaven Hill and bottled by Luxco, St. Louis, MO.

My Score

Notes: _____

_____

_____

Appearance (1-5) ____   Nose (1-25) ____

Taste (1-25) ____   Finish (1-25) ____

Complexity (1-10) ____   Overall Impression (1-10) ____

SCORE ____

Ezra Brooks 80

Proof: 80
Age: NAS
Type: Straight
Style: Traditional

Mash Bill: Not available
Color: Light Straw
Price: $

Mike
Nose: Sweet corn and vanilla with a bit of sweet spices. Some oak in the background.
Taste: Caramel and pepper with a bit of honey. A bit thin, but still flavorful.
Finish: Dries out with oak tannins and sweet spice. Lasts fairly long. Pleasant.

Susan
Nose: Very light. Sweet corn and dry oak. A whiff of baking spices.
Taste: Roasted corn with a flash of apricot and sweet spice.
Finish: Warm with dry, peppery bite at the end. Heat lingers.

Notes
A very good bourbon for the price. Not bad neat, but would work well in a cocktail. Made by Heaven Hill and bottled by Luxco of St. Louis, MO.

My Score
Notes: _____

_____

_____

Appearance (1-5) _____   Nose (1-25) _____
Taste (1-25) _____   Finish (1-25) _____
Complexity (1-10) _____   Overall Impression (1-10) _____
SCORE _____

Ezra Brooks 90

Proof:	90
Age:	NAS
Type:	Straight
Style:	Traditional
Mash Bill:	Not available
Color:	Light Straw
Price:	$$

Mike

Nose:	Corn, vanilla and a hint of apple.
Taste:	Corn, vanilla, apple and cinnamon.
Finish:	Medium long with some dry oak spices.

Susan

Nose:	Very light. Some caramel and sweet mint.
Taste:	Light caramel with sweet spice and some apple.
Finish:	Medium long with dry pepper at the end.

Notes

Another Luxco production. Distilled by Heaven Hill in Louisville. An age statement of 7 years has been replaced by label copy reading "7 generations."

My Score

Notes: _____

_____

_____

Appearance (1-5) _____   Nose (1-25) _____

Taste (1-25) _____   Finish (1-25) _____

Complexity (1-10) _____   Overall Impression (1-10) _____

SCORE _____

Filibuster Duel Cask

Proof:	90
Age:	NAS
Type:	Straight
Style:	Special Finish
Mash Bill:	75% corn, 21% rye, 4% malted barley
Color:	Light Amber
Price:	$$

Mike

Nose: Caramel and vanilla with some apple and spice.

Taste: Corn and vanilla with nutmeg.

Finish: Dry with oak and spice.

Susan

Nose: Caramel, sweet spice, light oak and leather.

Taste: Ripe apples, bit of barnyard (in a good way) and sweet oak.

Finish: Dries to peppery oak.

Notes

From Filibuster Distillery, Mauretown, VA. A "master blender" choses whiskies for finishing in French oak after aging in charred oak. This was Small batch #2, bottle #866.

My Score

Notes: _____

_____

_____

Appearance (1-5) _____   Nose (1-25) _____

Taste (1-25) _____   Finish (1-25) _____

Complexity (1-10) _____   Overall Impression (1-10) _____

SCORE _____

Flatboat

Proof:	90
Age:	NAS
Type:	Straight
Style:	Traditional
Mash Bill:	Not available
Color:	Light Straw
Price:	$$$

Mike

Nose:	Honeysuckle and bananas with a hint of spice.
Taste:	Sweet honey and apples with baking spices.
Finish:	Long. Starts sweet and dries nicely with some oak.

Susan

Nose:	Bananas and some vanilla.
Taste:	Banana carries through to the palate with some light caramel and fruit.
Finish:	Hot on the tongue.

Notes

Bottled by The Founders Company, Louisville, KY. Sourced from Barton, Bardstown, KY.

My Score

Notes: _____

_____

_____

Appearance (1-5) _____   Nose (1-25) _____

Taste (1-25) _____   Finish (1-25) _____

Complexity (1-10) _____   Overall Impression (1-10) _____

SCORE _____

George Remus

Proof:	90.7
Age:	NAS
Type:	Not Straight
Style:	Small Batch
Mash Bill:	Not available
Color:	Light Straw
Price:	$$$$

Mike

Nose: Very young. Lots of fusel oil. Some corn vanilla.

Taste: Sweet corn and oak tannins. Corn with some pepper spice. Tastes young.

Finish: Astringent and dry with oak tannins.

Susan

Nose: Mineral oil. Needs more time in the barrel.

Taste: Corn, a little oak. Not much else.

Finish: Starts sweet. Ends hot.

Notes

Batch 1. Queen City Whiskey, Bardstown, KY. But it is sourced from MGP in Lawrenceburg, IN. Named for the famous Cincinnati bootlegger.

My Score

Notes: _____

_____

_____

Appearance (1-5)	____	Nose (1-25)	____
Taste (1-25)	____	Finish (1-25)	____
Complexity (1-10)	____	Overall Impression (1-10)	____

SCORE ____

George Remus Straight

Proof: 94
Age: NAS, but "over 4 years" according to distillery
Type: Straight Bourbon
Style: Traditional

Mash Bill: Not available
Color: Straw
Price: $$$$

Mike
Nose: Berries and vanilla with some spice.
Taste: Caramel and berries with nutmeg and oak.
Finish: Sweet notes with a little oak.

Susan
Nose: Berries, caramel, and baking spices.
Taste: Caramel and nuts, Some underlying astringency.
Finish: Black pepper with a surprising sweet note at the end.

Notes
Brand acquired by contract distilling giant Midwest Grain Producers of Lawrenceburg, IN. Named after an infamous Cincinnati bootlegger.

My Score

Notes: _____

_____

_____

Appearance (1-5) ____   Nose (1-25) ____
Taste (1-25) ____   Finish (1-25) ____
Complexity (1-10) ____   Overall Impression (1-10) ____
SCORE ____

Hirsch Reserve

Proof:	86
Age:	Mingling of 4-6 year-old
Type:	Straight
Style:	Small Batch
Mash Bill:	Not available
Color:	Straw
Price:	$$$$

Mike

Nose: Very light. Vanilla and corn and a hint of tobacco.

Taste: Sweet corn and vanilla with some pepper complex.

Finish: Dry oak, almost astringent. Moderate Length, but not complex at all.

Susan

Nose: Orange zest and light caramel.

Taste: Caramel on the palate with some spice. Not sweet spices. Not complex.

Finish: Starts sweet. Ends hot.

Notes

Bottled by Meier's Distilled Products Company, Silverton, OH. (Distilled in Kentucky) for Anchor Distilling, San Francisco, CA. "Inspired by the quality of A.H. Hirsch." Pleasant, but too expensive for what you get.

My Score

Notes: _____

_____

_____

Appearance (1-5) ____   Nose (1-25) ____

Taste (1-25) ____   Finish (1-25) ____

Complexity (1-10) ____   Overall Impression (1-10) ____

SCORE ____

Hooker's House

Proof:	100
Age:	6 years
Type:	Straight
Style:	Special Finish
Mash Bill:	High rye
Color:	Light Amber
Price:	$$$$

Mike

Nose: Caramel and fruit with some tobacco and leather.

Taste: Caramel and berries with nutmeg and cinnamon.

Finish: Long and spicy with some oak and fruit.

Susan

Nose: Vanilla, caramel, orchard fruit.

Taste: Caramel and ripe berries. Touch of baking spices.

Finish: Peppery. Water releases fruit.

Notes

Finished in pinot noir barrels and bottled by Prohibition Spirits, Sonoma, CA. Distilled in Indiana. (Probably MGP, but not stated.)

My Score		
Notes: _____		
_____		
_____		
Appearance (1-5) ____	Nose (1-25)	____
Taste (1-25) ____	Finish (1-25)	____
Complexity (1-10) ____	Overall Impression (1-10)	____
SCORE ____		

James E. Pepper 1776

Proof:	100
Age:	NAS
Type:	Straight
Style:	Small Batch
Mash Bill:	38% rye
Color:	Dark Straw
Price:	$$$

Mike

Nose: Corn and vanilla with some oak. Old leather and nutmeg.

Taste: Candied fruit – berries and cherries some pepper spice, leather or tobacco and oak.

Finish: Sweet to start, but dries out nicely with some oak tannins.

Susan

Nose: Caramel and a little licorice. Some faint mint.

Taste: Vanilla, licorice, sweet spice. Adding with water releases nuttiness, but no fruit.

Finish: Starts sweet and ends with spice Not as long as expected from the proof.

Notes

Jas. E. Pepper and Co., Bardstown, KY. But sourced from elsewhere, possibly MGP in Lawrenceberg, IN.

My Score

Notes: _____

_____

_____

Appearance (1-5) _____   Nose (1-25) _____

Taste (1-25) _____   Finish (1-25) _____

Complexity (1-10) _____   Overall Impression (1-10) _____

SCORE _____

Jeffer's Creek

Proof:	80
Age:	6 years
Type:	Straight Bourbon
Style:	Small Batch
Mash Bill:	Proprietary
Color:	Pale Light Straw
Price:	$$

Mike

Nose: Not complex. Vanilla and a hint of leather and spice – anise?

Taste: Not hot at all. Sweet vanilla, liquorice and some other sweet spice – cinnamon – and some oak.

Finish: Medium long and turns dry with oak and some spice.

Susan

Nose: Candy corn, light wood smoke, not complex.

Taste: Wood smoke, caramel, honey.

Finish: Short, but warm with a little sweet spice at the end.

Notes

Label states that it is bottled by King's Mark Co. of Louisville. Might be more interesting at higher proof.

My Score

Notes: _____

_____

_____

Appearance (1-5) _____   Nose (1-25) _____

Taste (1-25) _____   Finish (1-25) _____

Complexity (1-10) _____   Overall Impression (1-10) _____

SCORE _____

Jefferson's

Proof:	82.3
Age:	NAS (website states 8-12 years)
Type:	Straight
Style:	Small Batch
Mash Bill:	Not available
Color:	Light Straw
Price:	$$$

Mike

Nose: Corn and vanilla with a hint of tobacco and oak.

Taste: Corn and vanilla with some sweet spice. Clove? A bit of apricot and oak.

Finish: Starts sweet with the caramel/spice, but dries out some with oak tannins. Not overly long.

Susan

Nose: Sweet corn, vanilla, some oak.

Taste: Corn, vanilla and sweet oak. Not complex, but has a rich, creamy mouthfeel.

Finish: Medium length. Dry, and smooth

Notes

Uncomplicated bourbon makes a pleasant, simple sip. Serve neat or with a single ice cube. Sourced from unknown distillery. Distributed by Castle Brands.

My Score

Notes: _____

_____

_____

Appearance (1-5) _____   Nose (1-25) _____

Taste (1-25) _____   Finish (1-25) _____

Complexity (1-10) _____   Overall Impression (1-10) _____

SCORE _____

Jefferson's Ocean

Proof: 90
Age: NAS
Type: Straight
Style: Small Batch

Mash Bill: Not available
Color: Light Straw
Price: $$$$$

Mike
Nose: Vanilla, oak, and sea salt. Very light nose.
Taste: Vanilla and corn with some ocean air – salt and iodine. Some oak spice.
Finish: Long and dry with oak and sea salt.

Susan
Nose: Hard candy, vanilla, ripe cherries and oak.
Taste: Light vanilla and, believe it or not, a little sea salt. Sweet caramel and a touch of orchard fruit. Very smooth.
Finish: Long and a little salty. Unexpectedly pleasant change from pepper.

Notes
Put on a ship and aged at sea. This was from Voyage Three, Barrel 54. A gimmick? Perhaps, but the light salt aromas are certainly present. Very interesting.

My Score

Notes: _____

_____

_____

Appearance (1-5) ____   Nose (1-25) ____
Taste (1-25) ____   Finish (1-25) ____
Complexity (1-10) ____   Overall Impression (1-10) ____

SCORE ____

Jefferson's Presidential Select

Proof:	94
Age:	18 years
Type:	Straight
Style:	Small Batch, Wheated
Mash Bill:	Uses wheat in place of rye
Color:	Light Amber Red
Price:	$$$$$

Mike

Nose: Caramel and apples with some hazelnuts. Not complex, but full-bodied.

Taste: Caramel, chocolate and a bit of sweet spice – cinnamon and nutmeg. Fine tobacco and honey.

Finish: Long, sweet and pleasant. Not complex, but flavorful.

Susan

Nose: Apricot and dried mint. A little new leather.

Taste: Dried fruit, toffee, caramel with hazelnuts and buttered popcorn.

Finish: Long and smooth. Initial fruit gives way to dry oak at the very end.

Notes

Very limited release of bottling from the closed Stitzel-Weller Distillery in Louisville. We tasted the 18-year-old. The 17-year-old is pictured. Distributed by Castle Brands

---

My Score

Notes: _____

_____

_____

Appearance (1-5) ____   Nose (1-25) ____

Taste (1-25) ____   Finish (1-25) ____

Complexity (1-10) ____   Overall Impression (1-10) ____

SCORE ____

Jefferson's Reserve

Proof: 90.2
Age: 15 years
Type: Straight
Style: Small Batch

Mash Bill: Not available
Color: Light Straw
Price: $$$

Mike
Nose: Sweet caramel corn with fine tobacco and leather.
Taste: Caramel and fruit – apricot. A bit of pepper spice and tobacco.
Finish: Starts sweet but dries out. Fairly short. I hoped for a better finish.

Susan
Nose: Caramel, vanilla, toffee and note of new leather.
Taste: Candied corn, caramel and sweet spices with whiff of oak.
Finish: Starts sweet and ends dry and smooth. No heat.

Notes
Works very well in a classic Manhattan. Distributed by Castle Brands.

My Score		
Notes: _____		

Appearance (1-5) ____ Nose (1-25) ____
Taste (1-25) ____ Finish (1-25) ____
Complexity (1-10) ____ Overall Impression (1-10) ____
SCORE ____

Jefferson's Reserve Groth Reserve Cask Finish

Proof: 90.2
Age: NAS
Type: Straight
Style: Special Finish, Small Batch

Mash Bill: Not available
Color: Light Straw
Price: $$$$$

Mike
Nose: Fruity. Berries and vanilla. Grape popsicle.
Taste: Grapes and vanilla with sweet spice and oak.
Finish: Starts sweet and get some nice oak and spice.

Susan
Nose: Sweet wine notes. Fruit dominates with some sweet vanilla.
Taste: Wine, vanilla, cinnamon.
Finish: Long and warm and fruity.

Notes
Very small batch. Bottle 3711 of batch No. 1. Finished in French oak Groth cabernet sauvignon barrels. Might be a very good sip with pork tenderloin.

My Score

Notes: _____

_____

_____

Appearance (1-5) _____   Nose (1-25) _____

Taste (1-25) _____   Finish (1-25) _____

Complexity (1-10) _____   Overall Impression (1-10) _____

SCORE _____

Jesse James America's Outlaw Bourbon

Proof:	80
Age:	At least 36 months
Type:	Not Straight
Style:	Traditional
Mash Bill:	Not available
Color:	Pale Straw
Price:	$

Mike

Nose: Very light and young. Not much here but corn and vanilla.

Taste: Very light. Sweet corn vanilla. Hint of oak.

Finish: SShort and slightly dry with oak Tannins.

Susan

Nose: Faint vanilla and a little cinnamon. Very light.

Taste: Smooth and sweet on the tongue. Light caramel, a little honey. No bite.

Finish: Very short, sweet.

Notes

Londonderry, N.H., but distilled in Kentucky by an unnamed distiller. Singer Jesse James Dupree founded the brand. Pretty mild to be named after a tough guy.

My Score		
Notes: _____		
_____		
_____		
Appearance (1-5) ____	Nose (1-25)	____
Taste (1-25) ____	Finish (1-25)	____
Complexity (1-10) ____	Overall Impression (1-10)	____
SCORE ____		

Jethro T. Boots

Proof:	80
Age:	NAS
Type:	Straight
Style:	Traditional
Mash Bill:	Not available
Color:	Very Light Straw
Price:	$

Mike
Nose: Candy corn with a hint of oak.
Taste: Sweet honey and pepper. Hint of fruit.
Finish: Starts sweet and dries to light oak tannins.

Susan
Nose: Simple. Light vanilla, sweet corn.
Taste: Sweet corn, vanilla, faint candied apple.
Finish: Surprisingly long and warm. Oak at the end.

Notes
Bottled by the Legacy Distilling Company, Louisville, KY.
Sourced from Barton 1792 in Bardstown, KY.

My Score
Notes: _____

_____

_____

Appearance (1-5) ____   Nose (1-25) ____

Taste (1-25) ____   Finish (1-25) ____

Complexity (1-10) ____   Overall Impression (1-10) ____

SCORE ____

John B. Stetson

Proof: 84
Age: 4 years
Type: Straight
Style: Pot Stilled

Mash Bill: Not available
Color: Light Straw
Price: $$$

Mike

Nose: Corn and yeast. Very light.
Taste: Candy apple with some pepper spice, a hint of oak and tobacco. A bit hot.
Finish: Long and peppery.

Susan

Nose: Very light. Vanilla and corn.
Taste: Vanilla, some apple and honey. Black pepper.
Finish: Fades quickly to black pepper.

Notes

Frank-Lin Distillers, Fairfield, CA. This facility sources bourbon from undisclosed distilleries in Kentucky and bottles it under several labels.

My Score	
Notes: _____	
_____	
_____	
Appearance (1-5) ____	Nose (1-25) ____
Taste (1-25) ____	Finish (1-25) ____
Complexity (1-10) ____	Overall Impression (1-10) ____
SCORE ____	

J.R. Ewing

Proof:	80
Age:	4 years
Type:	Straight
Style:	Traditional
Mash Bill:	Not available
Color:	Light Straw
Price:	$$$

Mike

Nose: Very light. Very yeasty – bread dough or malt. Hint of vanilla and corn.

Taste: Very light. Slightly sweet with some caramel and light fruit – pears and apricots.

Finish: Short and sweet. Not much to it. Corn sweetness on the finish.

Susan

Nose: Very light, biscuit. With touch of corn. Not complex.

Taste: Light and sweet. Vanilla and pear.

Finish: Sweet. Short.

Notes

Made by Strong Spirits of Bardstown, KY for Southfork Bottling Company, Dallas, TX.

My Score

Notes: _____

_____

_____

Appearance (1-5)	____	Nose (1-25)	____
Taste (1-25)	____	Finish (1-25)	____
Complexity (1-10)	____	Overall Impression (1-10)	____

SCORE ____

Kentucky Owl

Proof: 118.4
Age: NAS
Type: Straight
Style: Small Batch, Barrel Proof

Mash Bill: Not available
Color: Dark Amber
Price: $$$$$$

Mike

Nose: Caramel and molasses with some nutmeg, Fine leather and tobacco. Water brings out some berries and dates.
Taste: Candies cherries and caramel with some sweet spice, tobacco, and oak. Water brings out caramel, but lessens fruit.
Finish: Long and dry with oak tannins. Water makes the finish more tannic.

Susan

Nose: Vanilla, caramel, sweet oak, cinnamon, cherries. Very rich. I could nose this all day.
Taste: Rich and smooth mouthfeel. Water reveals cinnamon, cherries and lots of vanilla.
Finish: Long and rich, with cinnamon, vanilla and lingering caramel.

Notes

A mingling of cask strength bourbons sourced from more than one Kentucky distillery. This is a resurrection of a brand the Dedman family (owners of Beaumont Inn in Harrodsburg, KY) made at their pre-prohibition distillery. Batch No. 1. Bottle 1235/1506.

My Score		
Notes: _____		
_____		
_____		
Appearance (1-5) ____	Nose (1-25) ____	
Taste (1-25) ____	Finish (1-25) ____	
Complexity (1-10) ____	Overall Impression (1-10) ____	
SCORE ____		

Lexington

Proof: 86
Age: NAS
Type: "Straight" not on label
Style: Traditional

Mash Bill: Proprietary
Color: Light Straw
Price: $$$

Mike

Nose: Very light. Sweet corn. A little vanilla. A little floral note.

Taste: Thin and watery. Corn and a little vanilla.

Finish: Not much. Very short and sweet. Brown vodka.

Susan

Nose: Light. Caramel, apple, sweet corn.

Taste: Very light. Some sweet spice and peaches with the vanilla.

Finish: Very short. Practically none.

Notes

Named for a famed racehorse, who appears on the label. Bottled by Western Spirits Beverage Co., Bowling Green, KY. Kentucky-sourced.

My Score

Notes: _____

_____

_____

Appearance (1-5) ____   Nose (1-25) ____
Taste (1-25) ____   Finish (1-25) ____
Complexity (1-10) ____   Overall Impression (1-10) ____
SCORE ____

Medley Bros.

Proof:	102
Age:	NAS
Type:	Straight
Style:	Small Batch
Mash Bill:	77% Corn, 10% Rye, 13% Malted Barley
Color:	Straw
Price:	$$

Mike
Nose: Vanilla and caramel with apricot and fine leather.

Taste: Vanilla and corn with oak wood and fruit – apricots – and tobacco.

Finish: Long and dry with oak tannins and spice.

Susan
Nose: Floral notes with caramel and some nutmeg.

Taste: Sweet corn, a smidge of mint, vanilla.

Finish: Long and warm. Peppery, as one of pepper might expect from the proof.

Notes
Kentucky sourced bourbon bottled by Frank-Lin Distillers, Fairfield, CA. A big-shouldered sip. Well-balanced for the proof.

My Score

Notes: _____

_____

_____

Appearance (1-5) _____   Nose (1-25) _____

Taste (1-25) _____   Finish (1-25) _____

Complexity (1-10) _____   Overall Impression (1-10) _____

SCORE _____

O.K.I.

Proof:	97.7
Age:	8 years
Type:	Straight
Style:	Small Batch
Mash Bill:	Not available
Color:	Amber
Price:	$$$$

Mike

Nose: Vanilla and caramel with candy corn and honeysuckle. Sweet spices and oak in the background.

Taste: A bit thin in the mouth, but sweet with fruit – cherries and with whipped cream. Very subtle apricots – with some nice pepper spice.

Finish: Long and peppery with oak tannins and pepper spice. Well balanced.

Susan

Nose: Peaches first, then a little mint followed by caramel and some vanilla.

Taste: Silky mouthfeel. Peach cobbler vanilla and mint at the back of the tongue.

Finish: Long and warm. Peppermint at the end.

Notes

Made for New Riff Distillery, Newport, KY by MGP in Lawrenceburg, IN. The names stands for "Loved in Ohio, Bottled in Kentucky, Made in Indiana." This was Small Batch #3, Bottle 296/402.

My Score

Notes: _____

_____

_____

Appearance (1-5)	____	Nose (1-25)	____
Taste (1-25)	____	Finish (1-25)	____
Complexity (1-10)	____	Overall Impression (1-10)	____
	SCORE ____		

O.K.I. Reserve

Proof:	100
Age:	9 years
Type:	Straight
Style:	Traditional
Mash Bill:	Not available
Color:	Light Amber
Price:	$$$$

Mike

Nose: Peaches ad caramel with baking spices. Peach cobbler in a glass.

Taste: Peaches and caramel with nutmeg and cinnamon.

Finish: Dry oak and spice, very nice.

Susan

Nose: Vanilla, apricots, dates.

Taste: Vanilla and oak with apples and spice.

Finish: Short and oaky, but not hot.

Notes

Bottled by New Riff Distillery, Newport, Kentucky. Age and proof can vary slightly by batch. New Riff is in the process of making and aging its own bourbon for release in 2018.

My Score

Notes: _____

_____

_____

Appearance (1-5)	____	Nose (1-25)	____
Taste (1-25)	____	Finish (1-25)	____
Complexity (1-10)	____	Overall Impression (1-10)	____

SCORE ____

Old Ezra

Proof:	101
Age:	7 years
Type:	Straight
Style:	Traditional
Mash Bill:	Not available
Color:	Dark Straw
Price:	$$

Mike

Nose: Caramel and vanilla with tobacco and leather and sweet spices – nutmeg?

Taste: Nice mouthfeel. Almost chewy with caramel and peppery spices. Apple fruit.

Finish: Medium long with sweet fruit at first drying to oak tannins.

Susan

Nose: Fruity. Light caramel and roasted corn and pie spices.

Taste: Caramel corn, pitted fruit with a bit cocoa and pepper.

Finish: Long and warm and chewy without being hot. Ends in oak.

Notes

Not especially complex, but a satisfying sip. Certainly would make a reliable, and potent, cocktail. Produced by Heaven Hill in Louisville. Bottled and distributed by Luxco of St. Louis.

My Score

Notes: _____

_____

_____

Appearance (1-5)	____	Nose (1-25)	____
Taste (1-25)	____	Finish (1-25)	____
Complexity (1-10)	____	Overall Impression (1-10)	____

SCORE ____

Old Forge Reserve

Proof: 89
Age: 9 years
Type: Not Straight
Style: Single Barrel

Mash Bill: Not available
Color: Straw
Price: $$$$

Mike
Nose: Maple smoke with vanilla and buttered corn.
Taste: Maple syrup, corn, vanilla, and oak.
Finish: Long lasting maple smoke.

Susan
Nose: Maple, corn, some cinnamon.
Taste: Sweet apples, sweet oak, flash of maple and smoke.
Finish: Warm, smooth, smoky.

Notes
A Tennessee bourbon (probably from George Dickel) bottled by Old Forge Distillery, Pigeon Forge, TN. Barrel #16-773.

My Score

Notes: _____

_____

_____

Appearance (1-5) ____   Nose (1-25) ____

Taste (1-25) ____   Finish (1-25) ____

Complexity (1-10) ____   Overall Impression (1-10) ____

SCORE ____

Old Kentucky

Proof: 80
Age: 4 years
Type: Straight
Style: Traditional

Mash Bill: Not available
Color: Straw
Price: $$

Mike

Nose: Light. Very young. Some vanilla and and corn.
Taste: Thin and watery. Some vanilla and corn, a hint of oak. Not much else.
Finish: Short and slightly oaky, but disappointing.

Susan

Nose: Light. Some mint. More tobacco. A little vanilla as it sits.
Taste: Roasted corn and some candied nuts. Simple, but pleasant at 80 proof.
Finish: Smooth, no burn. But short.

Notes
Bottled by Distiller Products, LTD., San Jose, CA. Sourced from Kentucky, but no indication from whom.

My Score

Notes: _____

_____

_____

Appearance (1-5) _____   Nose (1-25) _____

Taste (1-25) _____   Finish (1-25) _____

Complexity (1-10) _____   Overall Impression (1-10) _____

SCORE _____

Old Medley

Proof:	86.8
Age:	12 years
Type:	Straight
Style:	Extra Aged
Mash Bill:	Proprietary
Color:	Dark Straw
Price:	$$$$

Mike

Nose: Caramel and apples with some fine leather and oak.

Taste: Caramel and fruit. Apples and pears with some pepper spice on the end. Nice mouthfeel. No burn and some warmth in the throat.

Finish: Long and dry with oak tannins balanced by a bit of sweet caramel.

Susan

Nose: Lovely honey nose with caramel and some cherries.

Taste: Vanilla, pecans, a little new leather, some orange peel and black pepper. Pepper definitely in the background.

Finish: Fruit gives way to soft oak. Long and warm with no burn at all.

Notes

Very elegant sip. Kentucky-sourced. Distributed by the historic Charles Medley Distillery, Owensboro, KY, which is in the process of beginning to make bourbons again.

My Score	
Notes: _____	
_____	
_____	
Appearance (1-5) ____	Nose (1-25) ____
Taste (1-25) ____	Finish (1-25) ____
Complexity (1-10) ____	Overall Impression (1-10) ____
SCORE ____	

Old Scout

Proof:	99
Age:	2 years
Type:	Straight
Style:	Small Batch
Mash Bill:	High Rye
Color:	Light Amber
Price:	$$$$

Mike

Nose: Sweet caramel and spice. Nutmeg and and allspice. Some fine tobacco and leather.

Taste: Sweet fruit – very ripe apples and pears with vanilla and caramel.

Finish: Long and dry. Starts spicy, then oak kicks in with nice dry finish.

Susan

Nose: Spicy. A little peach and a lot of oak.

Taste: Some apple and oak. A little vanilla.

Finish: Long and peppery.

Notes

Smooth Ambler, Maxwelton, WV. Sourced from MGP, Lawrenceburg, IN. Good bourbon to sip with a steak. This was Batch 87, bottled August 26, 2014.

My Score	
Notes: _____	
_____	
_____	
Appearance (1-5) ____	Nose (1-25) ____
Taste (1-25) ____	Finish (1-25) ____
Complexity (1-10) ____	Overall Impression (1-10) ____
SCORE ____	

Old Scout Single Barrel

Proof:	109.8
Age:	8 years
Type:	Straight
Style:	Single Barrel
Mash Bill:	Not available
Color:	Amber
Price:	$$$$$

Mike

Nose: Nice nose with caramel, molasses, dates tobacco and hint of chocolate. Water brings out the chocolate.

Taste: Sweet caramel and cherries with tobacco and sweet spice. Water brings out the fruit – cherries and dates.

Finish: Very long and dry. Water makes the finish a bit less woody, but nice.

Susan

Nose: Alcohol, then some peppermint and vanilla.

Taste: Vanilla, some nuts and caramel. Water amplifies these and reveals a little fruit.

Finish: Long and peppery, ending in oak.

Notes

Smooth Ambler, Maxwelton, WV. Sourced from MGP, Lawrenceburg, IN. Would be nice with a cigar.

My Score

Notes: _____

_____

_____

Appearance (1-5) _____   Nose (1-25) _____

Taste (1-25) _____   Finish (1-25) _____

Complexity (1-10) _____   Overall Impression (1-10) _____

SCORE _____

Old Scout 10-Year-Old

Proof:	100
Age:	10 years
Type:	Straight
Style:	Small Batch
Mash Bill:	Not available
Color:	Dark Straw
Price:	$$$$

Mike
Nose: Caramel and molasses with tobacco, pecans and spice. Water brings out some chocolate.
Taste: Sweet caramel and apricots. A bit of oak and tobacco. Add water for fruit.
Finish: Medium long and oaky.

Susan
Nose: Vanilla, pitted fruit, toasted nuts, tobacco. Very nice.
Taste: Caramel, dates, ripe peach. Water adds some sweetness.
Finish: Medium long with pepper at the end.

Notes
Smooth Ambler, Maxwelton, WV. Sourced from MGP, Lawrenceburg, IN. Small Batch No. 23, bottled 11/18/2014.

My Score
Notes: _____
_____
_____

Appearance (1-5) ____   Nose (1-25) ____
Taste (1-25) ____   Finish (1-25) ____
Complexity (1-10) ____   Overall Impression (1-10) ____
SCORE ____

Old Williamsburg

Proof:	80
Age:	36 months
Type:	Straight
Style:	Traditional

Mash Bill:	Not available
Color:	Extremely Pale Straw
Price:	$$

Mike
Nose: Very light, some corn and vanilla.
Taste: Very light. Some sweet corn and vanilla. Brown vodka.
Finish: Short and sweet.

Susan
Nose: Almost nonexistent.
Taste: Astringent! A little corn.
Finish: Mercifully short.

Notes
Old Williamsburg Products Co., Princeton, MN. Ginger ale has more color than this stuff. Sourced from Kentucky. (Some distiller's rejects?)

My Score

Notes: _____

_____

_____

Appearance (1-5) ____   Nose (1-25) ____

Taste (1-25) ____   Finish (1-25) ____

Complexity (1-10) ____   Overall Impression (1-10) ____

SCORE ____

Old Williamsburg No. 20

Proof:	101
Age:	36 months
Type:	Straight
Style:	Traditional
Mash Bill:	Not available
Color:	Very Pale Straw
Price:	$$$

Mike

Nose: Corn and vanilla with just a hint of flowers.

Taste: Corn and vanilla with some pepper spice.

Finish: Medium long and spicy.

Susan

Nose: Faint vanilla, carnations. Very light.

Taste: Some vanilla and oak, but very.

Finish: Medium long, hot.

Notes

Old Williamsburg Products Co., Princeton, MN. Sourced from Kentucky. (Really?)

My Score

Notes: _____

_____

_____

Appearance (1-5) _____   Nose (1-25) _____

Taste (1-25) _____   Finish (1-25) _____

Complexity (1-10) _____   Overall Impression (1-10) _____

SCORE _____

OYO Bourbon Whiskey Michelone Reserve

Proof:	90
Age:	NAS
Type:	Not Straight
Style:	See notes
Mash Bill:	See notes
Color:	Dark Straw
Price:	$$$$

Mike

Nose: Very light. Vanilla and honey. Water brings out fruit.

Taste: Vanilla and peaches with some nutmeg and cinnamon. Water brings out vanilla.

Finish: Long and dry with pepper spice and oak. Water sweetens the finish.

Susan

Nose: Candy corn, sweet spices. Very light. Water amplifies alcohol.

Taste: Initially sweet corn and fruit, but quickly becomes peppery hot.

Finish: Long and hot. Water tames heat resulting in a nutty finish.

Notes

Midwest Spirits, LLC, Columbus, OH. This is a mingling of a Kentucky sourced rye recipe bourbon with a wheat whiskey made at the distillery. While it says "bourbon" on the label, by law this cannot be called bourbon because something, namely wheat whiskey, has been added to it. Interesting whiskey, but not bourbon. We have included it to illustrate the distinction.

My Score		
Notes: _____		
_____		
_____		
Appearance (1-5) ____	Nose (1-25)	____
Taste (1-25) ____	Finish (1-25)	____
Complexity (1-10) ____	Overall Impression (1-10)	____
SCORE ____		

Paddleford Creek

Proof:	93
Age:	NAS
Type:	Not Straight
Style:	Small Batch
Mash Bill:	Not available
Color:	Almost None
Price:	$$

Mike

Nose: Corn and vanilla, but very light.

Taste: Thin and watery. Beige vodka.

Finish: Hint of vanilla and oak. Most of its flavor is in the finish.

Susan

Nose: Very, very faint.

Taste: Some pear and vanilla, but very light.

Finish: Very short.

Notes

Produced and bottled by Paddleford Spirits, Princeton, MN. No indication of source.

My Score

Notes: _____

_____

_____

Appearance (1-5) _____   Nose (1-25) _____

Taste (1-25) _____   Finish (1-25) _____

Complexity (1-10) _____   Overall Impression (1-10) _____

SCORE _____

Penny Packer

Proof:	80
Age:	NAS
Type:	Straight Bourbon
Style:	Traditional
Mash Bill:	Proprietary
Color:	Straw
Price:	$$

Mike
Nose: Sweet vanilla and cherry. Hint of tobacco.
Taste: Very light. Sweet vanilla and cherries, dates. A bit of pepper spice.
Finish: Starts sweet, but gets peppery and dry with oak tannins.

Susan
Nose: Sweet corn and vanilla. Light, sweet fruit.
Taste: Sweet corn and cherry. Very lightly spicy.
Finish: Medium long. Very nice for low proof. Sweet corn dries to light oak.

Notes
This is distilled by Heaven Hill in Louisville for export to Germany where it is bottled. It has now found its way back to the U.S. Distributed by Niche Import Co. Limited availability.

My Score
Notes: _____

_____

_____

Appearance (1-5) ____   Nose (1-25) ____

Taste (1-25) ____   Finish (1-25) ____

Complexity (1-10) ____   Overall Impression (1-10) ____

SCORE ____

Pinhook

Proof:	90
Age:	NAS
Type:	Straight
Style:	Small Batch
Mash Bill:	75% corn
Color:	Straw
Price:	$$$$$$

Mike
Nose: Caramel and baking spices with hint of oak.
Taste: Corn husk and caramel. Some pepper.
Finish: Long and dry with oak tannins.

Susan
Nose: Light toffee with underlying corn and some orchard fruit.
Taste: Sweet entry, but then an odd mustiness.
Finish: Bitter oakiness.

Notes
CJS Beverage Group. Batch #140. Nose is its best aspect.

My Score

Notes: _____

_____

_____

Appearance (1-5) ____   Nose (1-25) ____

Taste (1-25) ____   Finish (1-25) ____

Complexity (1-10) ____   Overall Impression (1-10) ____

SCORE ____

Prestige

Proof:	80
Age:	36 months
Type:	Straight
Style:	Traditional

Mash Bill:	Not available
Color:	Light Straw
Price:	$

Mike

Nose: Very light corn and vanilla.
Taste: Thin and watery, but some nice buttered corn and vanilla.
Finish: Short with a hint of oak.

Susan

Nose: Sweet mint, light caramel corn.
Taste: Carmel apple and sprinkling of sweet spice.
Finish: Dries to black pepper.

Notes

Sourced from Kentucky. Bottled by J. Harrison Co., Mira Loma, CA.

My Score

Notes: _____

_____

_____

Appearance (1-5)	____	Nose (1-25)	____
Taste (1-25)	____	Finish (1-25)	____
Complexity (1-10)	____	Overall Impression (1-10)	____

SCORE ____

Rabbit Hole Straight Bourbon

Proof: 95
Age: NAS
Type: Straight
Style: Wheated

Mash Bill: 70% corn, 10% malted wheat, 10% honey malted wheat, 10% malted barley
Color: Light Straw
Price: $$$$

Mike

Nose: Butter and caramel with malt.
Taste: Apples and caramel with some baking spices.
Finish: Citrus and spices.

Susan

Nose: Distinctly sweet malt, almost like a fruity Scotch.
Taste: Some chocolate notes, but mostly grains with a touch of spices.
Finish: Warm and lingering.

Notes

Currently contract distilled by New Riff in Newport, KY. Rabbit Hole is building a distillery in downtown Louisville, scheduled to open in early 2018.

My Score

Notes: _____

_____

_____

Appearance (1-5) _____   Nose (1-25) _____
Taste (1-25) _____   Finish (1-25) _____
Complexity (1-10) _____   Overall Impression (1-10) _____
SCORE _____

Rabbit Hole Sherry

Proof: 93
Age: NAS
Type: Straight
Style: Wheated, Special Finish

Mash Bill: Uses wheat
Color: Straw
Price: $$$$$

Mike

Nose: Raisins and dates with vanilla and a hint of baking spice.
Taste: Raisins and berries with caramel corn and baking spices.
Finish: Short and fruity sweet with oak and spice.

Susan

Nose: Sherry predominates. Some vanilla, dried fruit.
Taste: Really, this whiskey tastes like sherry, complete with the sweet nuttiness.
Finish: Sweet with raisins and touch of spice.

Notes

Contract distilled to the owner's specifications. No point of origin on the label, and "Kentucky" is absent. Finished in 30 year-old PX sherry casks. The company is building a distillery in downtown Louisville.

My Score

Notes: _____

_____

_____

Appearance (1-5) ____   Nose (1-25) ____
Taste (1-25) ____   Finish (1-25) ____
Complexity (1-10) ____   Overall Impression (1-10) ____
SCORE ____

Rebel Reserve

Proof:	90.6
Age:	NAS
Type:	Straight
Style:	Wheated
Mash Bill:	Not available
Color:	Pale Straw
Price:	$$

Mike

Nose: Simple. Caramel and vanilla with bit of oak. Very light cotton candy in the background.

Taste: Caramel corn and ripe apples with a bit of hazelnuts or pecans.

Finish: Long and dry with oak tannins and pepper spice.

Susan

Nose: Very light. Vanilla and faint corn. Sugar is lurking underneath.

Taste: Caramel candy corn, sweet cereal. Faint nuttiness and dash of pepper.

Finish: Fairly long, drying to pepper spice.

Notes

Moderately-priced bottle will be interesting to compare to other wheated bourbons. Bottling to which cherry and honey have been added are also available. Produced by Heaven Hill in Louisville. Bottled and distributed by Luxco of St. Louis. Distributed by Luxco Brands of St. Louis.

My Score

Notes: _____

_____

_____

Appearance (1-5) _____   Nose (1-25) _____

Taste (1-25) _____   Finish (1-25) _____

Complexity (1-10) _____   Overall Impression (1-10) _____

SCORE _____

Rebel Yell

Proof: 80
Age: NAS
Type: Straight
Style: Wheated

Mash Bill: Not available
Color: Pale Straw
Price: $

Mike

Nose: Very simple. Vanilla and corn with a hint of oak.
Taste: Thin and watery. Vanilla and corn with some hazelnut.
Finish: A bit dry with oak tannins. Lasts longer than expected.

Susan

Nose: Very light, with notes of vanilla, candy corn, perhaps a whiff of mint.
Taste: Light nuttiness and faint spice support the vanilla.
Finish: Medium long with pepper spice.

Notes

Once upon a time, this was a 90 proof bourbon. The Yell's volume has been turned down. Distilled by Heaven Hill in Louisville. Distributed by Luxco Brands of St. Louis.

My Score

Notes: _____

_____

_____

Appearance (1-5) _____   Nose (1-25) _____

Taste (1-25) _____   Finish (1-25) _____

Complexity (1-10) _____   Overall Impression (1-10) _____

SCORE _____

Rebellion

Proof:	90
Age:	8 years
Type:	Straight
Style:	Traditional
Mash Bill:	Not available
Color:	Light Straw
Price:	$$$$$

Mike

Nose: Corn, vanilla, and smoke with a hint of cherries.
Taste: Corn, vanilla, maple smoke. Hint of fruit.
Finish: Long and dry with oak and smoke.

Susan

Nose: Honey, caramel corn, woodsmoke.
Taste: Oranges, caramel, some roasted corn.
Finish: Dries to oak.

Notes

Distilled in Tennessee. Bottled by Market Street Spirits, Bardstown, KY. This was bottle #10,106 of batch #1.

My Score

Notes: _____

_____

_____

Appearance (1-5) _____   Nose (1-25) _____

Taste (1-25) _____   Finish (1-25) _____

Complexity (1-10) _____   Overall Impression (1-10) _____

SCORE _____

Redemption

Proof:	92
Age:	3 years
Type:	Straight Bourbon
Style:	Small Batch
Mash Bill:	60% corn, 30.2% rye, 1.8% barley
Color:	Dark Straw
Price:	$$

Mike

Nose: Corn and vanilla with a bit of honey. Very simple nose.

Taste: Corn and vanilla with some pepper spice. A bit thin.

Finish: Long and spicy with pepper spice and oak tannins.

Susan

Nose: Caramel and vanilla. A little sweet spice.

Taste: Vanilla, corn, some spice. Rather simple.

Finish: Long and warm. Peppery ending.

Notes

Rather surprising that the spice one expects from a high rye bourbon only comes to the fore in the finish. Distilled in Indiana and bottled in Bardstown, KY by Strong Spirits.

My Score

Notes: _____

_____

_____

Appearance (1-5) _____   Nose (1-25) _____

Taste (1-25) _____   Finish (1-25) _____

Complexity (1-10) _____   Overall Impression (1-10) _____

SCORE _____

Rod & Rifle

Proof: 80
Age: 4 years
Type: Straight
Style: Tennessee Bourbon

Mash Bill: 70% Corn, 25% Rye, 5% Malted Barley
Color: Very Light Straw
Price: $$$$

Mike

Nose: Very young. Corn with a hint of cherries.
Taste: Sweet corn and vanilla with a bit of pepper spice.
Finish: Slightly sweet with corn and dries out with some oak.

Susan

Nose: Caramel and corn. Some mustiness. Alcohol.
Taste: Sweet on the tongue. Very smooth. Vanilla predominates. Very simple.
Finish: Short, but smooth and warm. A little honey emerges at the very end.

Notes

Georgia Distilling Company/Prestige Imports. Expensive, but part of the proceeds go toward preserving hunting and fishing habitats.

My Score

Notes: _____

_____

_____

Appearance (1-5) ____   Nose (1-25) ____
Taste (1-25) ____   Finish (1-25) ____
Complexity (1-10) ____   Overall Impression (1-10) ____
SCORE ____

Rough Rider

Proof: 90
Age: Minimum 2 years
Type: Straight
Style: Small Batch, Special Finish

Mash Bill: Not available
Color: Straw
Price: $$$

Mike
Nose: Fruity with grapes and pine wood.
Taste: Sweet vanilla and grapes with some spice. Water takes the spice out.
Finish: Short and peppery. Water lessens the pepper and brings out more oak.

Susan
Nose: Caraway, rye, raisons, dates.
Taste: Caramel and cashews. Water reveals dates fruit and amplifies nuttiness.
Finish: Short and smooth. Bit of pepper at the end.

Notes
Long Island Spirits, Baiting Hollow, NY. Sourced from MGP, Lawrenceburg, IN. Second barreling in French oak casks that have rinsed with high proof brandy.

My Score

Notes: _____

_____

_____

Appearance (1-5) ____   Nose (1-25) ____

Taste (1-25) ____   Finish (1-25) ____

Complexity (1-10) ____   Overall Impression (1-10) ____

SCORE ____

Spring 44 Single Barrel

Proof: 100
Age: NAS
Type: Straight
Style: Single Barrel

Mash Bill: Not available
Color: Straw
Price: $$$$$

Mike
Nose: Caramel and leather with some berry fruit.
Taste: Berries and apples with caramel and baking spice.
Finish: Long with balance of caramel and oak.

Susan
Nose: Corn and bread dough. Faint vanilla.
Taste: Vanilla, some pear and sweet spices.
Finish: Long and peppery.

Notes
Sourced from Kentucky. Bottled by Spring 44 Distillery, Loveland, CO. Proof adjusted with Colorado Rocky Mountain spring water. This was barrel #28.

My Score	
Notes: _____	
_____	
_____	
Appearance (1-5) ____	Nose (1-25) ____
Taste (1-25) ____	Finish (1-25) ____
Complexity (1-10) ____	Overall Impression (1-10) ____
SCORE ____	

Starlight Bourbon

Proof:	95
Age:	NAS
Type:	Straight
Style:	Small Batch, Special Finish
Mash Bill:	Not available
Color:	Amber
Price:	$$$$

Mike

Nose: Fruit and caramel. Not complex. Water opens the nose – fruit, spice, hint of oak.

Taste: Rich caramel and fruit. Strong not of the port wine Water brings added spice.

Finish: Dry and fruity. Water makes it spicy and brings out a little oak.

Susan

Nose: Rich chocolate note with vanilla and spice. Fruit revealed with water.

Taste: Vanilla and new leather. Caramel follows.

Finish: A little hot, but sweet before the tannins kick in at the end.

Notes

Huber's Starlight Distillery, Borden, IN. Label says that the bourbon is distilled in Kentucky (no distillery named) and aged and bottled at Huber's. Batch 1, Bottle No. 1348. Would make an excellent Manhattan.

My Score

Notes: _____

_____

_____

Appearance (1-5)	____	Nose (1-25)	____
Taste (1-25)	____	Finish (1-25)	____
Complexity (1-10)	____	Overall Impression (1-10)	____

SCORE ____

Stave & Barrel

Proof:	118.8
Age:	6 months
Type:	Not Straight
Style:	Single Barrel, Barrel Proof
Mash Bill:	21% rye
Color:	Straw
Price:	$$$$

Mike
Nose:　Corn, marshmallows, vanilla.
Taste:　Corn and vanilla with sweet spices.
Finish:　Medium long, spicy.

Susan
Nose:　Bananas, vanilla, some nutmeg.
Taste:　Banana pudding with nutmeg.
Finish:　Warm, drying to oak.

Notes
Distilled in Indiana. Bottled by Glenn Creek Distillery, Frankfort, KY. Barrel #2, bottle #128.

My Score

Notes: _____

_____

_____

Appearance (1-5) _____ Nose (1-25) _____

Taste (1-25) _____ Finish (1-25) _____

Complexity (1-10) _____ Overall Impression (1-10) _____

SCORE _____

The Steward's Solera Bourbon

Proof:	100
Age:	See notes
Type:	Straight
Style:	Small Batch
Mash Bill:	See notes
Color:	Light Amber
Price:	$$$$

Mike

Nose: Vanilla and caramel. Apricot and light oak.

Taste: Sweet caramel and apricot with a lot of oak tannins to the point of bitterness.

Finish: Long – oaky – bitter.

Susan

Nose: Very nutty. Toasted almonds with some vanilla notes.

Taste: Rich mouthful. Palate matches nose with nuts and vanilla.

Finish: Long and warm. Pepper and oak on the end.

Notes

From The Steward's Solera, Aurora, CO. Concept is to create a "meritage" of bourbon. Eight bourbons from four states are mingled. At least some of this whiskey comes from MGP in IN (put in barrels in 2000). Other barrels from Kentucky (2000, 2001, 2004) and Tennessee (2007) are added to new craft distillate from this Colorado distillery. Mash bills between 60 and 75% corn, 20% rye, 5% malted barley.

My Score		
Notes: _____		
_____		
_____		
Appearance (1-5) ____	Nose (1-25)	____
Taste (1-25) ____	Finish (1-25)	____
Complexity (1-10) ____	Overall Impression (1-10)	____
SCORE ____		

Straight Edge

Proof:	84
Age:	NAS
Type:	Not Straight
Style:	Special Finish
Mash Bill:	Not available
Color:	Dark Straw
Price:	$$$$

Mike
Nose: Vanilla and honey with a hint of banana.
Taste: Light, not complex. Corn and vanilla. A hint of oak.
Finish: Medium long and dry with oak.

Susan
Nose: Corn, bread dough, mint.
Taste: Sweet vanilla and caramel corn.
Finish: Long and warm, verging on hot.

Notes
"Finished and bottled" by Splinter Group, Napa, CA. Blend of 5, 7, and 8 year old Kentucky and Tennessee bourbons. Finished in cabernet sauvignon barrels.

My Score

Notes: _____

_____

_____

Appearance (1-5) ____   Nose (1-25) ____
Taste (1-25) ____   Finish (1-25) ____
Complexity (1-10) ____   Overall Impression (1-10) ____
SCORE ____

Tatoosh Bourbon

Proof:	80
Age:	3 years
Type:	Not Straight
Style:	Small Batch
Mash Bill:	Not available
Color:	Very Light Straw
Price:	$$$$

Mike

Nose: Maple smoke and vanilla.

Taste: Very light. Maple wood and vanilla with a hint of Flintstone chewable vitamins.

Finish: Quick and smoky.

Susan

Nose: Corn and light maple syrup.

Taste: Honeyed oak, sweet mint, hard candy.

Finish: Short and warm.

Notes

Finished and bottled by Tatoosh Distillery, Seattle, WA. No indication of source on the label.

My Score

Notes: _____

_____

_____

Appearance (1-5)	____	Nose (1-25)	____
Taste (1-25)	____	Finish (1-25)	____
Complexity (1-10)	____	Overall Impression (1-10)	____
	SCORE ____		

Temperance Trader

Proof:	98.2
Age:	NAS
Type:	Straight
Style:	Small Batch
Mash Bill:	Not available
Color:	Light Straw
Price:	$$$

Mike

Nose: Lots of corn. Hints of vanilla and oak.
Taste: Corn and vanilla with some pepper.
Finish: Lots of pepper and some oak.

Susan

Nose: Pecans, light oak, some sweet mint.
Taste: Nutty, with some vanilla. Very smooth.
Finish: Sweet with sweet oak and corn at the end.

Notes

Distilled in Tennessee. Bottled by Bull Run Distilling Co., Portland, OR. Batch #017 and bottle #04437. Enjoyable light sip. But even at 99.02 proof it would disappear in a cocktail.

My Score

Notes: _____

_____

_____

Appearance (1-5) _____   Nose (1-25) _____

Taste (1-25) _____   Finish (1-25) _____

Complexity (1-10) _____   Overall Impression (1-10) _____

SCORE _____

Trail's End

Proof:	90
Age:	NAS
Type:	Straight
Style:	Special Finish
Mash Bill:	Not available
Color:	Straw
Price:	$$$$$

Mike
Nose: Corn and vanilla. Hint of oak.
Taste: Corn and honey with oak tannins.
Finish: Dry oak and honey.

Susan
Nose: Figs, raison, toffee.
Taste: More figs with some oak and spice.
Finish: Oak and pepper.

Notes
Hood River Distillers, Hood River, OR. Sourced from Kentucky and finished in Oregon oak barrels.

My Score
Notes: _____

_____

_____

Appearance (1-5)	____	Nose (1-25)	____
Taste (1-25)	____	Finish (1-25)	____
Complexity (1-10)	____	Overall Impression (1-10)	____

SCORE ____

Temptation

Proof: 82
Age: 3 years
Type: Straight Bourbon
Style: Small Batch

Mash Bill: 75% corn, 20% rye, 5% barley
Color: Straw
Price: $$

Mike
Nose: Very light with corn and vanilla with a hint of spice and oak.
Taste: Sweet with sweet spices and corn. Just a hint of oak. A bit thin in the mouth.
Finish: Long and peppery turning dry with oak tannins.

Susan
Nose: Light nose. faint caramel, vanilla and spices.
Taste: Corn and pepper, some sweet spice. Not complex.
Finish: Hot and peppery. Dries quickly.

Notes
Distilled in Indiana and bottled in Bardstown, KY by Bardstown Barrel Selection.

My Score		
Notes: _____		
_____		
_____		
Appearance (1-5) ____	Nose (1-25)	____
Taste (1-25) ____	Finish (1-25)	____
Complexity (1-10) ____	Overall Impression (1-10)	____
SCORE ____		

Traverse City Whiskey Co. Bourbon

Proof: 86
Age: 4 years
Type: Straight
Style: Small Batch

Mash Bill: Not available
Color: Straw
Price: $$$

Mike
Nose: Very light with corn and oak.
Taste: Very light. Corn, vanilla, some spice.
Finish: Short with a hint of oak.

Susan
Nose: Light vanilla and apples.
Taste: Vanilla and apples. Whiff of cinnamon.
Finish: Ends in pepper and oak.

Notes
Traverse City Whiskey Co., Traverse City, MI. Sourced from MGP in Lawrenceburg, IN. The company is building a distillery where the bourbon will be produced. This was from small batch #5.

My Score
Notes: _____
_____
_____

Appearance (1-5) ____ Nose (1-25) ____
Taste (1-25) ____ Finish (1-25) ____
Complexity (1-10) ____ Overall Impression (1-10) ____
SCORE ____

Wathen's

Proof:	94
Age:	NAS
Type:	Straight
Style:	Single Barrel
Mash Bill:	Not available
Color:	Straw
Price:	$$$

Mike

Nose: Orange blossom, honey, corn and oak. Not complex, but very nice.

Taste: Sweet caramel, oak and a bit of citrus fruit. Peppery spices and fine tobacco.

Finish: Long and dry. Spicy with oak and pepper.

Susan

Nose: Fruity, with notes of banana and paw paw. Little bit of underlying sweet spice and a dash of cocoa.

Taste: Cinnamon and sweet caramel with peppery notes.

Finish: Sweet at the beginning, which gradually dries to pepper and oak.

Notes

A very pleasant single barrel to sip neat or with a chip of ice. Goes well with a cigar or steak. Distilled and aged in Kentucky and bottled by Charles Medley Distillery, San Jose, CA.

My Score		
Notes: _____		
_____		
_____		
Appearance (1-5) ____	Nose (1-25)	____
Taste (1-25) ____	Finish (1-25)	____
Complexity (1-10) ____	Overall Impression (1-10)	____
SCORE ____		

Whiskey Row

Proof:	88
Age:	NAS
Type:	Not Straight
Style:	Small Batch
Mash Bill:	Not available
Color:	Light Straw
Price:	$$$$

Mike

Nose: Cherries and vanilla with a hint of oak.
Taste: Vanilla and cherries with some baking spice.
Finish: Starts fruity. Balance out with some oak.

Susan

Nose: Corn, light caramel, some spice.
Taste: Vanilla, cherry juice, some cinnamon.
Finish: Medium long and smooth.

Notes

Whiskey Row Distillers, Crestwood, KY are housed in a former ice cream factory. Bourbon named for a section of Main Street in Louisville that historically was (and is once again) home to bourbon offices and distilleries. However, "Kentucky" appears nowhere on the label and we suspect this is sourced from MGP in Indiana. This was Batch 001, Barrel No. 002. The owners plan to distill their own product eventually.

My Score

Notes: _____

_____

_____

Appearance (1-5) ____   Nose (1-25) ____
Taste (1-25) ____   Finish (1-25) ____
Complexity (1-10) ____   Overall Impression (1-10) ____
SCORE ____

Whiskey Sister

Proof: 80
Age: NAS
Type: Not Straight
Style: Small Batch, Craft

Mash Bill: Not available
Color: Light Straw
Price: $$$

Mike

Nose: Very light. Corn and vanilla.
Taste: Sweet corn and vanilla with some honey apple.
Finish: Starts sweet and dries to oak and pepper ending.

Susan

Nose: Very light. Peaches and not much else.
Taste: Peaches on the entrance, then a mouthful of black pepper. Too hot for 80 proof.
Finish: Peaches, again, which linger to the spice.

Notes

Whiskey Sister, Fairfield, CA. Bottled by Frank-Lin Distillers, Fairfield, CA. Bourbon sourced from Kentucky and bottled in CA.

My Score

Notes: _____

_____

_____

Appearance (1-5) _____   Nose (1-25) _____

Taste (1-25) _____   Finish (1-25) _____

Complexity (1-10) _____   Overall Impression (1-10) _____

SCORE _____

Wildcatter Barrel Select

Proof:	90
Age:	8 years
Type:	Straight
Style:	Traditional
Mash Bill:	Not available
Color:	Straw
Price:	$$$$

Mike

Nose: Caramel and pears with a hint of oak.

Taste: A bit thin. Caramel and pecans with baking spice.

Finish: Dry with oak and spice.

Susan

Nose: Corn husk, some caramel and dates.

Taste: Burnt caramel and dark fruit.

Finish: Dry and peppery.

Notes

Sourced from Kentucky and bottled by Elite Brands, Fairfield, CA.

My Score

Notes: _____

_____

_____

Appearance (1-5) ____   Nose (1-25) ____

Taste (1-25) ____   Finish (1-25) ____

Complexity (1-10) ____   Overall Impression (1-10) ____

SCORE ____

Yellowstone Select

Proof: 93
Age: NAS
Type: Straight
Style: Small Batch

Mash Bill: Not available
Color: Straw
Price: $$$$

Mike

Nose: Corn and vanilla with a bit of tobacco. A bit yeasty.
Taste: Corn and vanilla with pears, oak, and spice.
Finish: Very nice. Starts dry with oak and gets spicy.

Susan

Nose: Mint, caramel, some orange zest.
Taste: Vanilla and caramel, some chocolate and pears. Rich mouthfeel.
Finish: Warm and smooth ending with a nice milk chocolate note.

Notes

Sourced from Kentucky and bottled by Limestone Branch Distillery, Lebanon, KY. It is owned and distributed by LUXCO, St. Louis, MO.

My Score		
Notes: _____		
_____		
_____		
Appearance (1-5) ____	Nose (1-25)	____
Taste (1-25) ____	Finish (1-25)	____
Complexity (1-10) ____	Overall Impression (1-10)	____
SCORE ____		

Zachory Boone

Proof:	80
Age:	NAS
Type:	Straight
Style:	Traditional
Mash Bill:	Not available
Color:	Light Straw
Price:	$

Mike

Nose: Very, very light nose.
Corn and vanilla with a hint of toasted marshmallow.

Taste: Sweet with vanilla and light fruit – bananas and pears.

Finish: Medium long and spicy with pepper spice.

Susan

Nose: Very light. Some oak, corn, and vanilla.

Taste: Ripe apples, vanilla, light pepper.

Finish: Short and oaky.

Notes

Bottled by Brookdale Ltd., Mira Lona, CA.

My Score

Notes: _____

_____

_____

Appearance (1-5) _____   Nose (1-25) _____

Taste (1-25) _____   Finish (1-25) _____

Complexity (1-10) _____   Overall Impression (1-10) _____

SCORE _____

Additional Independent Releases

Name: _____

Distillery: _____

Proof: _____ **Mash Bill:** _____

Age: _____

Type: _____ **Color:** _____

Style: _____ **Price:** _____

My Score

Notes: _____

_____

_____

Appearance (1-5) _____ Nose (1-25) _____

Taste (1-25) _____ Finish (1-25) _____

Complexity (1-10) _____ Overall Impression (1-10) _____

SCORE _____

Name: _____

Distillery: _____

Proof: _____ **Mash Bill:** _____

Age: _____

Type: _____ **Color:** _____

Style: _____ **Price:** _____

My Score

Notes: _____

_____

_____

Appearance (1-5) _____ Nose (1-25) _____

Taste (1-25) _____ Finish (1-25) _____

Complexity (1-10) _____ Overall Impression (1-10) _____

SCORE _____

ACKNOWLEDGMENTS

Many people helped in the preparation of the book. We received samples from several distilleries, as well as bottle photographs. We also appreciated information about ages and non-propriety mash bills. Thanks go to Ginger Flowers and Linda Hayes (Beam Suntory), Tracy Frederick, Phil Lynch, and Chris Morris (Brown-Forman), Amy Preske (Buffalo Trace/Barton 1792), Ellen King, Karen Kushner, and Al Young (Four Roses) Josh Hafer, Kelly Hubbuch, Larry Kass, and Niki King (Heaven Hill), Shelby Caret (High West Whiskey), Julian Van Winkle, III (Pappy Van Winkle), Tim Quinlan (River City Distributors), John Foster (Smooth Ambler) and Katrina Egbert and Rick Robinson (Wild Turkey).

And many thanks to the scores of craft distillers and independent bottlers who sent us photos and samples, not to mention our friend Julie Bartlett, who brought bourbons from her trip to Oregon.

The authors also tasted bourbons in several venues around Louisville and we enjoyed meals afterwards. Thank you Jason Brauner and John Morrison (Bourbons Bistro), Bonnie Eisert and Brian Sur (Charr'd Bourbon Kitchen and Lounge at the Louisville Marriott East) Anderson Grissom (The Dish), and Larry Rice (The Silver Dollar).

Many thanks also go to the bourbon lovers who occasionally joined us to taste and comment on the bourbons at hand (after we had made notes, of course). They were Dan Gardner, Joanna Goldstein, Sean Higgins, Renae Price, and Stacey Yates. Cheers!

THE AUTHORS

Susan Reigler
Bourbon Authority and Author

Award-winning writer Susan Reigler, author of *Kentucky Bourbon Country: The Essential Travel Guide, The Complete Guide to Kentucky State Parks, More Kentucky Bourbon Cocktails*, and co-author of *The Kentucky Bourbon Cocktail Book*, was born in Louisville the year Swaps won the Kentucky Derby. From 1992 to 2007, Reigler was a restaurant critic, beverage columnist and travel writer for the Louisville *Courier-Journal*. She is a Certified Executive Bourbon Steward by the Society of the Stave & Thief.

With her cat, E.T.

Reigler served as the President of the Board of Directors of the Bourbon Women Association from 2015 to 2017. She has presented workshops at the Kentucky Bourbon Festival, Bourbon & Beyond (Louisville), and bourbon festivals in Chicago, New Orleans, Oxford, MS, Smithfield, VA and others. She has lead bourbon tastings from Seattle to Savannah as well tastings to benefit non-profit organizations including Locust Grove, The Falls of the Ohio Foundation, and Shaker Village at Pleasant Hill. She has been a judge for numerous bourbon cocktail contests and has helped restaurants and retailers select barrels from Four Roses, Woodford Reserve, Knob Creek, and more, for private bourbon bottlings.

Reigler holds a bachelor's degree in music from Indiana University and a master's degree in zoology from the University of Oxford, which she attended as a Humphrey Scholar. She is a research associate in biology at Indiana University Southeast.

Michael R. Veach
Bourbon Historian and Author
The Filson Historical Society

Mike Veach is one of the foremost authorities on all things Bourbon, and has spent over 15 years with The Filson Historical Society serving in the role of historian and author. Veach possesses an unsurpassed wealth of knowledge and perspective on an industry that has Kentucky at the forefront of the Bourbon Boom occurring across the United States and abroad.

Mr. Veach is also a recognized author whose articles have been featured in publications such as *The Bourbon Review* and *The Louisville Encyclopedia*. He wrote the foreword for the release of Gerald Carson's *Social History of Bourbon in 2010*, and in 2013 published his own now-widely acclaimed book *Kentucky Bourbon Whiskey: An American Heritage*.

Prior to his long tenure at The Filson, Veach spent 5 years as the North American Archivist for United Distillers. Since then he has also provided research and consulting services for such institutions as the Oscar Getz Museum of Whiskey History, Brown-Forman, Buffalo Trace, Four Roses, and Heaven Hill Distillery.

In 2006, Mike Veach was publicly recognized for his knowledge, activities, and accomplishments surrounding bourbon by being inducted into The Kentucky Bourbon Hall of Fame. He has provided pro-bono services to many major non-profit entities such as The Black Acre Foundation, The Farnsley-Kaufman House, The Farnsley-Moreman Landing, Boy Scouts of America, Girls. Inc in Owensboro and many other organizations including The Filson Historical Society.

Veach holds a BA and MA in History from the University of Louisville. He travels across the country researching, lecturing, and hosting special seminars designed to spread the knowledge of Kentucky Whiskey products and enhance the appreciation of Bourbon. Mr. Veach resides in his hometown of Louisville, KY in the heart of Bourbon Country.

INDICES

Alphabetical
Proof
Special Style
Price

ALPHABETICAL

PROOF

SPECIAL STYLE

Age Accelerated
Cleveland Bourbon • 319

Barrel Proof
(No water added before bottling)
Angel's Envy Cask Strength Bottled 2012 • 290
Backbone Bourbon • 291
Balcones Texas Blue Corn Bourbon • 212
Barrel Bourbon • 293
Big Ass Bourbon Barrel Strength • 299
Booker's • 22
Bourbon 30 Single Barrel • 222
Bourbon 30 Small Batch • 223
Bulleit Cask Strength • 68
Col. E.H. Taylor, Jr. Barrel Proof • 171
Elijah Craig Single Barrel • 89
Evan Williams Barrel Proof • 95
Four Roses Elliott's Select • 80
Four Roses Single Barrel Private Selection • 83
George T. Stagg • 177
Heaven Hill Select Stock • 105
Jefferson's Reserve Groth Reserve Cask Finish • 340
J. Henry & Sons Cask Strength • 244
Kentucky Owl • 345
Maker's Mark Cask Strength • 34
Michter's US*1 Barrel Strength • 132
OCD #5 • 253
Old Forester 1920 • 54
Smooth Ambler Old Scout Single Barrel • 265
Stagg, Jr. • 191
Stave & Barrel • 374
West of Kentucky No. 2 Cask Strength • 277
Wild Turkey Rare Breed • 206
William Heavenhill Cask Strength • 115
William Larue Weller • 195

Bonded/Bottled-in-Bond
(Bourbon that is at least 4 years old, bottled at 100 proof, and produced by one distiller at one distillery in one season)
Col. E.H. Taylor, Jr. Bottled-in-Bond • 172
Col. E.H. Taylor, Jr. Single Barrel • 173
Evan Williams White Label • 97
Heaven Hill Old Style Bourbon Bottled-in-Bond • 103
Henry McKenna Bottled-in-Bond • 107
Jim Beam Bonded • 27
J.T.S. Brown Bottled-in-Bond • 108
Old Bardstown Bottled-in-Bond • 125
Old Fitzgerald Bottled-in-Bond • 110
Old Forester 1897 • 53
Old Grand-Dad Bonded • 39
Old Tub • 41
Very Old Barton 100 • 158
William Heavenhill Bottled-in-Bond • 114

Craft
(Distilled on-site. Not merely sourced and bottled by a company. Usually fewer than 100 barrels bottled per year.)
Berkshire Bourbon • 216
Big Bottom Small Batch • 217
Breckenridge • 224
C.W. Irwin • 228
Delaware Phoenix • 230
Garrison Brothers • 234
Hudson Baby Bourbon • 241
John B. Stetson • 343
Kings County • 246
McKenzie • 249
Neversweat • 251
Old Pogue • 257
Smooth Ambler • 262
Stillwrights Bourbon • 267
Thirteenth Colony Bourbon • 268
Tom's Foolery Barrel 11 • 269
Tom's Foolery Barrel 19 • 270
Tom's Foolery Barrel 118 • 271
Town Branch • 273
Waitsburg Bourbon Whiskey • 274
Whiskey Sister • 384
Widow Jane • 279
Woodstone Creek • 281
Wyoming Whiskey • 282

Single Barrel

(Bottled from a single barrel. Can yield ~ 60-150 bottles per barrel depending on how much evaporation took place during maturation.)

Blanton's Export • 168
Blanton's Gold Edition • 169
Blanton's Single Barrel • 166
Blanton's Special Reserve • 167
Bourbon 30 Single Barrel • 222
Col. E.H. Taylor, Jr. Single Barrel • 173
Corner Creek • 320
Eagle Rare 17-Year-Old • 175
Eagle Rare Single Barrel • 174
Elijah Craig 18-Year-Old • 91
Elijah Craig 21-Year-Old • 92
Elijah Craig 23-Year-Old • 93
Elijah Craig Single Barrel • 89
Elmer T. Lee • 176
Evan Williams Single Barrel 2004 • 98
Ezra B • 325
Four Roses Elliott's Select • 80
Four Roses Single Barrel • 82
Four Roses Single Barrel Private Selection • 83
Grand River Baby Bourbon • 235
Hancock's President's Reserve • 178
Heaven Hill Select Stock • 105
Henry McKenna Bottled-in-Bond • 107
Jim Beam Single Barrel • 31
John J. Bowman • 143
Koval • 247
Michter's 20-Year-Old • 136
OCD #5 • 253
Old 55 Bourbon • 254
Old 55 Single Barrel • 255
Old Forester Single Barrel • 56
Old Forge Reserve • 351
Old Scout Single Barrel • 355
Rock Hill Farms • 190
Russell's Reserve Single Barrel • 201
Smooth Ambler Old Scout Single Barrel • 265
Smooth Ambler Old Scout - The Lion's Share Collection • 266
Spring 44 Single Barrel • 372
Stave & Barrel • 374
Tom's Foolery Barrel 11 • 269
Tom's Foolery Barrel 19 • 270
Tom's Foolery Barrel 118 • 271
Wathen's • 382
Widow Jane • 279
Wild Turkey Kentucky Spirit • 204
Wild Turkey Master's Keep • 205
Woodford Reserve Double Oaked Single Barrel • 59
Woodstone Creek • 281

Small Batch

(This is a very slippery designation since "small" can be defined by distillers as anything from the batching of two barrels to a few hundred. So, caveat emptor.)

Andy's Old No. 5 • 211
Angel's Envy • 289
Angel's Envy Cask Strength Bottled 2012 • 290
Backbone Bourbon • 291
Baker's • 20
Barrel Bourbon • 293
Barton 1792 High Rye • 147
Barton 1792 Ridgemont Reserve • 149
Basil Hayden's • 21
Battlefield Bourbon • 294
Beanball Bourbon • 295
Belle Meade • 297
Belle Meade Madeira Finish • 213
Belle Meade Sherry Cask • 214
Berkshire Bourbon • 216
Bib & Tucker • 298
Big Bottom Small Batch • 217
Big House • 300
Bird Dog Small Batch • 302
Black Ridge Small Batch • 303
Blind Tiger • 218
Blood Oath • 305
Bluegrass Distillers Bourbon • 219
Bond & Lillard • 198
Booker's • 22
Bootlegger 21 • 220
Bourbon 30 Barrel Crafted • 221
Bourbone 30 Small Batch • 223
Bower Hill Barrel Reserve • 306
Bowman Brothers • 142
Breaker • 307
Breaking & Entering • 308
Breckenridge • 224
Broken Bell • 309
Buck • 310
Bulleit 10-Year-Old • 69
Cedar Ridge • 225

PRICE

Subject to change

$ ($15 and under)
Ancient Age • 162
Ancient Age 10 Star • 163
Ancient Age 90 • 164
Banker's Club • 292
Big Bottom Small Batch • 217
Bourbon de Luxe • 23
Cabin Still • 88
Colonel Lee • 151
Evan Williams Black Label • 96
Ezra Brooks 80 • 326
Heaven Hill Old Style Bourbon
  Green Label • 104
Henry McKenna • 106
Jesse James America's Outlaw
  Bourbon • 341
Jethro T. Boots • 342
Kentucky Gentleman • 152
Kentucky Tavern • 153
McAfee's Benchmark Old No.
  8 • 179
Old Charter 8-Year-Old • 181
Old Crow • 36
Old Crow Reserve • 37
Old Fitzgerald Prime • 111
Old Grand-Dad • 38
Old Taylor • 183
Prestige • 363
Rebel Yell • 367
Ten High • 154
Very Old Barton 80 • 155
Very Old Barton 86 • 156
Very Old Barton 90 • 157
Very Old Barton 100 • 158
Waitsburg Bourbon Whiskey • 274
Zachory Boone • 387
Zackariah Harris • 159

$$ ($16-$25)
Ancient Ancient Age • 165
Big House • 300
Bird Dog • 301
Buffalo Trace • 170
Bulleit • 67
David Nicholson 1843 • 322
Devil's Cut • 24
Early Times 354 • 49
Early Times Kentucky Straight
  Bourbon Whisky Brown
  Label • 47
Early Times Kentucky Straight
  Bourbon Whisky Yellow
  Label • 48

Evan Williams • 94
Evan Williams 1783 • 101
Evan Williams Single Barrel
  2004 • 98
Evan Williams White Label • 97
Ezra Brooks 90 • 327
Fighting Cock • 102
Filibuster Duel Cask • 328
Four Roses Yellow Label • 79
Heaven Hill Old Style Bourbon
  Bottled-in-Bond • 103
Jeffer's Creek • 335
Jim Beam • 25
Jim Beam Black • 26
Jim Beam Bonded • 27
Johnny Drum Green Label • 118
J.T.S. Brown Bottled-in-Bond •
  108
Larceny • 109
ld Forester • 50
Medley Bros. • 347
Old Bardstown 80 • 123
Old Bardstown 90 • 124
Old Bardstown Bottled-in-
  Bond • 125
Old Charter 10-Year-Old • 182
Old Charter 101 • 180
Old Ezra • 350
Old Fitzgerald Bottled-in-Bond •
  110
Old Forester Signature • 55
Old Grand-Dad 114 • 40
Old Grand-Dad Bonded • 39
Old Kentucky • 352
Old Weller Antique • 186
Old Williamsburg • 357
O.Z. Tyler Small Batch Reserve •
  259
Paddleford Creek • 360
Penny Packer • 361
Rebel Reserve • 366
Redemption • 369
Temptation • 380
Wild Turkey 81 • 202
Wild Turkey 101 • 203
Winchester • 280
W.L. Weller Special Reserve • 194

$$$
Angel's Envy • 289
Barton 1792 Sweet Wheat • 150
Benjamin Prichard's Double
  Barrel • 215

Bird Dog Small Batch • 302
Broken Bell • 309
Buck • 310
Charred Oak • 316
Cody Road • 226
Coopers' Craft • 46
Corner Creek • 320
C.W. Irwin • 228
Cyrus Noble • 321
Delaware Phoenix • 230
Elijah Craig 12-Year-Old • 90
Elmer T. Lee • 176
Flatboat • 329
Four Roses Fine Old Bourbon
   Black Label • 81
Four Roses Small Batch • 84
Four Roses Super Premium
   Platinum Label • 85
Henry McKenna Bottled-in-
   Bond • 107
I.W. Harper • 71
James E. Pepper 1776 • 334
Jefferson's • 336
Jefferson's Reserve • 339
Jim Beam Single Barrel • 31
John B. Stetson • 343
Johnny Drum Private Stock •
   120
J.R. Ewing • 344
Knob Creek • 32
Lexington • 346
Maker's 46 • 35
Maker's Mark • 33
McKenzie • 249
Neversweat • 251
Old Bardstown Estate Bottled •
   126
Old Tub • 41
Old Williamsburg No. 20 • 358
Rough Rider • 371
Russell's Reserve • 200
Smooth Ambler • 262
Stillwrights Bourbon • 267
Temperance Trader • 378
Thirteenth Colony Bourbon •
   268
Town Branch • 273
Traverse City Whiskey Co.
   Bourbon • 381
Very Special Old Fitzgerald •
   113
Wathen's • 382
Whiskey Sister • 384
W.L. Weller 12-Year-Old • 193
Woodford Reserve Distiller's
   Select • 57
Yellow Rose Double Barrel • 283

$$$$ *($36-$55)*
Amador Double Barrel • 288
Andy's Old No. 5 • 211
Backbone Bourbon • 291
Baker's • 20
Barton 1792 Full Proof • 146
Barton 1792 High Rye • 147
Barton 1792 Port Finish • 148
Barton 1792 Ridgemont
   Reserve • 149
Basil Hayden's • 21
Beanball Bourbon • 295
Beer Barrel Bourbon • 296
Belle Meade • 297
Berkshire Bourbon • 216
Big Ass Bourbon Barrel
   Strength • 299
Black Ridge Small Batch • 303
Black Saddle • 304
Blade and Bow • 65
Blanton's Export • 168
Blanton's Gold Edition • 169
Blanton's Single Barrel • 166
Blanton's Special Reserve • 167
Blind Tiger • 218
Booker's • 22
Bourbon 30 Barrel Crafted •
   221
Bourbon 30 Single Barrel • 222
Bower Hill Barrel Reserve • 306
Bowman Brothers • 142
Breaker • 307
Breaking & Entering • 308
Bulleit 10-Year-Old • 69
Bulleit Cask Strength • 68
Burnside Double Barrel • 311
Calumet Farm • 312
Cassius Clay • 313
Cedar Ridge • 225
Charles Goodnight • 315
CH Bourbon • 314
Chestnut Farms • 317
Chicken Cock Heritage
   Reserve • 318
Cleveland Bourbon • 319
Duke • 323
Eagle Rare Single Barrel • 174
Evan Williams Barrel Proof • 95
Ezra B • 325
Featherbone Bourbon • 232
F.E.W. • 233
Four Roses Single Barrel • 82
George Remus • 330
George Remus Straight • 331
Grand River Baby Bourbon •
   235
Hancock's President's Reserve •
   178

Additional Releases

Name: _____

Distillery: _____

Proof: _____ **Mash Bill:** _____
Age: _____
Type: _____ **Color:** _____
Style: _____ **Price:** _____

My Score

Notes: _____

_____

_____

Appearance (1-5) _____   Nose (1-25) _____
Taste (1-25) _____   Finish (1-25) _____
Complexity (1-10) _____   Overall Impression (1-10) _____
SCORE _____

Name: _____

Distillery: _____

Proof: _____ **Mash Bill:** _____
Age: _____
Type: _____ **Color:** _____
Style: _____ **Price:** _____

My Score

Notes: _____

_____

_____

Appearance (1-5) _____   Nose (1-25) _____
Taste (1-25) _____   Finish (1-25) _____
Complexity (1-10) _____   Overall Impression (1-10) _____
SCORE _____

Additional Releases

Name: _____

Distillery: _____

Proof: _____ **Mash Bill:** _____
Age: _____ _____
Type: _____ **Color:** _____
Style: _____ **Price:** _____

My Score

Notes: _____

_____

_____

Appearance (1-5) _____ Nose (1-25) _____
Taste (1-25) _____ Finish (1-25) _____
Complexity (1-10) _____ Overall Impression (1-10) _____
SCORE _____

Name: _____

Distillery: _____

Proof: _____ **Mash Bill:** _____
Age: _____ _____
Type: _____ **Color:** _____
Style: _____ **Price:** _____

My Score

Notes: _____

_____

_____

Appearance (1-5) _____ Nose (1-25) _____
Taste (1-25) _____ Finish (1-25) _____
Complexity (1-10) _____ Overall Impression (1-10) _____
SCORE _____

My Top 25 Bourbons

Name	Total Score	Page #
1.		
2.		
3.		
4.		
5.		
6.		
7.		
8.		
9.		
10.		
11.		
12.		
13.		
14.		
15.		
16.		
17.		
18.		
19.		
20.		
21.		
22.		
23.		
24.		
25.		